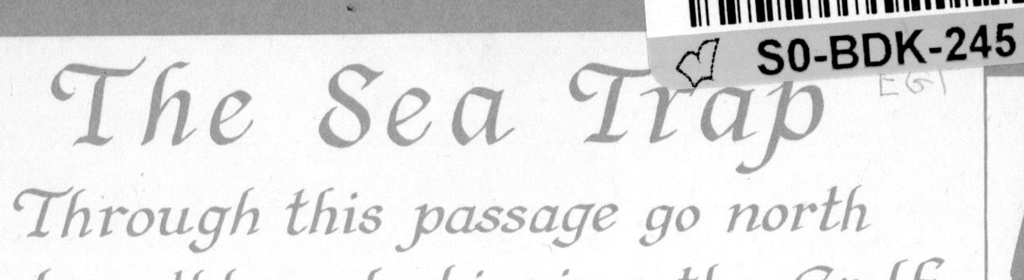
The Sea Trap
Through this passage go north and southbound shipping, the Gulf Stream and the tropical hurricanes

GRAND BAHAMA I.
BAHAMA
Hole in the Wall
HARBOUR I.
ELEUTHERA ISLAND
GISLANDS
Great
Nassau
NEW PROVIDENCE I.
ANDROS ISLAND
Tongue of the Ocean
Exuma Sound
Great Bahama Bank
Scale of Miles
0
20
40
60
80
100

Lore of the Wreckers

Lore of the Wreckers

by Birse Shepard

Cartography by Russell H. Lenz

Beacon Press Boston

Published simultaneously in Canada by
S. J. Reginald Saunders and Company, Ltd., Toronto

Library of Congress catalog card number: 61 - 6221

Printed in the United States of America

Acknowledgments

The author wishes to acknowledge with thanks the following for permission to quote from material under their control:
JEFFERSON L. BROWNE for excerpts from *Key West: The Old and the New* by Jefferson B. Browne.
THE NEW YORKER for excerpts from the article "Dragger Captain, a Profile," by Joseph Mitchell, which originally appeared in the magazine of January 11, 1947.

Photographs on the following pages were also supplied by The Mariners Museum, Newport News, Virginia:
11, 17, 18-19, 23, 26, 90, 100, 122, 183, 235

Contents

Fore Word

Peter Mark Roget, the man who first raised thesauruses commercially, was very nearly responsible for the scuttling of this chronicle before it was launched. The word "wrecker" he associates with thief, smuggler, poacher and kidnaper. The wreckers who stride across these pages were not like that — well, not many of them. But what author would be so brash as to build his craft on a definition in conflict with such an authority?

In mounting dismay I turned to Noah Webster, sturdy bulwark against the stresses of lexicology, and lo! the ship slid down the ways. The launch was done. A wrecker, declares Mr. Webster, is "one who searches for, or works upon the wreck of vessels, as for rescue or plunder." Rescue or plunder, that did it: the wreckers herein did one or the other of these things. Usually they rescued; but then again, they plundered. On this basis, we can put to sea.

Do you wish your wreckers to be scoundrels after the old tradition, battening on the lives and property of drowning seafarers? Then you probably won't like this book. The wreckers here were men on a wide, violent sea frontier — and they acted like men. Few were saints; some were sinners; but out of their composite humanity they left a brief, bright page in American history. Their story has too long been stained by popular prejudices and by pedantry. It is high time the record was set clean.

This book is not fiction, nor even fictionized history. It is the grist of happy days on the keys and the cays, of browsing in libraries and museums, and poking about the edges of the sea, listening to tales of the olden days. It is not scholarly enough to be called history, but is a lighthearted approximation of it, offered with clean hands and a frank warning that much of it can never be verified.

I dedicate it to the children of the wreckers — bronzed and brawny men, and women who hold their heads high — who still tread the paths of their island homes on both sides of the Bahama Channel and look out, sometimes restlessly, upon a more favored generation of shipping as it threads its confident way through the immemorial channels of the reefs.

Illustrations

The Five Wrecking Grounds
Ocean Currents
CANADA
NEWFOUNDLAND
CAPE BRETON
P.E.I.
NOVA SCOTIA
Halifax
SABLE I.
CAPE SABLE
UNITED STATES
Boston
CAPE COD
NANTUCKET
MARTHA'S VINEYARD
BLOCK I.
LONG I.
New York
NEW JERSEY
GULF STREAM
CAPE HATTERAS
DIAMOND SHOALS
FRYING PAN SHOALS
Charleston
St. Augustine
North Atlantic Ocean
BERMUDA I.
Miami
Nassau
BAHAMA ISLANDS
Dry Tortugas
Key West
FLORIDA REEFS
FLORIDA STRAITS
BAHAMA BANKS
Havana
CUBA
HISPANIOLA
JAMAICA
Caribbean Sea
SPANISH MAIN
CENTRAL AMERICA
Panama
SOUTH AMERICA
Scale of Miles
0 200 400 600
R. Lenz

A. M. Barnes Coll., Courtesy The Mariners Museum, Newport News, Va.
When the September gales of 1870 drove the brig *Poinsett* of Boston hard aground on Nantucket, wreckers improvised landing tackle and brought her cargo ashore through the surf.

1

Wreck Asho-o-re!

They were robust, rollicking men and proud women who built their homes on islands and outcropping rocks of the great reef, and wrested riches and adventure from the perilous seaways of the Atlantic shore. The world called them wreckers and held them in slight regard, but they wrote a page of reckless daring and skill in the early days of the New World that is seldom remembered and little understood. Unfortunately, there seems to have been no poet or historian among them to chronicle their exploits; but from the dry dust of old court records up and down the coast, their deeds cry for recognition.

The seventeenth century was a seagoing age. The cluster of seaport towns that was to become the nucleus of a new nation was, in the beginning, little more than a few convenient harbors to load and unload the cargoes that were the lifeblood of His Majesty's American colonies. Soon thousands of sailing craft were making their uncertain way up and down the coast from Halifax to the West Indies, and in and out of the Atlantic. Most of these craft were small: men feared that a vessel of over five hundred tons would break her back in a heavy sea. Some ships were staunch and seaworthy; many were not. Some, built on seaside farms after the crops had been gathered, had only a single thickness of wood to keep out the sea. Others were marvels of strength and beauty. Anything that could float went to sea, often overloaded or undermanned. (The Plimsoll mark, establishing a safe limit for the loading of a ship, did not come into use until 1875.) Nobody had ever heard of safety regulations, and little thought was wasted on such questions as whether a craft could take the stresses of an Atlantic crossing. She just went.

Trained navigators were rare. A ship got where she was going by sheer persistence, a magnetic compass and a few highly fanciful charts. Her master figured latitude with a cross-staff by angular distance of the sun from the celestial equator. This record was chalked up on a wooden board that folded together like a book; from it he estimated each day the position of the ship. If there was no sun for a week, he was in a bad way. Sometimes the ship's officers were the only persons on board who had ever been to sea.

In short, transport was an uncertain business, as likely as not to end in disaster. Ships ran aground innocently on hidden rocks and shoals, turned turtle because of clumsy or careless loading, went down in gales, came to grief because of unseaworthy condition or were lost through ignorant or faulty navigation. About half the casualties were the result of ignorance, incapacity or carelessness of crews and masters. As late as 1850, the Board of Underwriters of the Port of New York exhorted shipmasters to

carry adequate charts of the coast. The tragic toll of early steamboat fires and explosions too often pointed to criminal inattention to boilers and steam gauges.

Accidents upon approaching land were the most numerous. With plenty of sea room, a skipper could usually keep his ship afloat. But on narrowing seaways, the proximity of rocks and shoals, beaches, islands and other vessels brought on difficulties. All seacoasts had their shipwrecks, but when a dangerous locality lay directly in the sea lane to a busy port — as Nantucket Island with its shoals lay in the approach to New York; Cape Cod barred the way to Boston and Salem; and the gantlet of the Florida Straits lay in the path of every southbound skipper — *there* were the wrecking grounds. Since there was not a vestige of organized aid or rescue until well into the nineteenth century, thousands of ships were lost, many with all on board.

The Liverpool packet *Sheffield* had a rough westward crossing in the fall of 1843. She made her landfall off Long Island near the entrance to New York Harbor in high seas, wind and rain, on November 11, the thirty-seventh day of her passage. Worn and exhausted, her crew and passengers — 130 persons — hailed the coming aboard of the pilot with a cheer of relief and went below to make preparations for landing. The vessel's course was changed as the pilot headed her for Staten Island light. The *Sheffield's* officers did not like the change, but the pilot appeared confident, and they held their peace until a gentle nudge told them that their ship was on a shoal. Before she could be swung clear, there came a series of heavy thumps and, finally, a climactic crash that set her down on the hard-packed sand and gravel with a violence the strongest craft could not endure.

Passengers rushed from their cabins, and nearly a hundred immigrants poured from the steerage, frantically struggling to reach the lifeboats. A shouted command from the *Sheffield's* captain, backed up with a heavy fist, stopped the stampede in its tracks. The ship's officers held the crowd at bay until the first excitement abated. A flag, union down, was hoisted to the yardarm in sign of distress; and as soon as the seriousness of the situation was discovered, the crew set to work doggedly chopping at the three great masts. One after another they crashed down with their network of sails and rigging and were pushed overboard into the sea. For a brief moment the lightened vessel floated.

By this time a degree of calm had spread throughout the ship. Her master, Charles W. Popham, was a capable man, and the crew responded to his leadership. At his direction rockets and flares were sent up in an effort to attract attention from the

The deep-sea skipper disdained the puny craft that came to his aid, but the wrecker sailed blithely over reef or shoal in his schooner — seen at work in this old wood engraving.

Harper's New Monthly Magazine, April 1859

shore, which was not very far distant. But darkness closed down with no sign of aid, and the *Sheffield* again began pounding out her life as the high seas lifted her and let her down on the shoal. Because of the severe shaking and jarring, the women were placed on sofas in the cabin, and the men stretched out on the floor around them. Incoming water flooded the hold and rose into the cabin, driving everyone to the table tops, thence to the cabin aft, and eventually out onto the windswept deck.

About dinner time Captain Popham ordered tea and bread served to all — "And then, let us have prayers." Hot tea was followed by reading of the 46th and 130th Psalms and the Biblical account of the shipwreck and deliverance of St. Paul on Melita (Malta). The slight degree of cheer that followed was soon lost as the water rose higher and higher within the ship. The people huddled in a dense mass on the lurching deck in the darkness. By nine o'clock a change of wind set in; the rain ceased, and fitful moonlight gave glimpses of the heaving sea. The terrible pounding of the ship eased, but there was not the slightest indication that anyone from the shore or from passing vessels had observed her plight.

"The last hour was the bitterest, the most hopeless," wrote Dr. Cutler of St. Ann's Church, Brooklyn, in a statement to the press later. "The first hour on the wreck was one of excitement, agitation, lamentation, and visible and audible suffering. The last hour was one of silent and heart-rending but smothered agony. All had made up their minds. All had acquired fortitude — perhaps from different sources — all were subdued, affectionate, and respectful to each other."[1]

As the vessel heeled over on her side and seemed to be settling under their feet, someone appealed to the captain to try launching the lifeboats. "This kind man," the account continues, "after promising again and again that the boats should be ready at a moment's warning, at length said in a whisper, . . . pointing at the same time to the dark mass of steerage passengers around, 'Sir, do you not know, that the moment the word "boats" passes my lips, that mass will be in motion, and the most frightful confusion will ensue? There will be a general rush to this means of escape.' " He did not add, as he might well have, that a hundred and thirty persons could hardly be crowded into three small boats in a sea such as was still running. "It was now that the writer gave up all hope of life," declared another passenger, "and taking his seat beside one, from whom he did not expect to be seprated for a moment even in death . . . he endeavored to reconcile himself and others to the will of God."[2]

Late that afternoon Captain Earl, keeper of the Staten Island light, had climbed the spiral stairs to the light chamber and lit the big lantern. It was still daylight, and he lingered in the tower, peering out into the driving storm. Idly he watched a full-rigged ship beating its way in before the gale. He saw the vessel change its course and drive toward the light. Well he knew the habit of mariners to steer for a lighthouse — and the risks they often took, at times of low visibility, in getting too close to the very dangers the light was set to warn them off. Captain Earl's gaze was steady, and his eyes were strong from peering into the fogs of New York Harbor. He saw the *Sheffield* strike.

Staten Island was always a convenient rendezvous for wrecking vessels working in New York Harbor. As early as 1843, the Coast Wrecking Company, which was to evolve into the greatest salvage organization in America, had its headquarters there. The lightkeeper sent a messenger to spread the alarm that a ship had run ashore on Romer Shoal. Captain Oliver Vanderbilt, master of the little steamer *Wave* and brother of the famous Commodore Vanderbilt, fired up his boiler and prepared to put to sea, but another skipper was quicker on the take-off and sailed out into the gathering night. Precious time was lost as the other vessel felt its way about the edges of the shoal, decided the going was too hazardous and returned to its anchorage.

By this time the *Wave* was ready for sea, and Captain Vanderbilt had quite a head of steam up himself. The wind had changed into the northwest, and although it was still too rough for a small boat to live, the sea was falling. Patches of moonlight lit the troubled waters as the *Wave* steamed out, towing an empty lighter and carrying a crew of men and boys who had made up their minds they would swim the shoal if they could not reach the wreck in any other way. For two hours they coasted around the edges of the shoal, bucking heavy seas and feeling their way closer and closer in. But all was darkness, and the rescuers found no trace of a ship in distress until they came upon the tangle of rigging and the three masts drifting in the sea. Grimly they accepted the evidence that they had come too late. It appeared that the wreck had gone to pieces and its people had perished while their rescuers had been hunting blindly in the dark. Reluctantly the men on the *Wave* prepared to turn back and give up the search.

Meanwhile, the tide was dropping; but instead of receding within the *Sheffield*'s holds, as had been expected, the water continued to rise. A passenger looking at his watch found it had run down. He started to wind it, then stopped and thrust it back into his pocket, muttering, "I shall have no more use for time." Another man urged to captain to send up the last remaining rocket. Captain Popham — to comfort his passengers, but without hope himself — yielded to the request, but the rocket fizzled out on the deck. Then he lit a blue flare. In the despair of the moment, no one realized that the captain had set off the signal on the ship's lee quarter, which looked out to sea, instead of toward the land, whence they might expect help to come. But, strangely, this was the one spot on the *Sheffield*'s deck from which the blue light could be discerned at that moment by the men on the *Wave*. They headed their small steamer straight across the shoal.

Presently a steerage passenger on the wreck cried out that he saw something dark moving on the water. The *Sheffield*'s officers looked but saw nothing. Again the sharp-eyed passenger insisted there was something, and again he was silenced. The third time he shouted, the captain got out his glass and studied the sea. Yes, he admitted, it was just possible there might be something there. A moment later he lowered his glass and spoke a quiet word of reassurance to the frightened people. Some tiny sparks flew upward in the gloom. A shadow darker than the surrounding water moved across the shoal to within two feet of the stranded vessel. A young tenor voice rose above the cries and shouts of joy from the chanting deck of the *Sheffield*: "Praise God from whom all blessings flow. . . ." Steerage passengers began leaping across the narrow gap to the rescue vessel as scores joined in the familiar hymn: "Praise Him all creatures here below." Six hours later all were safely ashore at New York, and the *Sheffield*'s cargo was being transferred to the lighter which the *Wave* had left behind. A second craft arrived at daylight, and the work of salvage had begun.

Not all such disasters were man-made. Geography had a lot to do with the wreck of the *Alna* of Portland, Maine, in September 1838. On her way from Santiago de Cuba to Boston, she was caught in a northeast gale about fifteen miles off the Florida coast in the narrow Bahama Channel and swept relentlessly toward a lee shore. In her struggle to keep free, her bowsprit was carried away, and the sea made a clear breach over her. Her captain, Charles Thomas, realizing that he could not keep his ship off the land, made a bold decision and ran the *Alna* ashore, head-on, while it was still daylight. His strategy worked successfully: the breakers lifted the brig high on the beach, and her crew jumped safely ashore.

But her plucky captain had not counted on the Seminole Indian wars then in progress. Hardly had he and the five men from the *Alna* planted their feet on dry land when a war party of Indians attacked them and killed all but two. These men plunged into the undergrowth and got away, although one was shot in the hand and hip. The two followed different courses northward along the beach, each believing he was the sole survivor. From piles of wreckage strewn from other shipwrecks

On April 29, 1925, the three-masted schooner *Irma* was driven ashore on the North Carolina coast. Quarterboards, wheel and bell of a total wreck were often carried away as souvenirs.

IRMA
NEW YORK.

along the shore of this dangerous seaway at high-water mark, one of the men picked up a bucket to carry fresh water. Each wandered for days in the blazing sun, swimming rivers with a wary eye for alligators and eating dead fish found on the shore.

The wrecking sloop *Mount Vernon,* patrolling the reefs offshore, sighted one of the men from the *Alna* and sent a boat ashore to pick him up. The following day Captain Alden, continuing his search for survivors, found the other man. The castaways seem to have fared well at the hands of the wreckers, for in an account of their experience published in 1841 they declared:

> It is our humane and highly pleasing duty to say of Captain George Alden and his crew, of the wrecking sloop *Mount Vernon,* that our treatment was in the highest degree kind, hospitable, overgenerous — dressing our wounds, nursing us with parental kindness, giving us clothing, regretting, when we left, that they had no money to give us. . . .
>
> To correct wrong impressions and wicked prejudices, that exist against the wreckers on the coast of Florida, we feel bound by everything sacred to state, that instead of being "plunderers and pirates," as they are often represented, it is the height of their ambition to save lives and property.
>
> S. CAMMETT
> E. WYER, JUN. [3]

Other natural causes that brought many a bark to grief were fog, currents, lightning and watersprouts.

A bolt of lightning ran down the mainmast of the *Oglethorpe* en route from Savannah to Liverpool, on the afternoon of December 27, 1818. It went through the vessel's deck and set fire to her cargo of cotton, deep in the hold. Captain Jayne called out all hands, took in sail, laid the ship to and went to work on the fire. A gale was blowing, and the smoke was so thick that his men could not enter the hold, so he closed down the hatches tightly in hope of smothering the blaze. Then he ordered up a distress signal and called the crew together, frankly explaining the danger and the need for everyone to keep his head and for all to work together through the emergency. First he set them to readying the lifeboat with water and provisions in the event they should be forced to abandon ship. The crew responded willingly, and their confidence in Captain Jayne staved off panic.

At this point the decks — in a line directly across the ship — became so hot that pitch began to ooze out of the seams. As a last resort, axes were brought up and holes were chopped at the hottest places. Water was then poured directly onto the fire. After an hour or so the men were able to scramble into the hold, seize armfuls of the burning cotton, carry it on deck and dump it overboard. But it was difficult to toss the cotton into the sea; eddies of wind caught the loose burning stuff and blew it all over the ship, so that the *Oglethorpe* appeared to be afire from stem to stern. Soon the men had to come up from below and clear the burning cotton from the deck, while the ship herself had to be maneuvered free of the burning material floating in the sea around her.

About seven o'clock the crew returned to the hold and found the fire had gained in their absence. In two hours they had carried out most of the burning cotton, and by nine-thirty (according to the captain's log) the hold was clear. The exhausted men returned to the deck to clear it again and to navigate the *Oglethorpe* out of her surrounding ring of fire. Captan Jayne closed his log for the day simply: "The fire being arrested, we now took half an hour to refresh ourselves. . . ."[4] The danger was past.

Not all masters had the wisdom and skill of Captain Jayne of the *Oglethorpe* or Captain Popham of the *Sheffield.* Ships overturned because of their skippers' bad judgment in carrying too much or too high sail, or they were allowed to broach to by a careless or sleepy helmsman; sometimes they quietly sank in good weather because of worms boring into their wooden bottoms. Sound vessels were overwhelmed by sudden squalls when a captain neglected to put tarpaulins over the open hatches on a short voyage; or they ran aground because the compass was disturbed by a difference between the magnetic and the true axis. Then, too, there were many fraudulent disasters brought about by owners or masters wishing to exchange worthless, worn-out vessels for good coin of the realm, by means of marine insurance. The number of shipwrecks in American waters often reached over 1,500 in a single year. The wonder was that any windjammer ever made port at all.

Captain John Lowe, Jr.'s wrecking schooner, *Rollin B. Sanford,* was a familiar sight in Key West waters during the late 1800s. Lowe won his skipper's license at the salty age of thirteen.

2

The Wrecker, Hero or Knave?

Across this backdrop of dire circumstance strode the wrecker, a swashbuckling, ominous figure in the public imagination of his day. Before the formation of a coast guard or the first vestige of a lifesaving service on American shores — in days when charts of the coast were crude and scarce, and lighthouses little more than whale oil lamps set in two or three places along the coast — the wrecker was at sea, saving lives and property and rendering practical assistance to vessels in distress. He lived under a cloud of disrepute: scavenger of the sea, land pirate and mooncusser were some of the epithets applied to him. His calling was commonly believed to be akin to piracy. From the days of William the Conqueror, the wrecker has been a controversial figure. Old English folklore clothed him in the rig of a scoundrel; history passed him by; and fiction dealt with him irresponsibly.

What are the facts? The wrecker was sometimes merely a seaside farmer or fisherman, eager to help when calamity struck. Again, he was the master of a small vessel, ready, when employed by responsible persons, to sail out to a wreck and strip it of cargo, rigging and sails. But often he was a competent navigator and pilot with a fast, well-equipped vessel and a crew of skilled divers and salvage men, who put to sea voluntarily in all weather to snatch survivors or merchandise from a foundering vessel, pull a stranded ship off into deep water or dive for sunken cargo. As such, the wrecker was a daring and skilled adventurer of the sea, as truly a product of frontier days as was the cowboy or the Indian scout on land.

Nor was the American and Bahamian master wrecker always an unlettered fisherman striving to get up in the world. Many were mariners of broad experience and education, attracted by the speculative nature of wrecking, the life of excitement and the possibility of quick and spectacular profits. They were of the young, eager breed who in a few years would stampede westward at the cry of "Gold!" in that great surge that pushed the boundaries of the United States to the Pacific Ocean.

It is probable that no more reckless sailing of small craft has ever been seen than that of the wreckers of the keys and the cays, the hundreds of islands lying close to the Gulf Stream as it plunges around Florida and up the coast. These men scorned safety ashore and put to sea in any weather, hard-driving their trim, finely rigged craft without benefit of charts or lights. In old court records their exploits still glow with color and action. "Ship *Eastern Star* ashore in a hurricane," runs one such record. "A wrecker tried eighteen hours to reach her. Wrecker lost both masts, all anchors, cables, boats, and spare rigging. Made anchor

Prof. Collier Cobb, Courtesy Miss Mary Cobb

Photographs of early shipwrecks are rare. Only when a vessel was swept high on shore did she survive until a photographer could reach the scene. Such was the wreck of the *Priscilla.*

of old gun, rigged two jury masts, got to the wreck, and saved twenty lives and most of the cargo. Award, 30%." It was an epic in five sentences.[1]

Judge James C. Webb wrote in 1838 that wrecking was "an established and well defined profession, distinct from and unconnected with all other occupations . . . and honorable in itself."[2] It should not be confused with the common practice of beachcombing. On open beaches all along the coast, crowds gathered at times of disaster, helped with rescues and afterwards

made off with portions of the wreckage. These people were not wreckers, though often so called. They were the rank and file of the seaside community, ready and willing to lend a hand in time of need, but without the equipment or skill to render practical assistance to a vessel in distress.

Henry Thoreau recorded the thrill of the beachcomber. In his book *Cape Cod*, he wrote: "We saw this forenoon a part of the wreck of a vessel, probably the FRANKLIN, a large piece fifteen feet square and still freshly painted. With a grapple and a line we could have saved it. . . . It would have been a lucky haul for some poor wrecker, for I have been told that one man who paid three or four dollars for a part of the wreck of that vessel, sold fifty or sixty dollars' worth of iron out of it."

Professional wrecking reached its highest development in the wreckers' city of Key West. There it grew into an exciting, profitable and legally regulated industry. The Key West wrecker, unlike his New England kin, was not a beachcomber wading into the surf to snatch fragments from a hungry sea, nor was he a dealer in the residue of shipwrecks. He was a gay and clever adventurer, devoting full time to his work of rescue and salvage. By dint of enterprise and derring-do, he made himself the coast guard, lifesaver and ocean salvor of his day.

The early wrecker-pilots knew the geography of the great reef. They knew the currents and tides, and they knew their smart, well-fitted vessels. In 1830 every able-bodied man in Key West was a wrecker and proud of it. Some in their spare time were shopkeepers, warehousemen, fishermen, spongers, speculators in salvaged goods, grogshop operators and whatnot. But at the blast of a conch shell or the cry of "Wreck asho-o-re!" every man would drop what he was doing and sprint for the wharf, where a row of sloops and schooners rocked in the jade-green water.

It was a sporting event — the take-off to a wreck — trying the skill of every contestant. From all parts of the town, running men carrying Georgia bundles (spare clothing or hastily snatched-up food) converged on the waterfront. They sprang aboard their waiting craft, flung out jib and mains'l, slipped moorings and drew away from the wharf even as their slower shipmates leaped the widening gap to join them. The first man to speak the wreck became wreck master by the unwritten law of the community; he commanded that particular rescue and salvage venture, choosing whom he wished to assist him from among his eager competitors.

If they found a ship ashore, every man moved at top speed,

for all preparations had to be ready before the next high tide. Usually a casualty struck head-on and had to be hauled off stern first. If she was not bilged (broken below the water line), the wrecker would run out an anchor. In this operation, a heavy anchor attached to a steel cable was dropped into deep water well behind the grounded vessel. The cable was fastened to a winch on the stern of the wreck. When the tide was high and there was the greatest depth of water under the ship, the windlass would be manned and all hands would heave to the limit of their strength. If the grip of the anchor held and the cable did not break, the straining wreckers might haul the vessel off into deep water. If the rising water and the strain failed to loosen and lift the distressed vessel, or if she was large and heavily aground, she had to be lightened before the next tide. This was a fast and furious business — a race to tear open her hatches, thrust aside her top cargo, start to haul up her heavy goods, and get enough weight transferred to the wrecking craft (or jettisoned) to free the ship when the high water exerted its lifting power. Much could happen before another high tide. A suddenly rising sea could pick up the helpless craft and let her down with such force as to break her back, or even reduce her to a pile of wreckage that would slide off bit by bit into deep water and disappear. The job called for the last ounce of strength and nerve of every man. If the weather was bad — and it was apt to be — their chances of success were slighter.

If the wreckers did not succeed in refloating the casualty on the high tide immediately after striking, they were considered to have failed in skill, and the salvage fee for their work was substantially reduced. This fee was fixed by any one of three methods: direct agreement with the master of the distressed vessel, friendly arbitration or action of a court having Admiralty jurisdiction. It was this fee that brought down the wrath of ship captains on the wrecking business. It had to be high: neither the wrecker nor his vessel was subject to insurance of any kind, and the wrecker often lost valuable equipment — sometimes even his ship — in performance of his duties. Each wreck he served had to carry its share of the price of replacements if he was to remain in business. The courts recognized that it was to the advantage of all that he do so, for without his quick and energetic action, many a crew would have perished and many a cargo been lost.

The deep-sea skippers were the wreckers' immemorial adversaries. Tradition and necessity combined in giving the shipmaster complete command of his vessel. The very warp and woof of his position was confidence in his own skill and in his ability to exercise it in defiance of all that sea and wind could do. A moment of mishap or even of outright disaster was no time for a self-respecting skipper to admit his inability to get his ship out of trouble. He usually ordered away the wrecker and strove mightily, both to save his owners a salvage fee and to preserve his own good name as a competent and careful mariner. The wrecker was forced to stand by. "You go out uncalled for and remain even when help is refused," wrote Klaas Toxopeus, noted European salvor, in his great book *The Flying Storm.* "Some captains refuse to believe until the water is up to their necks."

The wrecker had little sympathy to waste on an obstinate skipper. His job was to get hold of the endangered vessel before his competitors arrived on the scene or the sea swallowed it up. He had his own ways of convincing a reluctant shipmaster of the seriousness of his plight. If, perhaps, he painted a grimmer picture than facts warranted, there was always the court to review the case and redress the scales of justice.

Every wrecker made it his business to know salvage law, and know it better than the skippers with whom he dealt. He had to, for without a legal base under his every act, he could easily have become the pirate he was so often supposed to be. Shipmasters derided his services; underwriters distrusted him; and lawyers vied with one another to trap him. Legally he might under some circumstances force his way onto a distressed vessel and take command, if the degree of peril warranted it and the captain showed reluctance to save the ship. With such commandeering possible, and both honest wreckers and crafty adventurers at work, it is not hard to see how wrecking became generally regarded as a shady business. "I was taught to believe that this class of men were an unprincipled set of beings who foraged on the misfortunes of others by plunder and depredation," wrote a correspondent in the *New York Enquirer* in 1827. But he added: "On the contrary, I find them to be decent men of good common sense." [3]

John James Audubon, the noted ornithologist, left an eyewitness account in his *Journal* of a visit with Florida wreckers in the early 1830s:

> Long before I reached the lovely islets that border the southeastern shores of the Floridas, the accounts I had heard of "The Wreckers" had deeply prejudiced me against them. Often had I been informed of the cruel and cowardly methods which it was alleged they employ to allure vessels of all nations to the dreaded reefs, that they might plunder their cargoes, and rob their crews and passengers of their effects. . . . with the name of "wrecker" there were associated in my mind ideas of piratical depredation, barbarous usage, and even murder.
>
> One fair afternoon, while I was standing on the polished deck of the United States revenue cutter, the *Marion*, a sail hove in sight, bearing in an opposite course . . . By and by the vessel, altering her course, approached us. . . . In a short time we were gliding side by side, and the commander of the strange schooner saluted our captain, who promptly returned the compliment. What a beautiful vessel, we all thought, how trim, how clean rigged, and how well manned. She swims like a duck, and now, with a broad sheer, off she makes for the reefs, a few miles under her lee. There in that narrow passage, well known to her commander, she rolls, tumbles, and dances like a giddy thing, her copper sheathing now gleaming, and again disappearing under the waves. But the passage is made, and now, hauling on the wind, she resumes her former course, and gradually recedes from the view. Reader, it was a Florida wrecker. . . .
>
> The duties of the *Marion* having been performed, intimation of our intended departure reached the wreckers. An invitation was sent me to go and see them on board their vessel, which I accepted. Their object on this occasion was to present me with some superb corals, shells, live turtles of the hawk-bill species, and a great quantity of

Many windjammers went down with all on board, leaving not so much as a plank to mark the site. Four crewmen survived the wreck of the *Priscilla*, which occurred near a lifesaving station.

eggs. Not a picayune would they receive in return, but putting some letters in my hands, requested me to be so good as to put them in the mail at Charleston, adding that they were for their wives down east . . . and with sincere regret, and a good portion of friendship, I bade these excellent fellows adieu. How different, thought I, is often the knowledge of things acquired from personal observation, from that obtained by report. I had never before seen Florida wreckers, nor has it since been my fortune to fall in with any. . . .

Mr. Audubon then quotes from a letter he received from a friend, Dr. Benjamin Strobel, who spent a few days with the wreckers:

On the 12th day of September, while lying in harbour at Indian Key, we were joined by five wrecking vessels. Their licenses having expired, it was necessary to go to Key West to renew them. We determined to accompany them the next morning, and here it will not be amiss for me to say a few words respecting these far famed wreckers, their captains and crews. From all that I had heard, I expected to see a parcel of dirty, pirate-looking vessels, officered and manned by a set of black-whiskered fellows, who carried murder in their very looks. I was agreeably surprised on discovering that the vessels were fine large sloops and schooners, regular clippers, kept in first-rate order. The captains generally were jovial, good-humored sons of Neptune, who manifested a disposition to be polite and hospitable, and to afford every facility to persons passing up and down the reefs. The crews were hearty, well dressed, and honest-looking men. On the 18th, at the appointed hour, we all set sail together, that is, the five wreckers and the schooner *Jane*. As our vessel was not noted for fast sailing, we accepted an invitation to go on board of a wrecker. . . . I can scarcely find words to express the pleasure and gratification which I this day experienced. . . . One would never have supposed that these men were professional rivals, so apparent was the good feeling that prevailed amongst them. About nine o'clock we started for supper. A number of persons had already collected, and as soon as we arrived on board the vessel, a German sailor, who played remarkably well on the violin, was summoned to the quarter-deck, when all hands with a good will cheerily danced to lively airs until supper was ready. The table was laid in the cabin, and groaned under its load of venison, wild ducks, pigeons, curlews and fish. Toasting and singing succeeded the supper, and among other curious matters introduced, the following song was sung by the German fiddler, who accompanied his voice with his instrument. He was said to be the author . . . the chorus was trolled by twenty or thirty voices, which in the stillness of the night produced no unpleasant effect.

Dr. Strobel transcribed the song "as it came on my ear":

THE WRECKERS' SONG

Come all ye good people one and all,
Come listen to my song;
A few remarks I have to make,
It won't be very long.
T'is of our vessel, stout and good,
As ever yet was built of wood;
Among the reefs where the breakers roar,
The wreckers on the Florida shore.

Key Tavernier's our rendezvous,
At anchor there we lie;
And see the vessels in the Gulf
Carelessly passing by.
When night comes on we dance and sing,
Whilst the current some vessel is floating in;
When daylight comes, a ship's on shore,
Among the rocks where the breakers roar.

When daylight dawns we are under weigh,
And every sail is set;
And if the wind it should prove light,
Why then our sails we wet.
To gain her first each eager strives,
To save the cargo and the peoples' lives;
Amongst the rocks where the breakers roar,
The wreckers on the Florida shore.

When we get 'longside, we find she's bilged,
We know well what to do;
Save the cargo that we can,
The sails and rigging too.
Then down to Key West we soon will go

When quickly our salvage we shall know;
When every thing it is fairly sold,
Our money down to us it is told.

Then one week's cruise we'll have on shore,
But we do sail again;
And drink success to the sailor lads
That are plowing of the main.
And when you are passing by this way,
On Florida reef should you chance to stray,
Why, we will come to you on the shore,
Amongst the rocks where the breakers roar.[4]

The Spanish brig *Augustina,* or *Agustina,* of Barcelona broke in two in the surf off Monmouth Beach Station on the wild New Jersey shore on February 3, 1880, becoming a total loss.

F. J. Watson, Jr.

3

Wreck and the Crown

The king has wreck of the sea, whales and sturgeons.
De Praerogativa Regis (17 Edward II) 1324

Before we plunge too deeply into the pleasantly befuddling subject of wrecking, a quick look in the direction of its origin may help explain how it got that way. If wrecking ever had a beginning, it was in the struggle out of the deep fogs of superstition that passed for thinking some time ago. Before the Romans took over the known world, the ancient Greeks believed it unlucky to rescue a drowning man. Early Romans put shipwrecked people to death or sold them as slaves, and plundered their belongings. Primitive Britons destroyed all stranded property belonging to those lost at sea. "Save a stranger from the sea, And he will turn your en-e-my," ran an old English rhyme.

The earliest sea laws seem to have come from Rhodes, the first great trade center of the Mediterranan world. As early as 900 B.C., the Rhodian common law of the sea made provision for payment of salvage awards for goods saved at sea.

Article XLV If a ship be surprised at sea with whirlwinds, or be shipwrecked, any person saving anything of the wreck, shall have one-fifth of what he saves.
Article XLVII If gold, or silver, or any other thing be drawn up out of the sea eight cubits deep, he that draws it up shall have one-third, and if fifteen cubits, he shall have one-half, because of the depth. And if anything is cast on the shore by the tide, and taken up only one cubit deep, the finder shall have a tenth part.[1]

There were penalties for looting and for molesting shipwrecked persons. Whoever took anything from a wreck was forced to restore its value fourfold.

The earliest sea trade was from city to city, and most of the Mediterranean ports used these Rhodian laws for hundreds of years. In Rome during the reigns of Tiberius, Vespasian and Hadrian, the imperial court referred maritime cases to Rhodian law. The emperor Antoninus was once appealed to by Eudemon of Nicomedia, whose vessel had been wrecked and plundered on the Italian coast. Antoninus replied: "I am the lord of the world, but the law is the master of the sea. Let thy plaint and controversy, Eudemon, be decided by the law of the Rhodians."

No one can justly say that wrecking was a lawless business. The Egyptians, Greeks, Venetians and Genoese all employed the Rhodian laws. Maritime and salvage codes became man's first halting step toward international law.

During the Dark Ages, sea traffic diminished sharply and from about 900 A.D. to 1100 A.D. died out. Only with the revival of trade following the first Crusades did other European cities begin to write their own sea laws, based on the Lex Rhodia. Barcelona was among the first, with a code known as the Consulate of the Sea. Eleanor of Aquitaine, mother of Richard the Lionhearted, secured a copy and referred it to a special court which met on the island of Oléron — a part of her domain — in the Bay of Biscay. The court accepted the Barcelona regulations and, on that framework, built up the Laws of Oléron, the medieval maritime code which formed the basis of the sea laws of Flanders and England, Lübeck and the other Hanse towns. There were, however, as many variations of this code as there were towns and cities that adopted it. One version, which was probably in use about the time the Normans crossed over into the British Isles, offers a gruesome picture of what the criminal wreckers of the eleventh and twelfth century could expect if they were caught. "If people, more barbarous, cruel, and inhuman than mad dogs, murdered shipwrecked folk,"[2] they were to be plunged into the sea until half dead and then drawn out and stoned to death. Another article provided that

Courtesy The Mariners Museum, Newport News, Va.

William Tracey proposed to "sling" H.M.S. *Royal George*, sunk in 1782 at Spithead, England, a method still used in modified form today. The Royal Navy refused cooperation, backing another plan.

"all false pilots shall suffer a most rigorous and merciless death, and be hung on high gibbots."[3]

Private landowners — the lords of the seacoast manors — employed pilots and set out the guiding lights along the coasts. Articles 35 and 36 declared that if pilots, to ingratiate themselves with their lords, should knowingly run ships upon the rocks, they were to be excommunicated, held accurst and punished as robbers. But the lords were also to be dealt with:

> The wicked lords are to be tied to a post in the middle of their own houses, which shall be set on fire at all four corners, and burnt with all that shall be therein; the goods being first confiscated for the benefit of the persons injured; and the site of the houses shall be converted into places for the sale of hogs and swine.[4]

Should a pilot cause a shipwreck by mere negligence, he was to make good the loss out of his own pocket. If he lacked means to do so, the aggrieved captain and crew were to cut off his head. The law seems to have gone a little soft at this point, however, for it admonishes: "Some care should be taken by the master and mariners that they should be persuaded that the man had not the means to make good the loss, before they cut off his head."[5]

Another code of about the same period — that decreed by the consuls of the old Roman city of Trani in 1063 — provided that anyone who found goods cast upon the sea should be rewarded for their safe return. Within three days of his find, he was to turn the property over to a court, together with a list of the articles retrieved. If the owner showed up within thirty davs, the finder was entitled to half of what he had saved. If not, he got it all.

These early regulations were strict and clear, but just how much attention was paid to them is questionable. Seacoast towns were ever the resort of the homeless, the lawless and the destitute. From every port in Europe, the plundering of vessels wrecked on nearby shores seems to have been carried on ruthlessly throughout the Middle Ages.

Pre-Norman English law gave to the Crown possession of property wrecked on the coasts of that country. Such goods were considered part of the royal revenue, and any rights of their true owner were supposed to have lapsed by action of the sea. This law is said to have been enacted as an effort to protect shipwrecked property from the common people, who were burning it under the superstitious belief that it would otherwise bring them bad luck.

Henry I, the younger son of William the Conqueror, who had a strange hobby of efficient government, was the first to recognize injustice in this arbitrary law of possession. He decreed that a ship should not be considered a wreck if any man on board escaped from it alive. His successor, Henry II, went a bit further and defined wreck of the sea as anything from which no creature, man or beast, had escaped alive.

This old definition was used in court as recently as 1864 when the *Margaret Quail* went aground near Clovelly on the Devonshire coast of England. The wreck was abandoned by her captain and crew, and the lifeboat men of Clovelly took charge of salvaging her cargo. She was a fulsome wreck, and the salvors applied to the court for a fee of £3,000 for their services. To their chagrin, the court ruled that the *Margaret Quail* could not be classed as a wreck, since the captain's dog had been left on board when the crewmen abandoned the ship and was saved alive. The salvors therefore received only £300 instead of the £3,000 for which they had petitioned.

Henry III continued to liberalize the law, ruling that if goods cast ashore had any identifying mark, they should revert to the true owner if claimed within a year and a day. Richard the Lion-hearted came all the way. About 1190, before setting out on the Third Crusade ("for the love of God," he declared, "and the health of his own soul, and the souls of his ancestors and successors, kings of England"), he issued a decree:

. . . all persons escaping alive from a wreck should retain their goods; . . . wreck or wreckage should only be considered the property of the king when neither an owner, nor the heirs of a late owner, could be found for it.[6]

Unidentified wreckage was still taken by the Crown, but the lords of the seacoast manors were soon vigorously contesting that ownership. In 1305, for example, on Tresco in the Scilly Isles, a mob of townspeople headed by the Prior of St. Nicholas locked up William Le Poer, the official coroner, who had come in the interest of the king to inquire about a wrecked ship. In time, some of the lords themselves got into the wrecking business by obtaining grants from the Crown allotting to each man his own "royalty of wreck" — a stretch of seacoast where he could claim the good things the sea tossed up. The law courts were soon busy adjudicating the disputes arising from overlapping jurisdictions of the seaside gentry.

In the same period, Edward III first legalized payment of a fee for the safe return of shipwrecked property to its true owner. By establishing the principle of compensation to persons saving and restoring property lost at sea, he opened the way for wrecking to become a legitimate occupation. But even with royal decrees and acts of Parliament, the return of shipwrecked cargoes to their true owners was easier legislated than enforced. In actual practice, the right of wreckage very often was exercised by the lord of the adjoining manor.

In 1526, for example, the *St. Andrew*, a fine vessel belonging to the king of Portugal, went on the rocks at Gunwalloe off Lands End. Her cargo included 8,000 cakes of copper and eighteen blocks of silver bullion, as well as silver vessels, jewels, tapestry, Flemish cloth, a chest of musical instruments, four sets of armor for the king and harness for his horses. The country people gathered on the beach from miles around, rescued the crew and brought ashore a good portion of the cargo. As the work of salvage was in full swing, three magistrates — representing the three leading families or lords of the manor residing in the

Courtesy The Mariners Museum, Newport News, Va.

The methods actually employed by the East India Company and the Royal Navy in removing the wreck of H.M.S. *Royal George* from anchorage at Spithead are shown in this contemporary lithograph.

district — marched down to the wreck at the head of fifty or sixty retainers armed with swords and bows. They attacked the shipwrecked sailors and their helpers, and made off with the merchandise.

This was the popular version of the affair. The three lords, on the other hand, claimed that one of their number had ridden into town to help in the rescues. Arriving on the scene, he found the ship's company destitute and very little of the ship's goods brought ashore. In an effort to help the shipwrecked crewmen, he and his two friends had paid the captain of the vessel twenty pounds — then a small fortune — in a lawful bargain, the captain turning over to them all the salvaged material. (It is a curious fact that the goods seized were the Portuguese wares and that early laws prohibiting the importation of goods or articles "fully wrought and ready made for sale" specifically excepted goods which came into the realm by way of shipwreck.)

So much for early efforts to regulate wrecking. Unlettered countrymen living on the islands and beaches of Cornwall knew little about the law and probably cared less. When news of a shipwreck sped from family to family up and down the shore, excited crowds gathered opposite the laboring vessel. Men and women came with pickaxes, hatches, ropes and crowbars. They waited only for the ship to strike, then fell upon her as fair plunder.

On the Cornwall coast and the Scilly Isles, where age-old poverty had been the lot of the tin miners, the avid plunderers stopped at nothing, but tore ship and cargo to pieces and dragged away the last plank. If the cargo chanced to be wine or spirits, as it often did, there was a frenzied scramble of half-drunken men and women wrangling and fighting to stave in the casks and fill pans, kettles, pails and pitchers. A local Parson Troutbeck is credited with a famous addition to the Litany: "We pray Thee, O Lord, not that wrecks should happen, but that if wrecks do happen, Thou wilt guide them into the Scilly Isles, for the benefit of the poor inhabitants."

In the reign of George II a new law was passed setting death as the penalty for placing false lights, killing or preventing the escape of shipwrecked persons, or stealing goods from a wreck, whether there was a living creature on board or not. Later the death penalty was changed to imprisonment. Penal servitude for life was prescribed for willfully scuttling, wrecking or setting fire to a ship in an effort to defraud insurance officers or owners.

Legends of intentional wrecking — the luring of ships to their destruction by various devices — are found in all English-speaking countries. They seem to have started on the Cornish coast of England, where the savage seas have driven so many ships to their doom on the rocky shore. There bodies of the drowned were sometimes stripped of clothing, dismembered and even beheaded by the action of the pounding surf. The legends of murdered seamen and plundered corpses probably stem from such tragic circumstances, for there is no historical record that false lights or intentional luring of a vessel onto the rocks ever actually occurred on that coast.

The half-starved miners did, however, often leave the mines and follow a ship along the shore in the hope it would strike. Men earning as little as sixteen shillings a month were taught from the cradle that they had a right to such spoils as the sea brought in. In their sight, only injustice — backed by local authority and sanctioned by law — would tear such booty from their grasp. Someone made up a rhyme when the ship *Good Samaritan* drove aground at Bedruthen Steps on October 22, 1846:

> The *Good Samaritan* came ashore
> To feed the hungry and clothe the poor.
> Barrels of beef and bales of linen,
> No poor man shall want a shillin'.

A long-famous "tea wreck" brought tea to people who had never been able to buy it, and a "coffee wreck" gave them their first taste of that beverage.

Cornishmen in general have always been ready to aid when

disaster struck their coast. In the wreck of the *Boscawen* at St. Ives on April 19, 1745, a vessel belonging to a well-known privateer, Commodore George Walker, crashed ashore in a great storm. In his journal the Commodore declared:

The people of the sea coast of Cornwall have for some years undergone the censure of being savage devourers of all wrecks, that strike against their coasts. How weak a creature is general belief, the dupe of idle fame! Humanity never exercised its virtues more conspicuously than in this instance, in the inhabitants and people of St. Ives. They flocked down in numbers to our assistance; and, at the risque of many of their own lives, saved ours. Mr. Walker would not be previled upon to quit the ship, till he had seen the sick lifted thro' the cabin windows into the boats; bidding all, without distinction, provide for themselves, as he was capable of swimming: but he was himself, at last, lifted out by two of the townsmen, strangers to him, who went upon the wreck to bring him off. . . . When they came into the town, every body's house was open to them in all the offices of assistance: but above all other instances which could be given of the generosity of the place, gratitude must here pay her greatest debt, in remembering John Stevens, Esq; whose unwearied activity, liberality, and prudence, in aiding, befriending, and directing our affairs, are without paralellel, [*sic*] except in other like actions of his own. . . . When we mention this gentleman as most distinguishable amongst many others, we do not forget to acknowledge the debts of obligations we owe to the mayor, the magistrats, and other gentlemen of the town, whose invitations, readiness to serve, and other acts of civility, rendered them ever worthy the best report of their deserving. The first night Mr. Walker made all his officers sleep under their arms, as he did the like, to be in readiness, in case of any attack against the wreck; and accordingly so it happened, for in the night the miners came down, and were setting about sharing the wreck amongst them. At the very first alarm, the mayor himself was up, and a party of the town, who went in arms with Mr. Walker against them, dispersed the croud, and took two of the men prisoners: these are a people the civil power are scarcely answerable for, at least for their good manners, as they live almost out of the districts of human society, and may be said to be no visible inhabitants of the earth, tho' they act in the world. The time during their stay, which was upwards of three weeks, was solely employed in taking care of the wreck; and thro' the assistance of the aforesaid gentlemen and others, every thing and matter was taken care of with as much and more exactness, than if the wreck had lain at the shore of Dartmouth, or the doors of the proprietors; and a great part was saved to a considerable amount.[7]

Local folk tales claim that false lights were displayed in a number of places overlooking the sea by avaricious landowners in order to bring about more profitable shipwrecks. These points include St. Donat's Castle, near Barry, and Dunraven Castle, high over the Oger estuary. A hill near Gilman Point is still called Beacon Hill, supposedly so named because wreckers exhibited their lights there.

In 1619 inhabitants of the Lizard, a peninsula just east of Lands End, petitioned against erection of a lighthouse, claiming that it would deprive them of God's special provision for their welfare — that is, of the shipwrecks which strewed their coast with supplies.

The noun "wreck" originally meant anything without an apparent owner that was found afloat upon, sunk in or cast ashore by the sea. As the seaside gentry increased their efforts to gain possession of property grounded on their domains, a distinction was made between "wreck proper" and other types of wreckage. Wreck proper was property left or cast upon the land by the sea — property on which no life had survived and which offered no means by which it could be identified. Such property could be claimed by the owner of the land upon which it was flung, providing he had obtained a grant from the Crown to his "royalty of wreck." Otherwise, the property went to the sovereign.

Other wreckage — known as flotsam, jetsam, ligan and derelict — only became wreck after it had been cast ashore. Flotsam was fragments of a ship or cargo afloat on the sea. Jetsam was goods cast overboard from a ship to lighten it when in trouble. Ligan was heavy articles allowed to sink to the bottom of the sea but attached to a buoy or float so they could be recovered. A derelict was a vessel abandoned by its crew at sea. The right to retrieve any of these was occasionally delegated by the king to his ministers or others.

Little by little, men learned to salvage and protect shipwrecked property. This activity became known as "wrecking" and the men who engaged in it "wreckers." It became the duty of the courts to award to the wrecker a suitable sum of money or merchandise for his services. This was known as salvage.[8] The true owner received the remainder of the property, less expenses, if he appeared and claimed it within a year and a day; otherwise his share went to the Crown (or, in later years, to the underwriters).

The granting of money awards to volunteer salvors is peculiar to maritime law and had its beginnings in antiquity. Anyone who at a risk to himself voluntarily saved another's property from peril at sea was to be rewarded by a bounty well in excess of the compensation that might be due him merely for the labor involved. In this way began the legitimate occupation of wrecking.

4

Mar Caribe: The Spanish Main

Early in the sixteenth century, the eyes of the Old World were turned hopefully to the newly discovered lands of the West. Long before any colonies were planted on the American mainland, the first trickle of what soon would be a flood of settlers — political and religious refugees, prison inmates and sturdy pioneer folk — had found its way across the Western Ocean, following Columbus' course into the islands of the warm southern sea. Among them were many homeless men, maritime stragglers and misfits, seamen set adrift when their ships were laid up, and irreconcilable survivors of the defeated Huguenot navy.

All who came into the Caribbean area, whether innocently or defiantly, fell under the long shadow of Spain that lay across the island-dotted sea. Columbus had arrived there ahead of them all, landing in the Bahamas in 1492. The following year, at Spain's prompting, Pope Alexander VI had issued a series of bulls confirming to Spain the ownership of whatever new lands might be discovered west of the meridian 360 leagues west of the Cape Verde Islands, and to Portugal everything new that lay east of it. On the strength of this claim, Spain had moved into the Caribbean as its sole proprietor. At once she had declared illegal — and classed as smuggling — any trading whatsoever by vessels of other nations. Non-Spanish settlers were adjudged enemies to be driven out or exterminated. These were brutal actions, but in line with the accepted colonial policy of the time.

Spain was not interested in planting colonies as such. Few Spaniards of that day wished to leave their homes to settle permanently in a far-off heathen land. They had a country of their own, uncrowded and united since the Jews and Moors had been expelled. What they sought was gold and silver with which to develop Spain and to build the strongest army and navy in Europe. Spanish settlements in the New World were little more than bases from which to seize the gold and ship it to the Spanish treasury, depleted by years of armed conflict at home. The gentle Arawak Indians, so easily enslaved, became another important source of income; and the slave trade rose in importance until it was second only to the plate fleets that yearly carried the treasure of the Mexican and South American nations to Spain through the perils of an unknown ocean.

As word got around Europe of what was happening in the Caribbean, the enemies of Spain (she was nearly always at war with somebody) sent privateers to the New World to prey upon the treasure fleets. These privately outfitted fighting craft were commissioned to act as men-of-war and to seize and plunder enemy shipping and settlements — a method of warfare then held highly respectable. This led Spain to build bigger and faster galleons and to sail them in convoy for protection.

Once a year the treasure-carrying armada crossed the Atlantic. Ships laden with precious metals from South America would meet at the Isthmus of Panama and sail together to Havana, Spain's greatest port in the New World. There they would join a second squadron carrying gold from Mexico, which the Spaniards called New Spain. The combined fleet then entered the bottleneck of the Florida Straits and the Bahama Channel, passing Cayo Hueso and riding the Gulf Stream north past Bermuda, then turning east as they approached Cape Hatteras on the Carolina coast. A very old map, believed to have been drawn in the sixteenth century, shows a line traced from the northern end of Cuba almost to Key West, then veering northeast to the "sea of the British Empire." Along this line is written: "The galleons and fleet usually leying at Habana and the whole Spanish armada sails for Spain by this line."[1] The Bahama Channel and the Straits had become the lifeline of Spanish conquest.

The Spanish admirals did their best in this danger-fraught passage but their best was not always good enough. The galleons were top heavy and unseaworthy, and many were lost. More than once an entire fleet, carrying a year's take of precious metals and jewels, ran into a hurricane and was scattered or sunk. In the sixteenth century, forty-one known treasure-filled vessels went to the bottom; in the seventeenth century, thirty-eight more joined them. The approximate locations of many of these plate wrecks were known, and they have presented a lure to the wrecker and the treasure-seeker from that day to this.

Spanish ships coming to the New World were usually too heavily laden with men, horses, arms and ordnance to carry supplies to the Spanish settlements. Luxuries, and even the necessities of life, often had to be smuggled in by traders of other nationalities. Such vessels were officially forbidden to come within fifteen miles of any Spanish shore; but they were secretly welcomed, and illicit trade was brisk. The smugglers had to go ashore furtively in remote places to obtain fresh water and shoot game for food, or to careen their ships, which had to be scraped clean of marine growth about three times a year. This led to the rise of smugglers' hideouts or gathering places at covert points throughout the islands.

On the American side of the Bahama Channel, no permanent settlements were established until well into modern times. Florida at that time was Spanish territory and extended from fifty leagues west of the Mississippi River to the Atlantic Ocean; northward it had no boundary.

After the early Spaniards there came into the Caribbean a variety of small ships — British, French, Dutch, Portuguese, Swedish and Danish — beating their way among the islands, innocent of what lay beneath the lime-green sea. Some were able to put their human freight ashore, but many were claimed by the reefs, the shoals and the storms. For a time, plantations began to take form here and there; land was cleared, and houses went up. Herds of cattle, goats and swine were turned loose to stock some of the islands with fresh meat, for Europeans had not learned to eat green food to any great extent. Then the Spanish ships came from Havana to raid the little, new villages, burn the plantations and kill or drive away the settlers. Those who escaped with their lives were mainly men and boys; either the women had not yet come in any great numbers, or they perished more quickly. The fugitives escaped to sea on whatever sailing craft was at hand, and became roving, outlaw bands of destitute and vengeful men.

As early as 1629, Spain was burning the plantations of the French and English on Santo Domingo and St. Kitts. Next she moved against the Dutch, Portuguese, Swedes and Danes, making fugitives of any who escaped her raiding parties. If their boats were destroyed, they hid in the forests and became hunters, living on game and fish. Few had the means to return to their native lands. These outcasts were tough, hardy men in a cruel age, drawn together by the camaraderie of misfortune.

Meanwhile the attraction of the New World was drawing new colonies across the sea. In 1647 the Eleutherian Adventurers, a party of about one hundred Protestant gentlemen with their families and servants, obtained a grant of land in the Bahama Islands from Oliver Cromwell's Parliament. As was customary with Englishmen leaving their country, the Eleutherians secured a permit to fish for sunken wreck and treasure in the seas adjacent to their new homes. It was their intention to set up a "re-public" in which all men would be equal and would enjoy a just government and religious freedom, including the very unusual right of individual dissent. Each family contributed £100 and signed a paper, the "Articles and Orders of the Eleutherians Adventurers," which deserves a place among the world's noblest documents. As to wrecking, the charter declared:

> That whatsoever Ordnance can be recovered of any wrecks, shall be wholly employed for the use of the public, and serve for the fortification of the Plantation. That all other wrecks which shall be recovered upon, or near the Islands . . . shall be delivered into the

custody of two such persons . . . as shall be yearly chosen by the said Company for that purpose.[2]

Provision was made to sell what could be salvaged from the wrecks and to divide the proceeds: one-third to the public treasury, one-third to the finder and one-third to be shared equally among the original Adventurers or their heirs.

The following year, the Adventurers reached the New World. Not surprisingly, the Eleutherians got themselves shipwrecked on the present site of Nassau, but finding the soil there unsuited to agriculture, they made repairs and sailed on until they came to Segatoo, a fertile island fronting on deep water. This they named Eleuthera (from the Greek *eleutheros,* the free) and here they cleared the land and built their homes. These people, the forefathers of American wrecking, were strong, law-abiding, friendly settlers — a remarkable gathering at a time of confusion and lawlessness, when honest men were few and hard to find.

The raiding Spanish soon found the Eleutherian colony and burned the houses and the standing crops. Some of the people fled, but others returned, replanted and stayed put. An early letter to England shows the character of the group: it urgently requested "small arms and ammunition, a godly preacher and a good smith."[3]

It was a far cry from the orderly affairs of these settlers to the violence, looting and outright piracy that swept the area in the next half-century. Bands of fugitives roving among the islands — drawn together by hunger, the need for companionship and shared resentment against the power that had outlawed them — congregated on the depopulated island of Hispaniola, where large herds of cattle and pigs ran wild. Here they encountered illicit traders, who stopped there to revictual their ships and who taught them the Indian method of sun-drying their meat by cutting it into thin strips and hanging it in a storage shed called a buccan.

There was an abundance of meat. Some of the fugitives tried curing a quantity of it and selling it illegally in the Spanish settlements. The meat was good, and the hungry people were eager for it. A brisk butcher trade soon sprang up which earned for the fugitives the name of buccaneers. Meat smuggling quickly became so extensive and brought the buccaneers so many recruits that they needed a storehouse which would be safely hidden from Spanish eyes. Just off the shore of Hispaniola lay the rocky little island of Tortuga (the turtle). High on its rocks was a cave and a spring of fresh water. Here, in 1629, the buccaneers built their storehouse, surrounded by a stockade. The only approach was a narrow cleft in the rocks which they destroyed with gunpowder, leaving no ingress except by a ladder let down from the top.

It was eight years before their enemies got around to attacking Tortuga. By that time it had earned the name of a piratical hideout. Picking a time when most of the buccaneers were away, the Spanish raiders destroyed the warehouse and killed the few settlers they found there. This disaster did not stop the buccaneers, but it changed the direction of their activities and brought them into open hostility with Spain. Soon they had banded into a rude organization, which they named "The Brethren of the Coast."

Contrary to popular belief, buccaneering did not grow out of sea robbery, but from the determination of tough frontiersmen to live in a hostile world by the only means left to them — violence. They set up a code of conduct by which they shared food, responsibilities and property. Each man pledged himself to deal fairly and honorably with the others. They all wore the same type of clothing: short pants, shirt belted outside, Spanish hat with the brim cut off except for a peak in front. They usually camped together in pairs. All forswore marriage: if one took a woman, he was driven out of the brotherhood. They became expert hunters, using Spanish dogs gone wild. Each morning they killed an animal for breakfast, sent a haunch back to camp for the midday meal and gave the remainder to the dogs.

The buccaneers were driven by three passions — hatred of

Spain, lust for wealth and love of adventure. But before very long, the first of these so outweighed the other two that a savage desire for vengeance led them into acts of inhumanity and utmost ferocity. As the brotherhood grew in numbers and strength, it withdrew from smuggling and began a series of armed reprisals against Spain — a sort of private war, in which its members seized and plundered her ships and burned and pillaged her settlements. The loot collected was sold at bargain prices in the American and British colonies on the mainland, all the way from Charleston to Boston, and even as far away as Ireland. This harassment continued actively from about 1625 to 1697.

The buccaneers were not pirates. They claimed the status of privateers and operated much the same way. The main difference was that a privateer carried letters of marque from its home government, commissioning it as an independent, privately outfitted man-of-war authorized to prey upon enemy shipping. A buccaneer captain had no such papers; but with the development of such capable leaders as Sir Henry Morgan, Pierre le Grand and Francois l'Ollonois, the buccaneers became strong, successful and, in time, greatly feared. They eventually built their own ships and used their own type of guns (called Buccaneer muskets), made in France by Brochire of Dieppe and Galin of Nantes.

In 1654 the British government under Cromwell sent Admiral Sir William Penn and General Venables to the West Indies in an attempt to crush Spanish power in that area. They were joined by a number of friendly buccaneer vessels, and the combined force attacked and captured the large island of Jamaica. This action gave the buccaneers harbors and bases from which they could carry on their war against Spain — a war in which they were joined by many British privateers, following the vengeful example of Sir Francis Drake. The privateers operated, under British law, which provided that enemy goods captured on the high seas during wartime by a properly commissioned privateer should be taken before a court, condemned and sold, with the proceeds to be divided among the captors.

But privateers or buccaneers could operate only so long as enemy shipping was plentiful enough to keep them in prize money or plunder with which to pay off their crews. When this supply failed, the honest ones turned back. But men who had become morally infected by the violence, brutality and power of buccaneering sometimes took the next easy step and attacked any merchant vessel that came their way, regardless of its nationality. These men had become pirates.

Piracy is a phase of maritime robbery through which many societies have passed. The Phoenicians and the Vikings were pirates, as were the Barbary Coast traders. The same word might have been applied to the early Normans and the Romans. In seventeenth-century England, the inhabitants of coastal towns thought nothing of sailing out to sea to attack passing ships. Indeed, English coastal towns have been known to attack and plunder each other. In Queen Elizabeth's reign it was difficult to distinguish piracy from legal warfare, the methods of action were so similar. Between 1563 and 1618, the number of known English pirates increased from 400 to nearly 4,000.

Conditions in the West Indies offered a training ground for piracy and nurtured it for several hundred years. Rich cargoes of silver and gold roused the rapacity of the unscrupulous. Piratical activity thrived on the chaotic condition of the small settlements and the inability of the European powers to police the western Atlantic coast. It was reinforced by buccaneers and privateers who lacked moral fiber to hew to their own rude honor; by the absence of women, children and family life; and by the large numbers of seafaring men thrown out of work in Europe when ships were laid up at the close of each war. These men soon became desperate enough to sign on for any sort of a voyage, on any terms — or no terms at all but a share in the profits of the expedition — and no questions asked. Piracy was operating on a global scale even before organized trade was set up between the Old World and the New.

A piratical venture was usually a one-man affair, the man being a daring scoundrel who held power over his crew by rousing their greed, or their fear, or both. When these two passions were spent, he usually lost control and the expedition came to grief. A successful pirate required three things—plenty of shipping on which to prey; a locality with an indented shore line or small islands, behind which he could lie in wait for passing ships; and a safe, remote market for his plunder. The West Indies provided all three, and suffered most. But for generations, the whole Atlantic coast was subject to piratical forays.

By 1700, there were few settlements, honest or otherwise, left in the Bahamas or on the Florida coast. The buccaneers had disappeared, merged with the legitimate navies of Spain's enemies. Outright piracy was riding the seas, and the few non-Spanish towns that were left were little more than gathering places for freebooters. To make matters worse, France and Spain united in 1703 to expel the English from Nassau. As neither country wished to occupy the city, it became another haunt for lawlessness, one more gathering place for pirate crews between voyages.

England, in the grip of commercial expansion, began to feel the pressure of piracy on her sea-borne trade. Lloyd's, even then the nerve center of British shipping, clamored for more effective action against the West Indian pirates, who were beginning to reach out into other parts of the world. Eventually the British government sent Captain Woodes Rogers, a renowned navigator and administrator, with orders to suppress piracy and establish a colonial government at Nassau. Rogers was well equipped for his job. As part owner and commander of two privateers, he had sailed around the world harrying Spanish commerce. His capture of a Spanish treasure ship had brought him wealth and made him a national hero. Today we know him best as the mariner who rescued Alexander Selkirk, the original of Defoe's fictional Robinson Crusoe.

Rogers' ultimatum to the pirates that they renounce lawlessness, take an oath of allegiance to the British Crown and be pardoned *or else* was successful, mainly because of the patience and ability of the man himself. Pirates by the hundred decided to call it a day. Some authorities claim that almost a thousand surrendered, sooner or later. With this dubious material and a sprinkling of second- or third-generation Eleutherians, Governor Rogers set up a representative govenment in Nassau in 1729 and stabilized the colony. In his House of Assembly he brought into being an approximation of the popular form of government envisioned in the Eleutherian charter.

As the false stimulus of piracy began to fade, the economic reaction was severe. Men accustomed to excesses of meat and drink were now forced to live on only the meager supplies sent from England. Even these were soon used up. Former seafarers — freebooters and maritime misfits — were forced to become self-supporting in an agricultural frontier community which had neither export crops nor raw materials. Life became very much a hand-to-mouth affair. A shipwreck producing food and supplies for free or a pirate selling his plunder for a pittance, were events of first magnitude. Governor Rogers once observed: "Thus they live poorly and indolently with a seeming content, and pray for wrecks or pirates."

This glance back along the vista of West Indian history explains why the skull and crossbones may be found even today in the closet of many a Bahamian family. It accounts, too, for the bold seamanship, hardihood and zest for danger which ran in the blood for generations from father to son. And it may offer a canny hint as to how those qualities, through the passage of time and the pressure of near starvation, were transmitted into a new and adventurous calling — a trade which was to reap as rich a harvest from the sea as ever a piratical ancestor dreamed about.

5

Packhorse of the King

British monarchs were generous in parceling out the waters of distant seas. James II, William III and Queen Anne dealt out such grants, regally appropriating the seas of the entire Western Hemisphere for the purpose. "The sea is the packhorse of the king" was a common legal concept. Sometimes a sovereign would lend a vessel and crew to a well-favored adventurer on the promise of a good slice of whatever he should bring home.

Even before the Spanish caravels or the first European colonists came to America, feeling their way along the coast of the new continent, the red men had learned to build seagoing canoes and sail them skillfully. As time went by, the men of the coastal tribes must have gathered in wonder around many a strange shipwreck on the beach, then swarmed over it and carried away the beautiful and unfamiliar objects they found among its broken timbers.

Oriental junks and fishing craft manned by dead men are known to have been carried by the Japan current across the Pacific and left on the shores of Oregon. Years before the first explorers entered the Columbia River, the Clatsop Indians came upon a waterlogged vessel wallowing in the surf south of the river's entrance. Two bearded, white castaways sat huddled before a fire on the beach. The Indians clambered onto the wrecked vessel, where they found bright beads and trinkets of trade goods. The white men were friendly and helped them remove everything of value. This accomplished, the Indians looked on in wonder as the castaways set fire to the wreck and carefully removed every piece of iron and copper it contained.

Clatsop tribal lore today tells of Konapee, the ironworker, who came out of the sea to live among them, and how his skill with metal won for him the respect and admiration of the tribe. Early explorers in Oregon came upon an elderly Indian who spoke broken English and showed plainly his white ancestry. This man claimed to be the son of a white man shipwrecked near the mouth of the Great River of the West. If he was indeed the offspring of the ironworker, his age would have dated the shipwreck at somewhere near 1725.

On the South Atlantic shores of the continent, the coastal Indians knew and sailed the deep waters of the Hawk Channel for centuries. When Anton de Alaminos discovered the passage in 1519 from one of Ponce de Leon's vessels, it became the official route of the Spanish plate fleets and the earliest settlers. Until late in the seventeenth century, the Indians of the area looted vessels they found wrecked along the shore. The Arawaks — gentle and handsome fisher folk who, according to Columbus, owned no weapons — and their more warlike neighbors, the Caribes, paddled their dugout canoes to the remains of many a brave ship, picked up bits of bright metal and puzzled over the drowned bodies of strange, pale men. The Spanish historian Fontaneda, writing in 1551, describes such an incident:

> I wish to speak of the riches that the Indians of Ais found, which must have been a million or more in bars, gold and things of jewelry made by the hands of the Indians of Mexico which the passengers were carrying, which were shared by the chiefs of Ais, Jeaga, Guacata, Mayajuaca, and Mayaca [places in Florida]. . . . They are rich as I have said, from the sea and not from the land. . . . But on all the coast . . . there is neither base nor fine gold because that which they have comes from the ships of Mexico and Peru which are wrecked on Cape Canaveral or in the Keys.[1]

The Calusas, so-called Spanish Indians of southern Florida, sometimes ventured as far as the Spanish settlement of Havana on trading expeditions. Some historians believe they maintained a rude ferry across the Straits to Cuba. The Indians brought as barter objects that could only have come from European ships wrecked on the reefs near their homes.

In 1605 several venturesome sea traders from London were stranded on the West Indian island of Santa Lucia. They were trading from their ship's small boat, laden with trade goods, when their crew mutinied and made off with the ship. One of the traders, John Nicholl, eventually made his way back to England by way of Mexico and Spain. In his account of his adventure, Nicholl lamented that he had been forced by circumstances to leave behind on Santa Lucia large quantities of shipwrecked goods salvaged by the Indians:

> A little before our arrivall, three Spanish ships were cast away, and much of the goodes these Indians had saved with their Boats, and hid it in the Woods, they had so much Roancloath, that all their Periagoes had sayles thereof. They also had great store of stuffe, Sirge, and Spanish woollen cloath, cloakes and apparell; insomuch that if we had had a Barke of fortie tuns burthen, wee could have loaden her home with such commodities as would have made a saving voyage. All which we could have bought for hatchets, knives, beads, fish-hookes, and thimbles, with other trifles.[2]

In 1624, four years after the landing of the Pilgrims at Plymouth Rock, the small English vessel *Sparrow Hawk* sailed with settlers and supplies for the Virginia colony. The voyage was prolonged by the mariners' ignorance of the coast, and scurvy broke out on board; the captain himself could only lie in his cabin doorway and give orders. The passengers became panicky and soon demanded that they be set ashore at the first sight of land, regardless of where it was.

That night the weather was rough. The tiny vessel touched land during the night and drifted ashore in the morning near the site of the present town of Orleans, on Cape Cod. As the passengers climbed down to the beach, a band of friendly Nauset Indians, led by Chief Samoset appeared and made them understand that there were other white men nearby. The Indians carried a message to Plymouth and led a group of Pilgrims back to the *Sparrow Hawk*. They brought corn, repair materials and tools; but before the vessel could be refloated, another storm drove her up on the shore, a complete wreck.

There she lay for 200 years. Salt meadows built up around her, and low dunes covered her completely. Only the fearsome power of the coastal storms, cutting new channels and stirring the sea bed to its depths, brought the *Sparrow Hawk* once again into the light. With gentle hands, she was taken from the sand bit by bit, carried to the Plymouth museum and reconstructed. She rests today in state, a true contemporary of the *Mayflower* and a tribute to the friendliness shown by Indians to the early invaders.

In 1657, Indians on Long Island were responsible for the rescue of all the Dutch immigrants on the *Prins Maurits,* which was lost on Fire Island. The red men served as guides, taking the distraught people safely to the Dutch city of Nieuw Amsterdam (now New York).

Fifty or sixty years later, Antonio Gomez, encouraged by visits of friendly Florida Indians bringing shipwrecked goods for barter to the Spanish city of Havana, set up the first trading post in Spanish Florida. For his site he chose Indian Key, an islet destined to loom large in the annals of wrecking.

By the mid-nineteenth century, the Calusa and Tequesta tribes of south Florida — or such remnants as had survived the long series of Indian wars by hiding in the mazes of the Everglades — became friendly with the keepers of the isolated Cape Florida lighthouse. When hunting was poor and hunger stalked the tribes, the Indians would visit the lighthouse and pitch camp at the base of the tower, sleeping at night in the empty lower rooms under cheesecloth mosquito nets. They brought bolts of water-soaked cloth, cooking utensils, Oriental rugs and other strange articles they had fished up from wrecked vessels in the area. These goods they offered the lightkeeper in trade for provisions.

Relations between the Indian salvors and the white families were cordial. In Miami the story is still told of one lightkeeper's wife who went to waken her children for breakfast on a chilly mid-winter morning and found an Indian brave peacefully asleep in bed with them. When indignantly routed out, the guest meekly explained that he had come during the night and, being cold, had crawled under the covers with the children to keep warm.

When the first British settlers arrived in the New World, they recognized in theory the traditional right of the Crown to unclaimed wreck of the sea. In practice, beachcombing was a favorite and profitable activity from Canada to Barbados. Weather-wise colonists along the waterfront knew when the wind and tide were right for flotsam and jetsam to wash ashore, and vied with each other to get down to the beach after a storm. If a spar or a good oak beam was too heavy for the finder to pick up and carry home, his initials plainly marked on it were respected by his neighbors until he could return with horse and cart to haul it away.

The well-known resistance of the Yankee colonies to British overlordship may have had something to do with their disregard of the king's right to what the sea brought in. From earliest times, each colonist took what drifted ashore as a stroke of fortune and let it go at that. Local officers who held authority under the Crown vigorously condemned such behavior, but they could do little to prevent it. A stranded vessel usually had been reduced to driftwood or to a sodden, overturned wreck before anyone in authority found out about it or could reach the scene. Its more or less valuable cargo had long since vanished into the sea — or into the barns of farmers and fishermen along the shore.

This was the state of the public conscience when the coastal trader *Marey* was blown ashore at Montauk Point, on the eastern tip of Long Island, in 1763. Captain Samuel Vetch, her master, had been "a-smuggling" — that is, trading illegally with "foreign plantations" in eastern Canada. To save themselves from the wreck, he and his crew abandoned the *Marey* and got safely ashore. When the wreck was reported, the king's revenue man promptly took charge of it and placed it in the custody of the local sheriff and several other substantial citizens living nearby. Then he set out for the city, where he would get horses and wagons to transport the *Marey*'s cargo to New York. The round trip took a number of days, and by the time he got back, much of her lading had disappeared. First the brandy, then the dress goods and other useful articles seemed to melt away.

The revenue officer and the sheriff stirred up a commotion, and an official search was carried out in a number of seaside homes. Portions of the *Marey's* lading were found in several houses. One indignant farmer declared that he had received seven pieces of cloth in payment for his services in relieving the wreck and that he had traded them for a bound boy to serve him thirteen years. The king's men seem to have gotten the worst of it, as usual. To mitigate their discomfiture they arrested the luckless master of the *Marey,* who, in addition to his other losses, was obliged to pay a fine for trading with the French and Indians.

Sea-borne commerce was the lifeblood of the early colonies. Though under British law they could exchange goods only among themselves, the colonists were out-and-out traders from the start. They built their own ships and ventured far afield in search of profit, blithely ignoring the laws intended to stop them, and fighting off Spanish men-of-war when necessary.

From 1620 to 1642, about 18,000 people migrated from Great Britain to the Virginia and New England colonies, and another 36,000 to the islands in the West Indies and Bahamas. These colonies were linked to each other and to the mother country by an ever-growing fleet of windjammers. When the civil war in England cut off American ships from British ports, the shipper-merchants of New England had to look elsewhere for markets for their fish, lumber and produce. As early as 1636, a son of Governor Winthrop of Massachusetts had sent a small sloop to Bermuda and found a ready market for the corn, smoked pork and cured fish she carried. Other enterprising traders followed, going farther and farther into the Caribbean area.

The West Indies were nearer New England by 1,500 miles than were the markets of Europe, and trade was soon looking southward. In 1676, Edward Randolph wrote:

The Massachusetts Bay colony owns 430 ships. . . . Most of these traffick with the West Indies and with most ports of Europe, freighting their own products and those of other colonies and distributing return cargoes among all the colonies and West Indies, so that there is little left for the merchants residing in England to import into any of the plantations . . . Boston may be esteemed the market town of the West Indies.[3]

In addition to the lucrative West Indies ventures, Providence Plantation (now Rhode Island) was soon up to its eyebrows in the slave trade. This involved carrying rum to Africa to exchange for slaves; taking the slaves to Jamaica to exchange for sugar; bringing the sugar to Newport to make more rum to get more slaves to exchange for more sugar to make more rum — with a sound profit at every stop. Soon frontier stores were showing signs that read: "We have West India goods," which meant a supply of rum and treacle. So much rum was coming into the colonies or being made there that a small, rural store in Maine sold ninety hogsheads of it in a single winter.

In time thousands of windjammers were sailing up and down the coast, through the Bahama Passage and the Florida Straits, with scant knowledge of where they were going or how they would get there. "Their skippers kept their reckoning with chalk on a shingle, which they stowed away in the binnacle," an old writer has recorded, "and by way of observation they held up a hand to the sun. When they got him over four fingers they knew they were straight for Hole-in-the-Wall; three fingers gave them their course to Double Headed Shot Key and two carried them down to Barbados."[4] Each voyage was an adventure. Some skippers came home with a fortune, such as the $100,000 Colonel Thomas Cutts of Maine made on a single cargo of molasses, which he exchanged for lumber and sold on a high market. Others, less fortunate, left their bones on a desolate islet and their goods scattered along a remote and uninhabited shore.

As colonial trade grew to rival that of Great Britain, restrictive laws were enacted to curb it. New Englanders ignored the laws or evaded them. Interference with their West Indies trade was a strong factor in the rise of anti-British sentiment in Boston and Philadelphia, and in the growth of smuggling as a respectable occupation. So high ran public feeling that in July 1769 the British ship *Liberty,* which was engaged in hunting smugglers, was wrecked and burned near Newport, Rhode Island — doubtless by colonists, though nobody was ever identified who took part in the deed.

Another kind of sea booty eagerly sought by early settlers was the whale. Numbers of these great creatures drifted ashore along the Cape Cod beaches. The Algonquin Indians, who lived along the shore, had long been experienced and skillful whale hunters. From them the settlers learned the craft of whaling, and the Algonquins' sharp, double-prowed whaling canoe was the original of the Cape Codders' far-famed whaleboat.

But the Indians did not surrender their ancient rights to the whale without a struggle. Their sachem, Cheesehahchamuk, selling tribal land to the white newcomers in 1642, demanded and got a recorded agreement that "four spans around the middle of every whale that comes upon the shore . . . and no more" would go to the white men. The remainder of the whale would belong to the tribe. As time passed and the Indians were driven inland, drift whales became the common property of the settlers, as they had been common property of the tribesmen.

Later, when seaside property changed hands, the right to fish and whales was sometimes arbitrarily demanded and included in the terms of sale. As a result, the question of who owned the whales vexed the men of the Cape all down the years. In 1693 the king's sheriff seized two captured whales in behalf of the Crown, under the old English law which gave "wreck of the sea, whales and sturgeons" to the king as royal revenue.

At one time, the tail of every whale caught by an English crew was preserved for the Queen. In 1705, William Clapp applied to "Squier Dudley" for the job of "water balif" on Cape Cod to see that the Queen got her share of the whales. His application read in part: "i have liveed hear at the Cap this 4 year, and I have very often every year sien that her Maiesty has been very much wronged of har dues by these country people." The document, still preserved, carries a notation that Clapp got the job.[5]

But wrecking during the colonial period was not all beach-combing. On the American mainland every settlement faced deep water or a navigable stream. Farms and plantations lay close to the shore, as there were few roads or trails through the wilderness. The grower depended on ships to market his surplus, and the coastal trade grew mightily. Dangerous waters on the approaches to the trade centers took the greatest toll of ship-wrecks — Long Island and the New Jersey coast, on the sea lane to New York; Cape Cod, barring the way to and from the thriving ports of Salem and Boston; Cape Hatteras, with its frequent storms and deadly shoals; Sable Island, lying close to the great circle to Europe; and the Florida Straits, to be run by every craft bound for Gulf or West Indian ports or for South America. These were the danger spots, and the danger spots were the haunts of the wreckers.

Colonial records show that Vice-Admiralty courts handled many salvage cases, making disposition of shipwrecked cargoes and decreeing payments to wreckers for their services. The judges, though often natives of the colonies, received their commissions from England, and the rates of allowance were laid down in England. It is evident from the record of cases brought to trial in New York between 1729 and 1770 that American legal practice at that time was based on English law and, where precedent was lacking, on local conditions and circumstances. (There was no written work on American wrecking law until 1858, when Judge William Marvin of Key West published *A Treatise on the Law of Wreck and Salvage.* This remained the authoritative textbook until 1958, when Martin J. Norris' comprehensive modern discussion, *The Law of Salvage,* was published.)

In the seventeenth century, sunken cargoes presented a tempting lure. They were sought and fished for, sometimes by specially equipped expeditions. As such cargoes were legally the property of the king, a commission or license was usually obtained from the Lord Admiral or some other official who acted for the sovereign. Commissions were granted to almost any seagoing adventurer who applied. The favorite fishing grounds was, of course, the Caribbean, where even at that time a number of treasure-laden Spanish vessels were known to be lying on the bottom.

On March 8, 1670, such a commission was granted to Edmond Custis of London by His Royal Highness James, Duke of York and Albany, Lord High Admiral of England and Ireland, granting him

> full power & free Liberty & Authority to Search for, fish for and recover, at, upon or neare the Sea or Sea Coasts belonging to his Maiesty in the West Indies, or the Bermudas, all such Shipps, Vessells, Treasure, Goods, Gunns, or Merchandizes, whatsoever which have been or shall be dureing the continuance of this Contract, Sunck, lost or Cast awaie in all, or any of the said places, And which are of Right belonging to his R:Highness as Lord High Admirall of all his Ma'ties Dominions beyond the Seas.[6]

The agreement was to be effective fifteen years. Custis and his partners were empowered to sell or dispose of all ships and materials they discoverd and salvaged, after delivering at a specified place the portion belonging to His Royal Highness. The duke agreed that, during the term of the commission, he would not authorize anyone else to go treasure fishing at any of the places mentioned. One-fourth of all the materials recovered were reserved for the royal treasury, "the dangers of the sea excepted." A representative of the Crown was to be on board each vessel to watch and report on what was salvaged.

One of the best wreck stories of all time revolved around a commission granted by Charles II to an unknown Yankee skipper who came to him young and starry-eyed, talked him out of an old ship and a crew of daring and faithful men, and set sail for the Spanish Main.

6

"Phipps Rack"

In 1651 in rural Maine, a boy was born who was to become the most fabulous wrecker of the New World. Historians do not describe Sir William Phipps, first royal governor of Massachusetts Bay Colony, in such terms; but wrecker he was — for all that. As a lad he had left his father's farm to seek what formal education he could wangle for himself; he is said to have walked to Portland barefoot, carrying his only pair of shoes over his shoulder to save them. Phipps was ambitious and energetic, and lived in an age of opportunity. He married well and was soon commanding his own small vessel, doing comfortably in the West Indies trade.

While calling at ports in the Caribbean, he sometimes met seamen who told tall tales of sunken Spanish treasure ships. Some had actually sailed on board one or another of them and knew approximately where they had been lost. Phipps listened to these tales with care and discrimination and, from time to time, wrote down bits of apparently reliable information. Eventually he had collected so much lore of sunken treasure that he became bold enough to sail to England and take his information to the king.

Charles II received the unknown Yankee skipper with curiosity and was impressed by his attitude and his story. The royal treasury was in desperate need of funds, and the king evidently decided that William Phipps was worth the risk of a very old ship and a small crew. He proceeded to outfit an expedition and to award Captain Phipps a royal commission to go wreck-fishing in the Caribbean Sea. After returning to Boston, Phipps finally sailed to the Bahamas on January 15, 1683.

Unfortunately, the expedition was not a success. It brought the royal treasury £470 19*s.* 8½*d.* Phipps did bring with him, however, something of value — highly trustworthy data on the position of three other Spanish vessels that had gone down in the hurricane of 1642 with a great treasure, somewhere between Turks Island and Cape Cabron on the northeastern coast of Hispaniola (now the Dominican Republic). He was convinced that he could find the place and recover much of the abandoned gold and silver.

A contemporary account of the venture, published in London by a member of the expedition, reports:

> Captain Phipps having for some years pursu'd the Art of weighing of Wrecks, and not without considerable progress; and having good information of a Spanish Galion, that was cast away among the Rocks and Shoals of the Bahama Islands about the year 1643 not only by some Spaniards that were aboard her when she was lost, but also by observation of others that had been in search after her, but all miscarried in the point: The Captain had almost certain Knowledge that he might discover the place; and so like a good Subject acquainted His late Majesty first with the design, proffering his Life and Fortunes at his Princes Service to search after it.[1]

But Charles II had died; and his successor, James II, disappointed by the small return from Phipps's first expedition, was not interested in financing another. The enterprising young skipper then took his scheme to certain well-known members of the British nobility. Christopher Monck, Duke of Albemarle, one of the Lords Proprietors of the Carolina Company, was either a man of vision or a hard-bitten maritime gambler, for he listened to Phipps's story, was duly impressed by it and formed a company to finance an adequate expedition to search for the Spanish wrecks.

His friends — Lord Falkland, Sir James Hayes, Sir John

Narborough, Francis Nicholson, Isaac Foxcroft and John Smith — among them raised £2,400 and agreed to share in the profits proportionally. Albemarle obtained a three-year patent from the king, dated March 4, 1686, to salvage "all flotsam, jetsam, lagan, bullion, plate, gold, silver, coin, bars or pigs of silver, ingots of gold, merchandises and other goods shipwrecked and lost before July 16, 1689 on the north side of Hispaniola, about the Bahamas, on the Gulf of Florida" — with the proviso that one-tenth of everything recovered should be reserved for the royal treasury and one-sixteenth for Phipps.

Two small vessels, the *James and Mary* and the *Henry of London,* were well outfitted; and their crews, including experienced divers, were carefully chosen. A stock of trade goods was placed on board so that, if the hopes of treasure should not be fulfilled, the adventurers might do some trading and bring back at least a moderate profit. The expedition sailed on September 12, 1686, did some trading along the way and arrived at what was believed to be the site of the wrecks during Februry. Phipps, after satisfying himself that the location was correct, took one of the ships to nearby Puerto Plata and traded. His two lieutenants stayed on the site and began underwater work with four divers, using watertight helmets with long tubes that floated to the surface for air. Soon they located wreckage thirty-five to fifty feet underwater, on a slope which was known locally as Ambrosia Bank.

Cotton Mather, telling the story of the treasure hunt, reports that after a few days the men sailed to Puerto Plata to report to their chief. They wore an air of disappointment and, with long faces, told Phipps a story of discouragement and failure. At that moment Phipps chanced to glance under the ship's table at which they were sitting. At his feet was a "silver sow," which could only have come from the submerged hoard. "Thanks be to God. We are made!" he cried, as the men laughed merrily over their jest. For they had succeeded beyond their dreams.

With every man pledged to secrecy, the expedition remained at work for about six weeks, bringing up bars and ingots of gold, as well as sowboys, pigs and sows of silver, loose coins and pieces of fine gold plate. Work was discontinued on Sabbaths and on days when too much wind might endanger the safety of the divers. At other times everyone worked frantically, despite sickness and exhaustion, to raise all the treasure they could before the weather should become too stormy, the provisions run too low or privateers from a nearby French base discover them. The divers located no slightest scrap of the wooden hulls of the vanished Spanish ships. They had either broken up and drifted away or been consumed by sea worms, which abound in the warm waters of the Caribbean. Much of the silver from the wreck had merged into solid masses, on which white coral grew in branches and clusters. The men even brought up valuable brass cannons from the galleons.

Phipps exercised good judgment in deciding to sail away before the job was completed. Every man knew there were more precious metals and jewels still embedded in the coral. But they cheerfully obeyed him, and on May 2 the expedition weighed anchor and bore away for London, each man pledging utmost secrecy as to the location of the remaining hoard. They reached England without mishap a month later. As the ships came in sight of the coast, word was passed to London, and the Duke of Albemarle sailed eagerly down the Thames to meet them. It is said that he found all things so mightily to his satisfaction that "his Grace Generously oblig'd every Man and Boy of the Ships Crew to Drink his Health."[3] He could well afford it, for the two small vessels carried twenty-seven tons of treasure, worth at that time about three hundred thousand pounds.

In the whole undertaking not a man or boy was lost. All returned to share the wealth and fame of the venture. James II knighted Phipps and presented him with a medal and gold chain, and Albemarle gave him a gold cup for "Lady Phipps." True, the Spanish ambassador promptly claimed the entire treasure for the king of Spain, but nobody paid much attention to him.

Word of Phipps's sensational success quickly spread throughout Europe, America and the West Indies. Here was a form of salvage that roused the interest and support of everyone, high and low. Bahamian planters and New England fishermen, accustomed to scramble for the meager remains of coasting traders scattered on reef and islet, saw in Phipps's wreck the promise of sudden wealth. Kings and nobles jumped at the chance to gather into their coffers the remnants of the gold and silver loot that was fast being stripped from the Indian civilizations of Peru and Mexico and bringing death at sea to so many of their Spanish conquerors.

A few months after Phipps's triumphal return, he was again at sea — this time accompanied by the Duke of Albemarle himself, who had been named governor of Jamaica — hurrying back to complete the salvage of the Hispaniola treasure. But upon arrival at the wreck site, they were dismayed to find that their well-guarded secret was neither well-guarded nor a secret. About twenty-five sail of plantation boats were hove to on the wrecking grounds, busily diving and raising anything they could find on the bottom.

It is believed that the son of a Bermudian who had been with Phipps on his successful voyage had been forced to betray the secret of the location of the great wreck. Immediately, so many Bermuda vessels took part in the gold rush to Ambrosia Bank that Governor Robinson met with his council on July 24, 1688, to decide how many men could be spared without "Debilitating ye Country." There were times when trade was at a standstill while most of the merchants — with divers, rakes and diving tubes — were away "on Phipps rack." Other expeditions arrived from Jamaica and neighboring islands, from New York and New England. In Britain and western Europe, a veritable hysteria of treasure hunting fever had set in. Love of adventure and visions of wealth combined to lure high and low to the wrecking grounds. Phipps and Albemarle drove off the vessels they found on the site and went to work, but they soon gave up the quest and left the scene. The wreck had been fished out.

Some of the expeditions to Ambrosia Bank had been authorized and commissioned by persons in authority. To them were added many private and unauthorized ventures — so many, in fact, that in 1687 William Constable was appointed commissioner of the king for the collection of royal dues, with power to collect a moiety of the treasure taken up. For his services Constable was to receive one-tenth of what he collected. This arrangement was based on new ordinances of the British Admiralty which required unauthorized salvors henceforth to pay one-half of all they took up from the sea, instead of the royal tenth which had been the former tax. News of this law had not reached the West Indies or Bahamas in time to secure James II his moiety on the expeditions to Ambrosia Bank: honest salvors had reported their finds, paid their royal tenth and gone their way. The king, no doubt chagrined at losing the fortune that could have been his, decided it was a good time to prosecute his claims. All colonial governors were alerted that collections were under their jurisdiction. To enforce the law, they might have the assistance of the chief judge, the attorney general, the marshals and naval captains. It was a nearly impossible assignment, but there was one place it might work — the Bermudas.

In those islands the effort raised a great deal of dust and some money. The judge issued a summons to all who had gone to the wreck to step up and pay their full moiety, regardless of what they had paid before. When nobody came forward, he sent soldiers armed with search warrants into all the houses, looking for treasure, and rode grandly up and down the streets on his horse shouting instructions. After three strenuous months he had raised £6,128 for the king, which he forwarded with the comment that private theft and official embezzlement in the Bermudas were rampant and that he suspected even the governor was withholding the king's just share of the loot. When a final checkup was made, Bermudians were found to have stashed away £47,880 of bullion and coins fished from Ambrosia Bank. In Barbados a small amount was found, and at the site of the wreck itself the king's commissioner collected £500 or £600 moiety.

Wreck recovery schemes began to bloom in all countries. Stock companies were formed, and shares were easily sold, for all sorts of fantastic expeditions and for the manufacture of newly invented diving and salvage gear.

By 1692, William Phipps, the most talked-of man of his time, had been sent back to New England, his birthplace, as the first royal governor of Massachusetts.

7

Cape Hatteras and the Bankers

In 1663, Charles II granted a large area of the American shore, known as the Carolinas, to five Lords Proprietors, one of whom was that same Christopher Monck, Duke of Albemarle, who later sponsored William Phipps in his great treasure hunt. These Lords Proprietors were given sole and complete control of whatever colonies they planted and were held responsible only to the king. Reluctant to gamble their own lives on a venture into the unknown, the Lords Proprietors sent other valiant souls across the seas to pioneer for them, while they ran the show by remote control.

The Carolina colony, like the older Bermuda Company and the Eleutherian Adventurers in the Bahamas, was authorized to keep as public revenue all returns from the salvage and sale of sunken ships and cargoes found on its shores. The Fundamental Constitution of Carolina, written by John Locke in 1669, stated (Section 114): "All wrecks, mines, minerals, quarries of gems and precious stones . . . shall wholly belong to the Lord Proprietors." These gentlemen instructed their military commander in Carolina on February 19, 1679:

Knowe yee that wee Doe hereby (During our pleasures) constitute apointe authorize and Impower Robert Houlden for us in our names and to our uses to look after Receive and Recover all Wrecks Ambergrice or any other Ejections of the Sea that by Virtue of his Majestie's letters pattents doe to us apertaine or belong and if needs be to sue for and Recover the same and . . . Doe hereby strictly Injoine all persons whatsoever from Intermeddling herein unless thereunto comistionated or deputed by the said Rob't. Houlden.[1]

Later instructions authorized Houlden to send all the money he collected for rents and wrecks to the Earl of Shaftsbury and Sir Peter Colleton, retaining for his pay one-tenth of what he reported.

One wonders if the noble lords ever dreamed of the harvest of shipwrecks that would in time attach the dread name of "Graveyard of the Atlantic" to the Hatteras coast of North Carolina, and that would weave about its salt marshes and islands the legends of criminal wreckers, who plundered the luckless ships that came ashore there and forced their half-drowned survivors to walk the plank.

Hatteras is conceded to be the most dangerous bit of coastline on the whole Atlantic shore. At that point the northbound Gulf Stream runs head-on into the cold current of the Arctic, tossing sand and spray high into the air on a stormy day. From this turbulence were formed the dreaded Diamond, Lookout and Frying Pan Shoals, where the sands (like those surrounding Sable Island, another murderous spot in the North Atlantic) are continually shifting beneath the conflicting currents and never-ending storms. The early Spaniards followed the current of the Gulf Stream up from the Caribbean; as they passed the Bermudas and approached Cape Hatteras, they would turn east and cross the Atlantic to Spain. Vessels coming from Europe sailed — after the pattern of Columbus — to the Canary Islands, then rode the Equatorial Current to the West Indies and followed the Gulf Stream up the coast. Thus stormy Hatteras saw early sea traffic coming and going between the Old and New Worlds.

A few miles seaward of the Carolina coast runs a line of narrow, sandy islands known as the Outer Banks. Here lived the "bankers," the traditional wreckers and pilots of the Carolina seaboard from earliest times. It is unfortunate that no record remains of the early days of these upstanding, self-sufficient folk. Later generations received a valiant heritage from them: the sons and grandsons who manned the coastal lifesaving stations up and down the shore with unforgettable heroism.

The earliest settlers on the banks were smugglers. In the

eyes of most American colonists before 1700, smuggling was a respectable and enterprising business, one of the few that earned a good living. Under the British Navigation Acts the colonists were obliged to exchange goods only with the mother country. This state of affairs not only encouraged smuggling; it made smuggling inevitable. A colonial governor of Carolina wrote to London that the tobacco raised in his province, instead of being marketed according to law, was shipped to the islands near "Connecticut Colony" and from there sent to Scotland. "Which fraud," he declared, "ought speedily to be prevented."[2] The isolation of the banks formed a perfect base of operation for illicit trade; in time the population increased with the coming of more shipwreck victims and pilots — and customs inspectors.

From the beginning of the colony, these rugged frontiersmen took to themselves the good things the sea washed up on their shores. This practice ran head-on into the old English law which gave disposition of shipwrecked goods to the Crown or, in this case, to the Lords Proprietors. Probably the bankers gave little heed to the edict of the Lords Proprietors, for wreckage was their chief source of income. Governor Gabriel Johnston may have had reason to refer to them as "indigent, desperate outlaws or vagabonds": they supplied him with the only militia he had along the coast, but he admitted in writing that he was reluctant to call upon them for support, as he feared he would not get it. As the governor did a bit of high-class wrecking himself now and then, he no doubt recognized the futility of expecting aid from the bankers.

The most renowned of Governor Johnston's exploits took place in 1750, the twelfth year since he had received any pay for his services as governor. His financial status at the time was most depressing. That autumn a Spanish treasure *flota* of five galleons — carrying the annual take of gold, silver and gems from Mexico and South America — rendezvoused as usual at Havana. Its commander, Captain Don Juan Manuel de Bonilla, was either ignorant or strangely unconcerned about weather conditions at that season, for he led the convoy to sea in his flagship, the *Nuestra Señora de Guadalupe,* at the beginning of the hurricane season. Grandly the galleons sailed through the Florida Straits and into the Bahama Channel, riding the current of the Gulf Stream north. As the fleet approached Cape Hatteras a few days later, a hurricane overtook it and scattered the ships along the Carolina banks. Three vessels were lost: one at Currituck Inlet, one at Cape Hatteras and a third at Topsail Inlet. Some of the crews and passengers were saved and taken to Norfolk. History is silent as to the fate of the gold, cochineal (a valuable red dye), cocoa and balsam they carried, though the British governor seems to have assumed that the bankers got them. A fourth vessel was aided by wreckers; her crew and passengers were saved and sent to England, taking with them the 32,000 pieces of eight she was carrying.

The flagship, however, the staunch galleon *Nuestra Señora de Guadalupe,* lost masts and rudder and was driven in a shattered and dangerous condition into the Ocracoke River. The cargo of this vessel was valued at a million pieces of eight.

Peace between England and Spain had just been declared by the Treaty of Aix, but it was still a very uneasy peace. Six weeks after the date it was to go into effect, a Spanish squadron appeared off the Carolina coast, entered the Cape Fear River and destroyed the English settlement of Brunswick, carrying away all movable property and slaves. Some time before this, Spain had made herself unpopular with the bankers by landing men on the out islands and seizing their cattle and hogs.

The disabled treasure-ship lay in the Ocracoke River for a month without making an official gesture in the direction of the British. During this long wait, Governor Johnston appeared surprisingly sensitive to the international situation and concerned for the welfare of Captain Bonilla and his treasure. The Spaniards kept strictly to themselves, repairing their vessel and occasionally trading out of her cargo with passing ships. When he could endure the situation no longer, the governor sent a member of his council who spoke Spanish to confer with Captain Bonilla and assure him of his welcome in British territory.

The envoy painted a strong picture of the danger to the Spaniards if the bankers should decide to raid the stranded ship in reprisal for past Spanish visits to their islands. Bonilla seems to have been impressed. Gratefully he agreed that Governor Johnston might send for a British frigate, the *H.M.S. Scorpion,* to stand by to protect him.

The Spanish crew, however, had no confidence in their traditional enemies, the British. While the *Scorpion* was on its way, they mutinied. The boatswain, Pedro Roderiguez, with most of the men supporting him, forced Captain Bonilla to permit 106 chests of money and thirty bags of cochineal to be transferred from the disabled ship to two strange sloops—probably manned by fishermen or wreckers—that suddenly appeared from Bermuda. The governor's envoy, who was present at the time, offered to take over the sloops officially and proceed with them up the river. Captain Bonilla was willing, but the suspicious mutineers objected. With the best of grace possible in an ugly situation, the Spanish captain left the ship and went with the British envoy, instructing his officers to place ten men on each of the Bermuda sloops for safety and to unbend their sails so they could not get away. His orders, however, were ignored, and both sloops put to sea in the night, one running aground and the other getting clean away.

Captain Bonilla, with suave diplomacy, offered Governor Johnston a reasonable salvage fee in recognition of his services. He then requested the transfer of his remaining cargo to the *Scorpion* and offered to pay regular freight rates to that vessel to carry it to Europe. Before anything could be done, however, there was one more effort to grab the treasure under a cloak of official procedure. The local customs officer, claiming the Spanish vessel had ignored the law by breaking bulk and trading within a British port, proposed to seize the *Nuestra Señora de Guadalupe.* The governor refused permisson, claiming that such action might imperil the treaties between the two countries. The customs officer then appealed to the surveyor general of customs, who approved the seizure. When the governor learned of this, he instantly took the treasure-ship into his own custody to "protect" her from his own customs. Fortunately, the *Scorpion* arrived promptly, and the treasure cargo was placed on board. Captain Bonilla paid the governor 11,444½ pieces of eight and signed a paper designating that sum as Johnston's commission for the protection and preservation of his cargo. But the governor was not to enjoy his sudden affluence. When the Spanish captain was safely home with his specie, he complained to his government about the British action, and Spain lodged a protest through its ambassador to Britain. The case was referred to the advocate attorney and the solicitor general of England. After a thorough study, these officials ruled that Governor Johnston had been out of order in taking money from the Spanish captain, as no salvage was due a British official under the circumstances. He was ordered to restore to Captain Bonilla "whatever you or any persons under your Government shall have unwarrantedly exacted from them." (One wonders how much of Johnston's 11,444½ pieces of eight ever got to Spain.)

Succeeding British governors were never able to do much about the disposition of wrecked vessels and cargoes on the Outer Banks. The bankers were strong-willed and independent villagers, descendents of shipwrecked people. When disaster came, they rescued whom they could, treated survivors kindly and buried the dead. But the remains of the ship and its cargo were another matter.

The schooner *Enterprise* from Charleston, with fifteen passengers and a horse, struck on the Outer Banks on a stormy night and bilged. She carried a cargo of rum, lime, crockery and lumber. All hands climbed into the rigging to escape the fury of the waves breaking over her decks. The lime in the cargo caught fire, and the crew and passengers soon felt they must make their choice between drowning or burning to death. At the climactic moment, a passenger shouted for everyone to start praying. (It is easier to pray after all hope is gone.)

"I told them not to despair," William Gardiner wrote in a letter afterward, "that the Lord was a prayer hearing and a prayer answering God, and I still cherished the hope we should escape."

The answer came in a homely way. Somebody remembered the horse that was plunging about the deck, half-drowned by the boarding seas, and suggested that they push him overboard. If the horse could swim ashore, there was hope that the men could follow him. With difficulty they managed to hoist the frightened animal over the side. He floundered for a moment, then scrambled to his feet in the surf, shook the water out of his eyes and walked ashore, none the worse for it. Abashed, the crew and passengers descended from the rigging and followed the horse to land. On the beach were tracks of a cart or wagon. The shipwrecked men followed these until they met three men on horseback, who took them to a village and hired a boat to convey them safely across the sound to Ocracoke. The horse joined the wild ponies that have roamed the Outer Banks since the earliest settlers arrived. What happened to the wreck and its contents remains one of the mysteries of the lonely Hatteras shore.

Later generations told the old tales of false lights and ships lured to destruction by the bankers. They claimed that the towns of Nags Head had been named for an old horse the bankers used to carry their lantern along the beach. Fortunately, historians had already heard the same tales attached to other localities; they declared that Nags Head had been named by homesick English settlers for the town of the same name in England. There is no doubt, however, that public auctions, or vendues, of shipwrecked goods took place under official supervision in Carolina for many years and that the bankers who brought in the goods did receive salvage awards for their services. Flotsam and jetsam coming ashore from the many wrecks near stormy Hatteras were a source of income, one way or another, to the island people for several generations.

No reference to the Carolina bankers would be complete without the celebrated story of the loss at sea of Theodosia Burr, daughter of Aaron Burr and wife of Colonel Joseph Alston, governor of South Carolina. On December 30, 1812, she and her little son — under the care of her father's friend, Timothy Green — sailed on the pilot boat *Patriot* from Charleston, bound for New York. Neither the *Patriot* nor anyone on board was ever seen again. The tragedy has been the basis for endless theories and speculations as to the fate of the lovely Theodosia. Soon after the loss of the *Patriot,* a wrecker on the Outer Banks named Mann gave his sweetheart, Lovie Tillet of Nags Head, a black lace shawl, a dress and the painted portrait of a beautiful woman that he had taken from the wreck of a pilot boat. Many years later, when Lovie was an old woman, a doctor attending her saw the portrait and, with her permission, took it to relatives of Theodosia Burr Alston. It was identified as indeed a portrait of that missing woman, and today it is listed in the Frick Art Reference Library as Theodosia Burr, painted by John Vanderlyn.

Lying approximately 580 miles southeast of Hatteras are the Bermuda Islands. They too had their wreckers from their earliest settlement. Their colonization came about because of a shipwreck in July 1609. The Bermudas had been known and feared for many years as a place of danger and violent storms, and the *Sea Venture* was not the first vessel to be lost there. But hers was probably the most famous wreck of the period. It may even have been the inspiration for William Shakespeare's *The Tempest.*

The ship, under the command of Sir George Somers and carrying 150 passengers, was on her way from London to the Virginia colony at James Towne when she became separated from the other eight vessels of the fleet. After three days of buffeting in a thrashing storm, she was in a sinking condition. Hope was abandoned, but Somers continued to drive the exhausted crew to pump and bail until land appeared and he was able to run the waterlogged craft ashore safely between two sheltering rocks. All on board accepted their deliverance as an act of Providence and went joyfully ashore, where they found an uninhabited paradise, with ample food and a pleasing climate.

The party remained on the islands for nine months, building two small ships. Then they continued on to James Towne, where they proclaimed the attractions of Bermuda; some passengers who returned to England spread the word there. Somers, meanwhile, returned to the Bermudas immediately to secure fish, wild hogs and other foodstuffs for the starving Virginia settlers. He died while on the islands, and it is said that his body was returned to England for burial, but his heart was placed in a grave on the island he loved. By July 11, 1612, the first settlers had arrived from England, and a successful colony was soon established on Bermuda.

The Bermuda Company, to whom the islands were granted by the Crown, had obtained the right to "wreck" as an Admiralty droit. If no owner appeared to make good his claim for wrecked property, it belonged to the company. But settlers paid scant attention to the law: England was a long way off, and each man took what he could find in or on the sea, as a natural right. Usually a shipwreck was picked clean long before officers of the company arrived on the scene. Sometimes a governor would post a proclamation forbidding the looting of shipwrecks, and at other times the government would attempt to prosecute violators. Neither course seemed to do much good.

The *Bermuda Gazette* of January 15, 1825, carried an account of the embarrassing predicament of some local wreckers who found, too late, that they had rushed to the assistance of a pirate ship in trouble. Early one morning, fishermen reported a vessel on the rocks at the eastern end of the islands. Several boatloads of Bermudians took off at once and discovered a long, low schooner of seventy or eighty tons, flying the colors of Spain, stranded on the rocks but not seriously damaged. As they came alongside to render assistance her crew, eighteen men armed with cutlasses and muskets lined up along the rail. They would permit only the pilot to come up her side. With some misgivings the pilot mounted the ship's ladder, noting as he did so that additional armed men were concealed below decks.

The pilot needed help and demanded that two of his companions be allowed to join him. This was permitted, and the three worked the vessel off the rocks and into deep water by skillful use of her sails and anchor. When she was quite clear, her commander handed the pilot $8 for his pay. This he indignantly refused, declaring it was too little for the services the three had rendered. At a signal from the ship's captain, each crewman then drew his cutlass menacingly. The captain then increased his offer to $20. The wreckers accepted without further argument, returned to their boats and made off with alacrity. The strange schooner was never seen again.

8

Block Island–Cape Cod–Nantucket

Wherever sail passed by a dangerous locality in great numbers, there was a wrecking ground. There men gathered to give aid or save life and property, and to such places were often attached the well-worn tales of false lights and contrived shipwrecks. Block Island, Cape Cod and Nantucket had their share of opprobrium. Long Island and the New Jersey shore were shunned by careful mariners, who not only believed firmly in mermaids but were also convinced that all wreckers were pirates and that no good could come through the services of "strangers" when they were in trouble at sea.

After the American colonies had fought their war and established their government, beachcombing was often condemned by those in authority and by the press of non-seafaring communities. Sometimes it was called wrecking, and reports carried more than a hint that the seaside community that profited from a disaster had something to do with causing it. No locality seems to have accused its own people of this; it was always some distant part of the country or some earlier generation on which suspicion fastened its fangs.

Early newspapers, poets and fiction writers doted on heartrending accounts of scenes that nobody had actually witnessed except the laboring boatmen along the coast or the victims they sometimes got ashore alive. There is no evidence that vessels were lured to their destruction or drowning people murdered on the American seaboard. On the contrary, there is proof up and down the coast of unselfish and often heroic exertions of the men from seaside farms and villages.

The poet John Greenleaf Whittier listened to a friend who told him a ghastly story of a shipwreck which had occurred a hundred years before, and immortalized the hokum in his poem "The *Palatine*":

> Into the teeth of death she sped;
> (May God forgive the hands that fed
> The false lights over the rocky Head!) . . .
>
> Down swooped the wreckers, like birds of prey
> Tearing the heart of the ship away,
> And the dead had never a word to say. . . .
>
> In their cruel hearts, as they homeward sped,
> "The sea and the rocks are dumb," they said:
> "There'll be no reckoning with the dead."

When friends protested, Whittier confessed frankly that he had believed the story to be true.

The "lost ship *Palatine*" to which the poem refers was the bark *Princess Augusta,* which sailed from Rotterdam to Philadelphia in 1738, carrying 350 religious refugees from the Palatinate, a state of the German empire. She had a nightmare voyage, during which most of the passengers and crew became ill from drinking contaminated water kept in moldy wine casks. Two hundred and fifty of the ship's company were buried at sea, including her captain.

Near the end of the terrible voyage, the ship ran into a gale with bitter cold and snow. According to one story, the *Princess Augusta,* leaking and with her mizzenmast cut away, became unmanageable and crashed ashore on Block Island, about twenty miles east of Long Island. The islanders gathered on the beach and helped the wretched passengers scramble ashore in the snow. They carried the weaker ones in blankets to nearby houses, but two elderly women died from exposure that night and over a dozen other passengers soon after. The acting captain, Andrew Brook, took his men and their luggage ashore and abandoned the ship, which drifted away at high tide. The following day she smashed ashore again and went to pieces. Her food and cargo lined the beach and were gathered up by the Block Islanders, who were able in some instances to restore luggage to its owners among the passengers.

A shock wave from the tragedy spread throughout the country, and soon there were many versions of what had taken place. Some said the wrecked vessel burned and sank at sea, with a helpless woman still on board. (A Block Island legend tells of the *Palatine* ghost light which appears over the sea at that spot on each anniversary of the tragic event.) Another version of the story has the passengers all murdered by wreckers who were supposed to have lived on Block Island; this seems to have been the version Whittier used for his poem. Edward Rowe Snow quotes a Block Islander who has done much research on the historic shipwreck; this authority believes that Brook starved and robbed the passengers and abandoned the ship, and that the deserted craft burned and sank with a woman on board.[1]

Block Island, lying amid treacherous tides, reefs and sand bars, has long been associated in the public imagination with the worst aspects of wrecking. Its lurid reputation may have started from the distorted tales of the wreck of the Palatine ship. Also, Block Island men, mainly fishermen, have long been noted for their lack of cordiality to outsiders. Mainland fishermen often sail out to drag in waters over which the islanders claim jurisdiction, and the islanders as often try to eject their unwelcome competitors. In retaliation for the lack of hospitality, mainland fishermen with gusty humor have long invented slanderous stories about the Block Islanders, based upon their alleged niggardliness and their assumed dependence on shipwrecks for livelihood. These highly imaginative yarns grew quite famous and gradually become known as "Block Islands." Here is a sample, quoted by Joseph Mitchell in *The New Yorker:*

"Old Chrissy was an old rascal of a woman that was the head of a gang of wreckers. They lured ships in with false lights, and they killed the sailors and passengers, so there wouldn't be any tales told. Old Chrissy took charge of the killing. She had a big club and she'd hist her skirt and wade out in the surf and clout the people on the head as they swam in or floated in. She called a wreck a wrack, the way the Block Islanders do. That's the way she pronounced it. One night, she and her gang lured a ship up on the reef, and the sailors were floating in, and old Chrissy was out there clouting them on their heads. One poor fellow floated up, and it was one of old Chrissy's sons, who'd left the island and gone to the mainland to be a sailor. He looked up at old Chrissy and said, 'Hello, Ma.' Old Chrissy didn't hesitate. She gave him a clout on the head with her club. 'A son's a son,' she said, 'but a wrack's a wrack.' "[2]

Along the more settled shores of New England, farmers and fishermen were the only lifesavers, alert to help when they found a vessel foundering offshore or hard on the rocks. On Cape Cod, these shore dwellers were often staunch and capable boatmen, able to give a good account of themselves in a stormy sea.

Until the first railroads were in operation, the North Atlantic ports were the main markets and distribution points in America for merchandise and produce, and the home ports of the lucrative West Indies trade. The shipping of the entire coast line converged at Salem, Boston, New York and Philadelphia. In stormy weather, which prevailed through the winter season, the toll of shipwrecks in the approaches to these cities ran high. There were no organized facilities for aid or rescue, and the loss of life was appalling. The victims perished not only from injuries, drowning and starvation on uninhabited banks and islands, but also — and perhaps most often — from cold or exposure.

It was inevitable that people living along the shore should develop a sense of responsibility toward the incoming ships. Every seaside garret held a spyglass lying ready at the top of the steps. Every house had its lookout, if only a rooftop scuttle where members of the family could scan the sea from time to time during daylight hours. When someone sighted a ship running too close to the beach or rocks, he blew the family's horn (the only means of communication from house to house), and his neighbor in turn passed the signal on. Men and women left what they were doing and ran for the shore.

More than 1,100 known shipwrecks have taken place on the shores of Cape Cod. An early post-Revolutionary law, effective throughout the Cape, provided that flotsam and jetsam picked up on the shore was to be reported to the nearest town clerk, who would advertise for its owner. If the owner did not appear within a year and a day, the salvaged material went to the finder. Some Cape towns still appoint a wreck master to take charge of shipwrecked goods until the owner appears; in other towns, finders are keepers. In strictest accuracy, few people have held closely to the letter of these laws. Beachcombers of yesterday and souvenir hunters of today have picked clean the bones of many a craft and carried away even its quarterboards, wheel and bell. Occasionally the owner of the shore property has tried to convince the crowds of beachcombers that whatever washes up on his land belongs to him, but nobody has paid much attention.

A pirate ship, the *Whidah,* drove ashore on the sands near Wellfleet in 1717. One wonders just what would have happened if the captain, Black Sam Bellamy, and his 102 men had not conveniently drowned. Only one pirate, Thomas Davis, and a Cape Cod Indian, John Julian, escaped from the wreck. They made their way to the home of Samuel Hardings in the darkness of early morning and woke him up. Hardings hitched up his horses and drove down to the wreck, and the three men got several wagonloads of loot safely tucked away in Hardings' barn before the neighborhood woke up. Quickly a crowd gathered on the shore, and it was every man for himself. When the news reached Boston, Captain Cyprian Southack was sent to Cape Cod to get the gold from the pirate vessel and take charge of whatever salvage work could be done. When he arrived, he found hardly enough of the *Whidah* left to recognize. He managed to get several cartloads of goods, but complained bitterly that people from twenty miles around interferred with his work. Years later a single gold doubloon was found on the beach — the only bit of the shipwrecked pirate gold ever known to have been found.

During the Revolutionary War, the British frigate *Somerset* was wrecked near Provincetown — the same vessel that figures in Longfellow's poem "Paul Revere's Ride": "Where swinging wide at her moorings lay The Somerset, British man-of-war." The frigate's officers and men were promptly pounced upon by the colonists and marched as prisoners of war to Boston. The war board stripped the vessel of her guns and ammunition. But a fine British frigate — enemy property and therefore fair game — had much more of value on board than guns and ammunition. The people of Provincetown and Truro laid aside their scruples and had a field day, swarming over the ship and taking away anything they could pry loose. "There is wicked work at the wreck, riotous doings," piously wrote Joseph Otis of Barnstable.[3]

Chatham, at the elbow of Cape Cod, once had its "wrecking gangs." Chatham is located on a particularly dangerous bit of shore; and these gangs of men and boys became expert in the use of dories, in which they rowed out swiftly to any vessel that showed a distress signal and that might be caught on the offshore sand bars and shoals. If they could reach the ship before the government men from nearby lifesaving stations, they could sometimes make a bargain with her master to maneuver his vessel into deep water for a specific price, or they could rescue the crew and make an agreement to bring the cargo ashore. But their activity was entirely local; they never went foraging for wrecks.

Joseph Lincoln tells of two Chatham boys who were too young to join the wrecking gangs. One dark night they took a long pole and a lantern and rowed across the sound to the outer beach, which was a string of small islands along the shore. There they lighted the lantern and waved it back and forth on top of the pole. To the people in Chatham, it looked like a distress signal in the rigging of a grounded vessel. All Chatham rose to the occasion and swarmed across to the beaches. But the boys were gone long before the wreckers arrived.[4]

South of Cape Cod lie two large islands, Martha's Vineyard and Nantucket, directly in the lane of shipping bound for New

York. Here is a dangerous locality where the encompassing sands hold hundreds of broken ships, most of which were inbound from the West Indies. In 1750, Martha's Vineyard had a cultured and aristocratic wrecker, John Cousens, who lived out his life on the island and never satisfied local curiosity by explaining why he came there or where he came from. Cousens salvaged the wrecks that took place with profitable regularity off Gay Head, a dangerous headland at the western tip of the island, where strong currents and hidden reefs took their toll.

Nantucket Island has a long history of maritime disaster. As early as 1678, a French ship loaded with hides, probably from French Canada, was lost on the shoals. The military governor, Tristram Coffin, ordered it wrecked and the cargo sold, at least insofar as local buyers could be found. This done, he abandoned the vessel, and the local people took over, carrying away whatever they could use. When the governor of New York learned of the incident, he was much displeased and ordered a court-martial for Coffin, who served under him. Coffin was found guilty, not of appropriating someone else's property, but of failing to advertise and sell the wreck.

Some years later, the fine new ship *Earl of Eglington* was caught in a heavy gale and driven aground close to the Nantucket shore. Her captain, John Niven of Greenock, Scotland, launched her two boats, but one was overturned in the boiling surf and the other very nearly lost. Villagers quickly gathered on the shore. They saw that no boat could live in the tempestuous seas breaking over the wreck. It was necessary to improvise a scheme for saving those of the crew who were still on board.

With gestures and pantomime, the Nantucketers instructed the sailors to toss overboard an oar with a line attached to it. When this was flung on the beach by incoming waves, a heavier line was attached and drawn ashore; and the first line, with a note of instructions tied to it, was hauled back to the ship. Next, by means of the heavy line, a cable was drawn ashore. One end was made fast to the timberheads of the *Earl of Eglington*'s forecastle, the other to a stake driven into the beach sand. A sling capable of holding one man was rigged and suspended from two hames, with a line fast to it from both ship and shore. With this primitive breeches buoy, all the remaining seamen were drawn safely ashore. It was three days before the seas had quieted sufficiently for men to board the ship. By then she was a complete wreck.

Typical of many Nantucket shipwrecks was that of the schooner *Caroline,* bound for Plymouth. She ran ashore in a gale on a bitterly cold day in February 1811, in a leaking condition, after losing her boats, cables and anchors. Her crew took to the shrouds to escape the icy waves rolling over the deck. The *Caroline* was too far out to be boarded by rescuers, so men on shore set out to get a rope. They had to walk four miles through the storm, and it took them four hours to return with it, during which one of the hungry, thirsty, half-frozen sailors let go and dropped into the sea. The others were hauled ashore with the rope. The schooner was a total loss, and her hull was sold for $40. Her cargo of tar was saved and sold at $2.25 a barrel.

Nantucketers had a Roman holiday during the War of 1812, when a rash of prizes captured by Yankee privateers was lost on their shores. One of the richest was the English ship *Queen,* which broke in two and strewed her cargo of bottled porter, sauerkraut, cheeses, hams, clothing, hats and trunks of costly goods along the beach. Hundreds of Nantucket people worked day and night to save the goods, each taking whatever he could get. Lanterns and bonfires burned all night, and carts piled with merchandise moved steadily to the nearest towns. Sometimes bodies washed up on the shore and were gently cared for.

The *Queen* was a prize of the American privateer *General Armstrong,* John Barnard, Master. Barnard's agents eventually arrived at Nantucket to claim the cargo, but found very little of it left. There were accusations among the islanders, quarrels, lawsuits and prosecutions. For months afterwards Nantucketers were not speaking to each other, and Barnard's divers were hard at it raising goods sunk beyond the line of breakers.

The story of the *Sarah Ann* was quite different. She was on her way from Savannah to Boston in 1828, with a cargo of rice and cotton, when she ran aground on the north side of the island. Several attempts to float her were unsuccessful, and she was finally sold at auction where she lay. Her hull brought $127 and her spars, rigging and sails $422.40. The buyer was a smart wrecker who managed to refloat and refit the ship; but when her original owners found out about it, they went to court to repossess the ship, claiming that the vessel's captain had had no right to sell it. The court, however, upheld the sale, ruling that since only one other wreck had ever been refloated from that perilous location, and since nobody else had been willing to pay any higher price for the wreck, the sale had been in good faith.

Whether the buyer of the *Sarah Ann* was Nantucket's famous peg-legged wrecker is not clear. In 1847 and thereabouts, Frederick F. Swain, a clever and successful wrecking captain with only one good leg, was active on the island. Local history records that he got off nearly every vessel that stranded on the south shore of the island.

While resourceful men along the coast line were doing their utmost to save life and property, thinking people in the cities were beginning to recognize the need for organized aid for the shipwrecked. This stirring of the public conscience was taking place at about the same time in England and other countries in many parts of the world. But Boston seems to have been the first city — in the New World, at least — to organize a benevolent society for the avowed purpose of rousing public interest in lifesaving.

The Humane Society of the Commonwealth of Massachusetts began its work about 1786 and was incorporated on February 23, 1791, "for the recovery of persons who meet with such accidents as produce in them the appearance of death, and for promoting the cause of humanity by pursuing such means from time to time, as shall have for their object the preservation of human life and the alleviation of its miseries."[5]

The society empowered its trustees to make rewards "not

exceeding three pounds lawful money" to anyone saving another from death, and secured the services of a prominent preacher to deliver once a year a sermon that would publicize its purposes. A collection was taken at this service for funds to continue the work.

Aid to the shipwrecked was a subject immediately appealing to the society's membership, who set up shelter huts in remote and exposed places along the seashore and furnished them with food and warm clothing. As early as 1787 there were three of these huts on the shores of Boston Harbor. By 1806 seventeen shelters were in operation on the Massachusetts coast. The following year the society built its first lifeboat, which it stationed at Cohasset. It is said to have been a copy of the English lifeboat — thirty feet long by ten wide, double-backed, with both ends alike — invented by Henry Greathead of South Shields, on the North Sea. The boat was rowed by ten men and steered by two men with oars, one at each end. It could carry twenty passengers. Other lifeboats were built and placed at dangerous places on the Massachusetts coast as rapidly as funds were available.

In 1840 the Humane Society appealed to the Massachusetts legislature and received a grant of $5000, with which it built eleven lifeboats. Each, with its equipment, was placed in a shed near the shore. It was understood that volunteers would man the boats and that the Humane Society would reward rescuers with cash or medals; a gold medal and $10 is the highest reward recorded. Humane societies were soon formed in New York and Philadelphia; and by 1869 the Boston society alone had nearly a hundred stations.

So much for the humanitarian endeavor. The saving of cargoes and the aiding of vessels in distress seem not to have achieved the social prestige of lifesaving. These services were undertaken cautiously and at an agreed price. Small wrecking companies were prepared to go out on hire to strip a stranded vessel of its metals and rigging or to bring in its cargo. Doane and Knowles of Eastham, Cape Cod, were a skilled and responsible firm of wreckers as early as 1820, and were equipped to give aid at sea. But professional wrecking on the northern coast had little romance. Few, if any, wreckers put to sea voluntarily to do whatever they could, regardless of remuneration. Nor did local salvage work attract the enterprising men who made fortunes at wrecking farther south. Such men left their homes and settled, either temporarily or permanently, along the Florida reef.

Wrecking, as it was known in New England in 1845, is described in a letter by James Lloyd Homer of Hull, Massachusetts, published in the *Boston Post*:

> Hull is a great place for wreckers, and for wrecks. Mr. Tower, Mr. Mitchell, and some others, whose exertions have often been witnessed amidst the tempest and the storm on Nantasket Beach and its vicinity, live in Hull. . . .
>
> Some of the Hullonians are in the habit of buying wrecks, and then breaking them up — saving the iron, copper, and such other parts as are valuable and using the wood for fuel. The wreck of the ill-fated *Massasoit,* and that of the brig *Tremont* . . . have been entirely broken up, and the materials are piled up mountain high before the house of Mr. Mitchell . . . who is a wholesale dealer in wrecked vessels — in old masts, spars, rigging iron and brass.
>
> The wreck of the old brig *Favorite* lies on the beach as does that of the schooner *Emmeline,* both of which vessels, heavily laden, were sunk, . . . and afterwards raised by Mitchell and others on shares, and towed into Hull Bay.[6]

At the beginning of the nineteenth century, beachcombing was common practice. Souvenir hunters were on the scene of every shipwreck, and so were canny villagers, unwilling to see good planks and cordage wash out to sea. Cape Ann, Tarpaulin Cove and Cuttyhunk have all been charged with wreck plundering, and this old seaside custom is not entirely unknown even in our own day. Bits of broken ships are still picked up and preserved. There is, for example, the wheel of the *Portland,* dragged up from the bottom by a fisherman and now a cherished adornment of a Cape Cod living room not far from where that famous ship was lost. At nearby Chatham, the spire of the Congregational church is tipped with a spar from the bark *R. A. Allen,* wrecked in 1887 on the shoals of Monomoy. And bed quilts of "wreck calico" are still in use on Long Island.

At the town of East Hampton, New York, the ship's bell of the *John Milton* hangs in the session house of the Presbyterian church. During a snowstorm, the master of that ill-fated vessel apparently mistook the lighthouse on that point for the Montauk light and drove his ship onto the rocks. All on board were lost. A big civic funeral was held when all the bodies and the wreckage had washed ashore. People came from miles around and formed a procession through the newly fallen snow. At the head were the men carrying the biers of the captain and mate. After them, the bodies of the thirty-one crewmen were borne through the deep snow on carts and wagons, drawn by the same men and boys who had struggled long and valiantly to save them from the icy sea.

9

Sable Island

Popular tradition has singled out Sable Island, remote and deadly sea-trap off the coast of Nova Scotia, as the number one haunt of land pirates or criminal wreckers on the northern coasts. For generations the people of Canada and the United States have woven half-truths about the place into fearsome tales of looting and murder. These were so generally believed that, in at least two instances, men shipwrecked on the island desperately attacked and beat off the very lifesavers who were working to save them. Even as they struggled through Sable's tumultuous surf, they were so possessed by the lurid tales they had heard of the wreckers of Sable Island that they had to be subdued by the government lifesavers, who were the only inhabitants of the place, before they could be gotten ashore.

Sable was known and had been visited as early as the beginning of the sixteenth century. It appears on an old Portuguese map dated 1505 and on the Cabots' map of 1544. The island lies in the Atlantic about 150 miles southeast of Halifax, in the sea lane between that port and Europe. It is also in the track of the trawlers crossing to and from the Grand Banks and between Europe and New York.

Sable is a thin crescent of rock and sand about twenty miles long and a mile wide, which is actually the exposed crest of a great bed of sand, shell and pebbles extending nearly 200 miles east and west under the surface of the sea. Like Cape Hatteras it marks the meeting pace of conflicting ocean currents — the Great Arctic Current, the Gulf Stream and the outflow of the Gulf of St. Lawrence, which sheers down the coast of Cape Breton Island and merges with another portion of the Great

Painting by Charles Robert Patterson

Inward bound fishing craft and towering square-rigger on its course to Europe often met, saluted and passed on the Grand Banks off Newfoundland.

Arctic Current. These currents, which have drawn many an unwary vessel onto the shoals, have been known to complete the circle of the compass around Sable in a single day, bearing bits of wreckage and bodies of drowned mariners round and round the low, treeless island.

Not even Hatteras has the desolate reputation of Sable. It is a place of sudden and violent storms, almost perpetual fogs, constant wind and great cold. In rough weather — that is to say, most of the time — it presents a fifty-mile line of breakers without a landing place or a channel through its three surrounding and constantly changing bars. It is possible to come ashore, but only from a vessel anchored two or three miles out, and only after several days of good weather have calmed things down. It is seldom tried except in surfboats.

Over 500 known shipwrecks are embedded in Sable's sands. About the only way to save a grounded ship is for a rescue tug to catch her when she first drives ashore, before she is swung broadside by crosscurrents and tides. Once the vessel yields to the currents, she is trapped: the flowing sands build up around her and quickly suck her down. Old wrecks are continually rising into the light or sinking down weirdly into these ever-shifting sands. There is little wonder that this setting of evil portent should become the background for sinister legends.

Sable's earliest known shipwreck took place during the sixteenth century. Its only record, found by later settlers, was a cluster of human bones, scraps of a British ensign and a few weapons and coins of the Elizabethan age. By 1801 an occasional settler lived on the island. Since fishing was impossible from its shores, it is likely that these adventurers located there to plunder the shipwrecked property that had accumulated during the centuries.

In that same year, a tragedy occurred which was to change the whole course of Sable Island's destiny. The Duke of Kent had been named the new commander of the military forces in Canada. He sent some of his stewarts ahead — with his household furniture, library, plate, horses and valuable collection of maps — to prepare his residence in the New World. They sailed on the ill-fated ship *Francis,* which was lost with all on board in the surf and sands of Sable Island. When news of the tragedy finally got to Halifax, stories of murderous wreckers living on the island were revived. It was freely surmised that there had been survivors from the *Francis,* but that they had been done away with so that the wreckers could plunder the duke's wealth. Fishermen claimed to have seen jewels and strange objects in the huts of other fishermen, which they firmly believed had come from the *Francis*' holds.

In the wave of excitement that followed, the legislature met and passed an act authorizing the governor of Nova Scotia to appoint an agent from time to time to visit Sable Island and see what was going on there. He would have authority to eject any persons he found living on the island without a license from the Canadian government and to confiscate any wrecked goods in their possession. Justices were to send such persons to jail, sell the goods and pay the proceeds to the rightful owner, or hold them for him. At his first visit, the governor's representative to Sable found a man and wife and a great herd of wild horses on the island. The couple, who were sent elsewhere, were the only known wreckers ever found on Sable.

The government then placed a superintendent and three families on the island, to be supplied with necessities and paid small salaries "to do their utmost to protect life and property."[1] (At this time the protecting of life and property was thought of as one activity, the salvor and the lifesaver being identical.) The families took with them a whaleboat, provisions, materials to build a house, a bull, two cows, two sows, one boar, a pair of goats, two rams, eight ewes and a horse. This was the beginning of the first lifesaving station in North America.

The first superintendent, James Morris, drew plans for two lighthouses for Sable Island, but seafaring men at first opposed such an innovation. They argued that if there was no light on Sable, seafarers would be encouraged to keep a safe distance. If there were a light, however, they would without doubt "run for it" and, before they realized it, would be drawn among the shoals and sand bars. It was also said that shipwrecks generally occurred at times of fog and storm, and that a light would be no good at such a time, anyway, as it wouldn't show.

The vicissitudes of the early lifesavers make interesting reading. Not the least of their hardships was the plague of ravenous rats come ashore from wrecked vessels. Cats were brought in to deal with them. Then the cats multiplied and became a nuisance, so dogs were imported to exterminate the cats. The families also stocked rabbits, but one day a single snowy owl arrived, took a look around and flew away, only to return later with a flock of owls that quickly made away with the rabbits. The wild horses, however, have persisted, and a few are still sold each year on the mainland. They are able to live on the natural fodder. During the wild winter storms they form a circle behind a sheltering dune, with the young and the weak in the center. It is generally believed that the herd was started from a cargo of animals placed on Sable in 1760 by Thomas Hancock, uncle of John Hancock, for the help of shipwrecked mariners.

By 1804 the keepers of the island reported five shipwrecks, forty-one lives saved and salvaged property on hand valued at £2300. When possible, wrecked vessels were preserved; but if too far gone, they were stripped of copper and iron, and their cargoes were landed and cared for. A government vessel visited the island every few months to land supplies and to carry away accumulated salvaged merchandise to Halifax, where it was sold. A portion of the proceeds was retained as salvage money, from which an allowance was made to the men on the island. Between visits of the government boat, the only communication the Sable Islanders had with the mainland was by carrier pigeon.

A story is told of James Miller, a customs officer who took fourteen days' leave from his job to represent the governor and visit Sable Island with supplies and mail. He sailed in a small schooner with a crew of three. The weather was so bad that he lost two of his crew in attempting to land. With only himself and one sailor on the schooner, he was forced to run before the wind, which persisted for days. At last he reached Antigua, in the Leeward Islands of the West Indies, and made port. It took him four months to get home to Halifax. Another supply ship, the *Ocean Traveler,* left the mainland for Sable Island on October 18, 1870, and was never heard of again.

Eventually the island had a barracks for housing shipwrecked seamen, a warehouse for salvaged goods, a flagstaff with a crow's-nest and lookout 120 feet high, and two shelter huts. In 1873 the two lighthouses recommended by the first superintendent were finally built. It is an interesting fact that, in the first fourteen years of the lights, there were exactly the same number of shipwrecks on Sable Island as during the previous fourteen years. The objections of the early mariners, which today seem so naïve, were perhaps not so far wrong at that.

In 1853, Dorothea Dix was a well-known reformer and lecturer in Boston. Her main activity was promoting interest in the establishment of public institutions for care of the insane. At that time it was not uncommon for hopelessly insane persons to be taken to remote places and left to shift for themselves; and when Miss Dix was lecturing in Halifax, she asked to visit Sable Island on the government supply boat. She had apparently heard that insane persons were abandoned on the island — and there actually was one. For the sake of this unfortunate, she braved the dangers of landing on Sable through the surf.

While she was there, Miss Dix had the experience of witnessing a shipwreck and seeing the lifesavers in action. The schooner *Guide* of London, bound from New York to Labrador with provisions, struck the inner bar on the south side of the island. The sea was too heavy for the *Guide*'s crew to run out an anchor and the master realized that his ship was doomed. In a last effort to save his cargo, he determined to make sail and run a cable and anchor ashore, to help the vessel beach higher on the sand. The maneuver was successful, and the *Guide*'s crew were safely brought ashore in the lifesavers' surfboat, together with their clothing and effects. What then took place is told in a letter written by an eyewitness and published during the lifetime of Dorothea Dix:

> The ship was abandoned by all but the captain. He had become a raving maniac, and would not leave. Miss Dix rode to the beach on horseback, as the last boat landed from the ill fated vessel, and learned the sad fate of the commander, who, the sailors said, was a kindhearted man. She pled with them to return to the wreck and bring him on shore, and to bind him if it was necessary for his safety. They obeyed her summons, and soon were again on the beach with their captain bound hand and foot. She loosed the cords, took him by the arm and led him to a boathouse built for the shipwrecked, and there by calm words calmed his mind and persuaded him to thank the sailors for saving his life. She trusted that rest and nourishing food would restore him to reason.[2]

From subsequent reference to the captain, it appears that she was right.

Dorothea Dix was a well-informed and observant woman. She saw that the men on Sable did not have the up-to-date life-saving gear which, by that time, was in use along the northern coast of the United States. There was no lifeboat, no wagon to carry the clumsy whaleboat along the beach, no mortar for throwing a line across a wrecked vessel, no breeches buoy. She returned to Boston and immediately set about raising money in that city, New York and Philadelphia to build three lifeboats for Sable Island and to equip them with the most modern apparatus. She enlisted the aid of Captain R. B. Forbes, then chairman of the Massachusetts Humane Society, to handle the construction and shipping of the boats. The project went forward without delay, and the first of the boats was rushed to Halifax with a letter of presentation:

NEW YORK, Nov. 28, 1853

TO HIS EXCELLENCY SIR JOHN GASPARD LEMARCHANT, K.C.B.
Lieutenant Governor of Nova Scotia

I have the honor and pleasure of consigning by this writing to your Excellency a lifeboat, the *Victoria of Boston* for the use of Sable Island, and which, with its appendages, is a gift to me for this sole purpose from Hon. Abbot Lawrence, Hon. Jonathan Phillips, Col. T. H. Perkins, Hon. Wm. Appleton, R. C. Harper, R. B. Forbes, and G. N. Upton, Esqrs., all of Boston.

To Mr. Forbes, who for courage and knowledge in nautical affairs has a wide reputation, I am especially obliged, since his judgment and experience have assisted me in effecting the completion of my wishes in this business in a satisfactory manner.

D. L. DIX [3]

In a postscript she promised the remaining boats and equipment would follow at once.

The boat arrived at Halifax safely, but the remaining two were shipped in the brig *Eleanor* which was wrecked near Yarmouth, Nova Scotia. The boats were saved, but in a damaged condition, and had to go back to New York for repairs. They finally reached Sable Island late in 1854.

The first new lifeboat had no sooner been installed than a great emergency arose. About six P.M. on November 26, a bitterly cold evening, the ship *Arcadia* of Warren, Maine — 715 tons; William Jordan, Master; carrying a general cargo, 147 passengers and a crew of twenty-one — struck the northeast bar, twenty miles from the lifesaving station, in a deep fog. The Sable Island crew did not learn of the wreck until nine o'clock the next morning. Immediately they hitched island ponies to the new car wagon and raced the new lifeboat to the beach as fast as the horses could draw it.

The *Arcadia* struck about 200 yards from shore, deep in the sand. She listed seaward with two masts gone, and great seas were sweeping over her bows, making hopeless any attempt to escape by means of her own boats. No boat ever used by the men on Sable before could have lived through the surf that was thundering in, but the crew bravely manned the new, untried lifeboat — and found she was good. Without even a rehearsal, they made six successful trips to the laboring *Arcadia* and brought in eighty of the passengers before darkness shut down. By that time the superintendent realized his men were utterly fagged; their clothing was freezing to them, and it was imperative that they have a rest. Reluctantly they withdrew, knowing that the weather might well destroy the wreck before dawn. The cries of the people still on the vessel, when they knew the lifeboat would not return again that night, were hard to endure.

Fortunately the wind abated, and the strength of the waves subsided. When morning came, the Sable Islanders returned and by ten o'clock had brought everybody safely ashore. In reporting the wreck, the superintendent wrote that the new lifeboat "had done what no other boat could do that I have ever seen. It was a fearful time, yet the boat's crew each took their stations readily, and soon showed that they felt the boat to be worthy of her name."[4] On the third night the *Arcadia* was smashed to driftwood, and only a few packages of her cargo and a few scraps of her material were ever saved.

This rescue was not only a triumph for a capable and valiant woman; it was the end of Canadian reluctance to let the United States share the work at Sable Island. Previous offers of assistance had been rejected, but this gift, free from any purpose other than love of humanity, was accepted in the same spirit. And Dorothea Dix never lost her interest in Sable Island. Sometime later she collected and sent several hundred books to start a library on the island.

Three hundred miles of rugged shore in the Canadian Maritime Provinces face the Atlantic. Newfoundland, Nova Scotia and Cape Breton have produced some of the finest seamen in the world. From early colonial days Halifax has been a port of refuge. Its people have always lived with one foot in the sea, ready to repair or refit a damaged vessel or to sail out on a mission of rescue at a moment's notice. The icy waters around Labrador and Newfoundland and the mouth of the St. Lawrence have seen many shipwrecks, and their people are traditional wreckers. As Farley Mowat wrote in his remarkable book *The Grey Seas Under:*

> There is an ancient tradition on the coasts of Labrador and Newfoundland that once a ship is beyond saving she belongs to the people of the shore. . . . There is no more honest race of men than these same fishermen, nor is there a braver race. When ships drive onto the hard rocks of their coasts the dory-men will put out in weather that would sink a well-found lifeboat, and will rescue crew and passengers at the most imminent risk to themselves. Afterward, while the stranded ship remains intact and while there is a possibility of refloating her, she will be treated as scrupulously as a bride. No fisherman will lay a hand on her even while food that would mean months of sure existence to the shore-dwellers rots in her holds. But on the day that she is pronounced doomed — then she belongs to those upon whose shore she lies.[5]

This custom, however, is not followed in other Canadian localities and probably never has been. The *Boston Herald* of

April 6, 1884, carried an account of the loss of the S.S. *Daniel Steinmann* on Sambro Island near Halifax during a stormy night. People on shore, unable to attempt a rescue, showed lights to guide any of the ship's boats that might try to make the perilous passage to land. At daylight a small boat put out from Halifax and rescued nine survivors, all that had outlived the night. Then, the article continued, "John A. Matheson, Capt. Jas. A. Farquhar and F. C. Stevens secured a contract for salvage of the wrecked goods and their vessels and wrecking steamer *Glendon* will be on the spot tomorrow to go at the work." The decks of the *Steinmann* were to be blown up with dynamite and her cargo transferred to the salvage craft, some of which were manned by wrecking crews from neighboring fishing settlements.

It seems to have been customary at that time for a salvor to secure a contract or agreement with the shipowners before moving to clear a wreck. Today, powerful and modern rescue vessels of Foundation Maritime and other salvage firms, operating under the watchful eyes of the London Salvage Association, are stationed up and down Canada's Atlantic approaches, ready to steam out upon receipt of an S O S. Probably some of the finest rescue and salvage work of the modern world has been done amid the rocks, ice and storms of this northern reach.

10

The Approaches to New York

Evil tales were in circulation for years among seafarers and landsmen about a small island lying near the entrance to New York Harbor. Vessels coming in from sea during the night often sighted huge fires on the island's beach, ships at anchor offshore and the silhouetted figures of many men looming darkly against the firelight. The place was widely known as a rendezvous of wreckers, and careful seamen gave it a wide berth.

But the legends of Fire Island were of the same stuff as those of the New Jersey shore, Cape Hatteras and other localities up and down the coast. Actually the island was a shore station for whalers; they brought whale blubber there in strips and rendered out the oil in great try-kettles on the beach. The wreckers were the product of public imagination.

Long Island was the nemesis of many an inbound vessel. Compass errors and careless navigation that neglected to take soundings when approaching land accounted for many casualties almost within sight of port. Gales, tides, rocks and blinding snow were also treacherous. In the great storm of December 23–24, 1811, between fifty and sixty ships were lost on the shores of the island or in the sound nearby. Early Long Islanders risked their lives without hesitation to help anyone in danger — and took without qualms the gifts the sea brought them. For generations they bore the stigma of "land pirates" in the metropolitan press and among those who read it.

Soon after New York ceased to be a colony of His Britannic Majesty and became part of the new Union, its legislature enacted a law giving the residue of all shipwrecks into the hands

F. J. Watson, Jr.

Volunteer lifeboatmen were local heroes when they were able to reach a wreck and bring off the survivors. The schooner *Thomas G. Smith* was an 1878 casualty of the New Jersey shore.

of certain officers, to be appointed by the governor and to be known as wreck masters or coast masters. One such officer, Thomas I. Strong, Gentleman, a Long Island seaside farmer, was authorized to serve as wreck master at Mt. Mersey Point:

> . . . to aid and assist all such ships and vessels as may happen to be stranded on the coast in the County of Suffolk, with full power and authority to give all possible assistance to all such ships and vessels, to all people on board the same. To use his utmost endeavors to save, preserve and secure the cargoes of all such ships and vessels and all goods and chattels whatsoever which may at any time be cast by the sea upon the land, and to employ such, and so many men for the purpose, as he may see proper.[1]

Usually the wreck master organized and directed the volunteer rescue work, took over all property from the wreck, identified and buried the dead, and reported all known facts concerning the wreck to his superior. In very early times he also sold the wrecked property, paid salvage to those responsible for saving it and turned over the remainder of the proceeds to the rightful owner or insurer. After 1820, when the Board of Underwriters of the Port of New York was set up to handle losses and report casualties, the wreck master cooperated with the underwriters and customs inspectors. He was more or less under supervision of a captain of the Revenue Marine Service, the forerunner of the United States Coast Guard.

At Southampton, Long Island, after a severe storm in the autumn of 1816, the wreck master was notified of a strange vessel, unlike the usual American coaster, adrift offshore and seemingly abandoned. The following morning he discovered the ship had gone ashore near Shinnecook Bay. Three men rowed to her and found no one on board, no ship's papers, no name or identifying mark of any kind. Food and clothing were scattered about as if the vessel had been abandoned in haste. The wreck master took charge and advertised the nameless, stranded vessel. Receiving no claim from her owners, he eventually sold her rigging at auction. On the day of the sale, someone noticed a Spanish piece of eight in the debris of her tilted deck; an eager search was made, but no other coins were located. The following day the material of the hull was sold where it lay. A second silver piece was picked up on the deck shortly afterward. Word of the find spread through the neighborhood, and again there was much fruitless searching of the wreck. At last all the searchers, including the ship's new owner, were convinced that no more coins would be found.

Some weeks later a whaleman named Henry Green and a friend made a secret trip to the wreck to satisfy their curiosity. They found still another Spanish coin, this time on the cabin floor. Convinced that there was money concealed somewhere on the nameless vessel, the two men went back for a thorough search after dark that night. By the light of a lantern carefully screened from view, they set to work, poking and prodding the rotten planks and timbers until they were weary with the effort. But the search was futile.

As they were about to give up and go home, a tiny flash of reflected light caught one man's eye. It seemed to come from above his head. Quickly turning the light of the lantern full on the overhead planking, he saw that the boards were warped and sprung slightly apart. Along the crack, the glinting edges of innumerable pieces of eight were plainly visible. A surge of excitement gripped the two men. Green recklessly pried loose a rotting plank, and down came a shower of coins on his head. He dropped the lantern and grabbed wildly for the money, but the lantern and most of the coins rolled down the slanting deck into the sea. On all fours in the dark, the men gathered all the money they could find and took it home, agreeing to return as soon as it became dark the following night. Again and again the two whalers made carefully guarded visits and carried away the treasure. Their luck eventually became known, but nobody ever knew just how much they found.

In time the old wooden hull broke up in a storm. Some pieces of eight were found in the sand, and farmers brought teams and plowed the sand at low tide. One man found sixty coins in a single day. Through the following year, "beach dollars" were occasionally turned up by the tide or by enterprising beachcombers.

Several versions of the story have been put forward. One declares that the money ship had taken part in the revolutionary movement in Mexico, but the dates of that movement and of the shipwreck do not seem to coincide. Deep-sea whalemen who saw the vessel before she broke up declared that she resembled ships they had seen on the Spanish Main, and off the coast of Africa. They judged her to be an ex-pirate or slaver. But this was rather late for piracy; only a few, third-rate freebooters were abroad after 1800.

Edward Richard Shaw, in his *Legends of Fire Island Beach,* tells of a tall, cruel-looking man who came ashore from a strange craft about the time of the "money ship wreck" and made observations on Montauk Beach, Long Island. He was recognized as a long-missing pilot of that place, whose wife and daughter still lived nearby. A sudden storm caught his vessel offshore, and seventeen men were seen to abandon her, carrying canvas bags which some thought might have contained money and jewels. Their small boat capsized in the surf as they struggled to reach shore, and only two of them, one the captain, got to land. He claimed the vessel had been captured from Spain by Mexican revolutionaries and that he was bringing her to New York to be refitted as a privateer. When, in the sudden storm, he had thought it necessary to abandon her, the money they had found on board had been divided among the crew members. He himself intended to turn over a big bag of gold and jewels to the Mexican leaders. Another version of the affair says that the captain lived ten years on the beach and never gave up hunting for gold near the site where the small boat had capsized. Finally he found a sealed jar full of money, and with it he built a ship which he named the *Turk*. There seemed to be little or no proof of either version.

For years the coverage of nearby shipwrecks in the metropolitan press was sensational and at times irresponsible. It often characterized the rescuers as "land pirates" and charged them with looting, robbery and even worse. Not all of these charges, of course, were undeserved. In 1835 a grand jury at Trenton, New Jersey, brought indictments against forty persons, two of them justices of the peace, for plundering the cargo of two wrecked vessels, the *James Fisher* and the *Henry Franklin*, which were driven ashore near Barnegat.

The small *Key West Inquirer* had an editorial field day when it learned of these charges through New York papers forwarded to its office. The islanders should have been warned by the injustices they had experienced themselves at the hands of a hostile press; but they seem to have accepted without question, and with some smugness, reports of the iniquities of their New Jersey brethren. The *Inquirer* of February 28, 1835, declared:

We have seen numerous accounts of the shocking depravity of the persons engaged in wrecking on the New Jersey shore, and we believe that those upon Long Island are not much better. Cargoes are pillaged, passengers and others robbed, and an utter disregard of all the moral qualities of our nature manifested, and that, too, in a section of country which is thought to be particularly enlightened, and where the laws are looked upon with peculiar reverence. Truly gratifying is it to have in our power to invite a comparison between the acts of those engaged in the same responsible business on the coast of Florida, and the acts of these wreckers of New Jersey and New York.

The editorial emphasized the custom among wreckers of the Florida reef to return, without salvage charge, rescued property belonging to the captain, passengers or crew of a wrecked vessel. In the case of the *Dumfries,* for instance, lost near Dry Tortuga, half of the cargo had belonged to the ship's captain and had been released without charge by the wrecker-captain who saved it. A valuable shipment of books consigned to a college in Alabama was also forwarded to the college without charge.

By 1886 the marine underwriters were largely directing salvage matters on the northeastern seaboard, and New York state abolished its office of wreck master. There were always persons and firms in the area ready to purchase stranded vessels and salvage their sails, rigging and metals. When possible, these were sold on the spot; in other cases, they were taken to New York City. A bit of old sailcloth heavily covered with paint was the early equivalent of linoleum floorcloth and often adorned a Long Island kitchen.

The loss of the bark *Elizabeth* near Point o' Woods in a gale on July 19, 1850, brought sensational newspaper headlines. Among her passengers were Margaret Fuller, the pioneer liberal writer and feminist, and her titled Italian husband and small son. All three were drowned with most of the other passengers and crew. The New York papers were vociferous in their denunciation of "land sharks" and pirates on the Long Island shore, claiming that such persons had not only made off with everything that drifted ashore from the *Elizabeth* but had even stripped the dead of their clothing. The reporters evidently did not know the facts of life regarding shipwrecks — that bodies are often tumbled about by the waves until all their clothing is shredded and torn away, and are then flung, broken and sometimes dismembered, onto the rocks. Some of the *Elizabeth*'s cargo was found; but whether the seaside villagers took it for their own profit, or to protect it temporarily from the elements, is anybody's guess.

There were 300 Irish immigrants and a cargo of soap, iron and salt on the *Catherine* of Liverpool, which stranded near Amagansett, Long Island, in August of the following year. The passengers were gotten safely ashore, and word was sent to New York City for a wrecker to race to the scene. She soon arrived and took the passengers and their baggage aboard. Before returning to port, the wreckers stripped the sails, rigging, anchor and chains from the stranded *Catherine* and loaded them on a lighter which they had in tow, along with all the cargo there was room to stow. Most of the *Catherine*'s cargo was lost before further help could reach the wreck.

In February 1846, a great storm swept northward up the Atlantic coast. It shattered nine vessels on the New Jersey shore and strewed their wreckage and cargoes southward from Barnegat for fifty miles. The loss of life and property was severe. The metropolitan newspapers ran lurid stories about the series of disasters, charging that criminal wreckers had refused to aid the victims, had plundered the dead and had demanded money for delivery of the bodies to friends or relatives. It was a shocking report. Some papers even accused the farmers and fishermen living along the New Jersey shore of placing false lights to decoy vessels onto the shore and of looting the wrecks.

Roused by the indignation that swept the state as a result of these inflammatory stories, the governor of New Jersey about a month later sent a commission to the scene of the shipwrecks to determine exactly what had taken place. The commission's report was printed in booklet form and has been preserved. It is a simple, unembellished transcript of the sworn testimony of scores of local people, eyewitnesses, public officials and survivors of the wrecks. The testimony was tragic and pitiful but a vivid tribute to the perseverance and self-forgetful service man has come to expect from his fellows at a time of disaster.

The report concluded:

> We therefore report to your Excellency that the charges in the resolutions under which we act, viz: "That at the time of the late distressing shipwrecks of the *John Minturn* and other vessels on the New Jersey coast, some persons on the shore neglected and refused to render relief and assistance to the perishing passenger and seamen, plundered the bodies of the dead of everything valuable found upon them, and in other cases exacted money for the delivery of the bodies," are according to the best of our judgment upon the evidence, each and every one of them utterly untrue; that there are no inhuman and guilty actors therein to be punished, and that the state ought to be relieved from the odium of such barbarity.[2]

Volunteer rescuers from the shore had saved all hands on four of the nine wrecks. On two more they saved all but a single man. Another ship, the *Alabama*, with seven or eight men on board, struck in the night at an uninhabited spot and was not discovered by persons on shore until too late. The other two craft were the centers of long, heartbreaking effort. Only forty or forty-five lives were lost in the whole series of wrecks.

The governor's investigators traced the handling of every body that washed ashore. The charge that articles of value had been taken from the dead proved to be a distorted rumor based on the work of the local coroner, who had preserved and catalogued everything of value that could be identified as belonging to each victim. The tale that money was exacted for delivery of the bodies to relatives was traced back to an official request for $2 or $3 from the family of each victim to help pay burial costs. And as for the charge that the cargo of one of the vessels was looted: of the $84,000 cargo which was strewn for eighteen miles up and down the beach and which lay exposed for weeks, only about $300 worth was missing when it was finally collected and warehoused. A single instance of the robbing of a trunk or sea chest was uncovered.

Shortly after this occurrence, and evidently inspired by the press coverage, an interesting bit of balderdash was published entitled *The Wreckers, or the Ship Plunderers of Barnegat.* It began:

> Bleak and bitter in the raging storm bristles the surf-foaming, rock-bound reefs of this far-famed beach, the celebrated locality of the notorious Barnegat piracies, which, within the past year or two, have thrown our whole populace into such a whirlwind of excitement; the scene of the dread deeds of death and depredation upon the unfortunate castaways of the seas, committed with such unparallelled enormities by the lawless wreckers of the Jersey Coast, with whose striking report of horrors the land still rings.[3]

The author, Charles E. Averill, a popular writer of his day, then lets his imagination riot among wreckers with gleaming swords and leveled pistols, a valiant maiden and Rudolph Raven, the wrecker-chief.

The early pilots of Cape May, New Jersey, combined wrecking and lifesaving with their duties, and were known for their skill and enterprise. They are said to have been always ready to face storm or freezing weather in order to rescue seamen in danger off their coast or to conduct a ship to safety.

Except for these Cape May pilots, there seem to have been no wreckers in the approaches to New York Harbor who put to sea in search of vessels in distress or did systematic patrolling of dangerous waters. The small wrecking companies no doubt worked hard and effectively, but they missed the flavor of adventure that was the daily bread of the voluntary wrecker—and they missed the big money.

The top echelon, the true elite of the wrecking fraternity, were the skilled and hardy men who lifted the business from the status of beachcombing or junk gathering into a new and exciting profession, based upon and buttressed by old English law. These were the men of the Bahama Islands.

Freddie Maura, Nassau, Bahamas

The streets of Dunmore Town have seen little change since the removal of most of Harbour Island's wrecking families to Key West, over one hundred years ago.

11

The 'Brilanders

Harbour Island — or 'Briland, as they say in good Bahama Cockney — was the point of origin of the Bahama wrecker and his American counterpart, the Key West Conch. 'Briland may not have created such a splash in history as Port Royal or Nassau, which were piratical joy spots, but it made its own small ripple as the spawning ground of the wrecking fraternity. Its sea-minded settlers — descendants of the Eleutherians, refugee planters from the rebelling American colonies and former pirates — in the process of time became welded into a brawny, self-sufficient community. They hewed out plantations on the fertile shores of Eleuthera, built sturdy stone houses on Harbour Island (off the northern tip of Eleuthera) and Green Turtle Cay, and looked to the sea for what it would bring. The answer that came back from the sea was — shipwrecks.

From earliest times the men on Harbour Island had kept a weather eye on the reef-strewn sea around them. Every family had a boat of some kind, and skill with wind and sail was a point of honor. Knowledge of the intricate channels and passes, the depths, shoals and pinnacles of the danger-fraught sea was a common heritage, passed from father to son; and many women-folk could handle a boat alongside their men.

The first Bahamians had come seeking freedom from oppressive political and religious conditions. Out of their solid religious convictions and love of freedom grew a broad-shouldered tolerance of the views and shortcomings of others — a tolerance that made them good citizens and friendly neighbors among the slave-holding planters and retired freebooters who came to live around them. Before the first Irishman set foot on Harbour Island, a little Anglican chapel was built and dedicated to St. Patrick. It was so mosquito-ridden that traveling missionaries who sometimes held services there had to lead the congregation out and finish their sermons on the open beach, where the sea wind could blow away the pests. Life on Harbour Island was never easy; and in the early years an occasional shipwreck, with the odds and ends that were to be recovered from it, brought sorely needed supplies and a little, very welcome excitement. But eventually the 'Brilanders were to make a startling discovery. It concerned geography.

Through the ages nature had been building a trap across the approaches to Cuba, the Gulf of Mexico and South America. She used limestone, sand and the sticky white marl of the shoals; coral polyps and the crustacean life of the teeming tropical sea; the quick-growing mangroves, and the thin coral cement that overspreads and binds and seals all together. From these elements came the rocks and shoals of the Bahama Islands and, across the channel, the Florida Keys. Between them slowly emerged the great reef, from twenty feet to scarcely one foot below the surface of the jade-green water. In some areas the reef extended nearly fifty miles out to sea. Here and there it dropped into deep gorges or rose to peaks or pinnacles so slender that with a single upthrust finger it could rip away the bottom of a vessel, at the very moment her leadsman was sounding a safe six fathoms over the side.

In the narrow space between reef and keys, a channel of safe navigation ran in a 200-mile, crescent-shaped curve through which funneled the northbound Gulf Stream. This was the waterway known to Indian and Spaniard, to coastal trader, pirate and buccaneer. As it narrowed, the water ran faster, creating an eddy that drove a strong southwesterly current over the reef — a current that on a windless day could carry a becalmed and helpless vessel to disaster. Prevailing winds were easterly, forcing northbound ships to keep near the center of the stream; but southbound traffic hugged the edge of the stream to avoid its full force and thus sailed dangerously close to the reef. As if these hazards were not enough, tropical hurricanes drove up from the Caribbean in July and October. These gigantic storms often stirred the ocean to its depths, changed the pattern of the sea bottom, overflowed islands, moved sand bars and swept the sea and sky clear of every living creature. Man had only to sail his fragile, wind-driven ships impudently into nature's trap for the shipwrecks to begin.

The sextant had been invented in 1730 and the chronometer sometime later, but they were slow coming into general use. As late as 1823, Bryant & Sturgis, a Boston shipping firm, wrote to one of its captains who had committed the extravagance of purchasing a chronometer: "Could we have anticipated that our injunctions respecting economy would have been so totally disregarded we would have set fire to the Ship rather than have sent her to sea."[1] Poor charts, the absence of lighthouses, irregular currents, a curved channel requiring repeated changes in the course of a ship, and the frequent and savage storms — all conspired to make the Florida Straits and the Bahama Channel a nightmare to the skipper who had been there before, and a booby trap to the uninitiated.

The first victims who coasted along the passage and into the trap were Spanish adventurers in quest of gold, which Columbus talked about so recklessly upon his return from across the Western Ocean. Between 1520 and 1820 it is estimated that about eight billion dollars in gold, silver and jewels sailed through this passage on its way to Europe or was lost en route. As long as the plate fleets were on the sea, violence and piracy ruled. When the Spanish power declined, plantations and settlements sprang up everywhere, and the little ships of trade and commerce followed. But the trap was set for all alike. Reef and key, shoal, current and gale claimed their toll of the evil and the good, the pursuer and the pursued. Fleeing merchantmen, Spaniard, pirate and peaceful trader — all were caught in the trap and left their bones to bleach on the sandy keys and their ships to rot in the clear green sea.

It took a little time for this state of affairs — and their own vantage point on the main stream of north-south sea traffic — to dawn on the Harbour Islanders. When it did, their enthusiasm for agriculture diminished rapidly. In the meanwhile, they were swept willy-nilly into the stream of political change.

The United States was young and lusty in 1776. Culture and education were in rugged flower among the rebelling colonies from Maine to Carolina, but the country was wild and woolly around the edges. Florida, not even a fringe settlement, was at the moment a loyal British colony. The lower peninsula and the keys held a few Indians, who had fled there from their enemies farther north. The keys were as little known to the average American as the ruined ships bleaching their bones on the sandy beaches or stranded high on the coral reefs.

British loyalists in the American colonies were having a hard time. Bills of attainder threatened banishment and confiscation of their property on mere suspicion of disloyalty to the new government, thus forcing them to flee by the thousands to Florida. Some went home after the dust had settled, and others sailed to Nova Scotia or Bermuda, but a substantial number accepted the invitation of the royal governor of the Bahamas and took permanent residence there.

A few good citizens were not all the Bahamas got from the American Revolution. In February 1776, in the very first foray of the infant United States Navy, Admiral Esek Hopkins sailed from Delaware Bay in an attempt to capture some much needed powder and shot from the forts at Nassau. The Americans seized Governor Montforte Brown, and raised a strange banner for a single day over the Bahamian capital: it carried the British union jack in the corner and thirteen white strips across its red field. The Bahamians, long experienced in raiding parties and outlandish flags, ransomed their officials philosophically with some good British sterling. The visiting Yankees sailed for home with a hundred guns, some powder and shot — and two hundred cases of smallpox, all picked up at Nassau.

A few years later, in 1783, word got around in Florida that

Nassau had fallen once again, this time to Spain. Colonel Andrew Deveaux — an ardent young loyalist refugee from South Carolina, with two brigantines, an English privateer or two, sixty-five men and a lot of nerve — set sail from St. Augustine to rescue the neighboring British colony. The party sailed bravely across the Bahama Channel and then seem to have realized their lack of prudence, for they weighed anchor off Harbour Island and went ashore to raise some reinforcements. When the loyal 'Brilanders learned the reason for the expedition, nearly 200 of them, white and black, swarmed aboard Colonel Deveaux's ships. One hundred and fifty men brought along their muskets; the others went for the ride; and the combined force did a good job of restoring British rule. (A peace treaty between England and Spain had already been signed at Versailles, but nobody in the Bahamas had heard about it yet.) The grateful governor rewarded the Harbour Islanders with fertile land on Eleuthera, to belong to them and their heirs as commonage forever.

The 'Brilanders dutifully planted their new land, sailing back and forth across the sound daily to cultivate it. They lived mainly on sweet potatoes, crabs, fish and pineapple tarts. On rare occasions a man led a goat with a bell hanging from its neck through the streets, shouting, "Mutton tomorrow!" The goat was butchered that night and the pieces distributed to the purchasers.

But 'Briland hearts were not in agriculture. It was inevitable that some ex-pirate, sailing his fishing smack out to the reef to catch a big one — or perhaps one of his respectable neighbors, pushing farther and farther out into the Bahama Channel — should come upon the harvest of stranded hulls . . . lonely, abandoned and laden with all manner of rich and interesting loot.

However it came about, the Harbour Islanders were soon building bigger and better shallops and schooners. Gradually they abandoned fishing and turtling and went in, all out, for relieving ships in distress — relieving them of everything that could be carried away. They did not confine themselves to Bahamian waters, their wrecking voyages eventually covered

Fashions may come and go, but pink limewashed houses and shops still line the streets of Nassau, capital of the Bahama Islands, adding to their Old World atmosphere.

all the important localities from the American coast to the West Indies. It did not take them long to learn that, by posting lookouts near dangerous places and cruising daily up and down the reefs, they could be on hand, in case a ship was in distress, early enough to do something useful. Sometimes they could work the vessel free of the reef and into deep water before it became hopelessly bilged. This type of service was highly profitable and well suited to their talents and temperament.

Men from Nassau soon joined in the new enterprise. An early letter written to Governor Johnson Wentworth complained that "In New Providence the young and able run a'coasting in shallops, which is a lazie course of life and leaveth none but old men, women, and children to plant. . . . All the Bahamas are healthy and the inhabitants have greater stomachs for the victuals than in any part of America."[2]

From such beginnings, wrecking evolved. From the mere looting of abandoned hulls, it grew into a primitive sort of pilotage, salvage and lifesaving service, with a wrecker showing up in his sloop almost as soon as a vessel struck the reef. If the disabled craft or its cargo was taken to port, it was placed in the custody of an English high court of Admiralty, which apportioned the ship and cargo between the wrecker (as compensation for his services) and the owner or underwriter. There seems to have been no reward, either in cash or in kind, for saving human life. Only if the life belonged to a slave was it considered property and assigned a cash value.

Business in Nassau never being very brisk, the merchants of that city soon began to follow the example of the 'Brilanders, outfitting vessels of their own and hiring anybody they could get to take them to sea as wreckers. "The usual custom in fitting out these small craft on a wrecking and turtling voyage (for they are usually combined) is upon shares," wrote Charles Blacker Vignoles in 1823. "The merchants of Nassau are chiefly the proprietors of the vessels, into which a few barrels of pork, and biscuit are put, the crews being supposedly able to subsist themselves by fishing and hunting, and these crews are composed of the pilots and fishermen of the islands."[3] These arrangements for a wrecking voyage were in some ways similar to those of the early buccaneers. The profits of each voyage were divided according to prearranged shares, and concealment of goods or private filching was forbidden. Each man was responsible for his own food and clothing.

Here let us pause and consider a subject of great but unrecognized importance to American wrecking: the green turtle. The contribution which this huge and succulent creature has made to the welfare of the New World has never been adequately heralded. Without the green turtle, history in the Caribbean would not have followed the pattern we know. Many an honest seafaring man would have become so weakened by lack of food that he could not have fulfilled his strenuous duties in the face of a sudden gale. Many a pirate would have risked capture and sailed smack into the hands of the law because of sheer starvation. And the well-being of the Bahamian wrecker himself would have languished.

Green turtles abounded in the warm seas of the area. They could be caught and kept on board a vessel alive, thus providing an inexhaustible source of fresh meat at a time when refrigeration was unknown and men were only beginning to learn from the Indians to eat green vegetables. The English trader John Nicholl, writing of his stay on Saint Lucia (in the Windward Islands) in 1605, may have been the first man in history to sing of the veal-like flavor of turtle steak sprinkled with "Guinnie pepper."[4] Today his song has swelled into a vast chorus of happy diners who have sampled the delicious meat of these great turtles as it is served all around the Caribbean.

By 1815 fifty or sixty Bahamian vessels and over 500 men were engaged in the business of wrecking, which had become the main industry of the "out islands." Nassau was gratified, but down at Havana the Spanish took a dim view of it. So far as they were concerned, a pirate under any name was still a pirate. No funny business such as an oath to support a British monarch had changed his status. Spain had suffered too long at the hands of West Indian buccaneers to accept a strange vessel, flying British colors, as a friend or salvor.

Curiously, Spanish captains have held firmly to this belief in piracy even into the present century. The famed Black Fleet, a group of Bahamian Negro wreckers, operated shortly after 1900 from Tabonas Island and Rodriguez Key, near the American coast. The Spanish rated them as freebooters and charged them with boarding becalmed and helpless vessels and taking unauthorized control.

This lingering distrust of the British wrecker is also illustrated by a story told by W. C. Albury of Nassau. Albury, the third generation of a family of wreckers, spent fifty years as commissioner of education for the Bahamas, sailing from island to island in his own small sloop. He was born and grew up on Harbour Island; the family lived in a big stone house close to the sea, and the children slept in the attic on the third floor. One of the boys in the family got his first whipping for telling the neighbors he had seen his father dividing a pile of "brass dollars" with his crew upon returning from a wrecking voyage to Spanish America. Albury himself saw the men go out of the house carrying the gold doubloons in their hats.

One night when Albury was about eight years old, he was awakened by the sound of a conch shell blown in the street. He hopped out of bed and ran to the window. It was storming outside and very dark. Men were running from house to house knocking on doors and shouting "Wreck asho-o-re!" Out in the blackness that he knew was the sea, a rocket streaked up into the sky, arched over and dropped back in a shower of sparks. Lamps began to show in the neighbors' houses. The town was in an uproar. The children grabbed their clothes and rushed downstairs, where they found some men urging their father to go out to the wreck with them. He steadily refused, insisting that he had not been wrecking for years and that his boat was in no condition to take out on such a night. The others soon went away and left him.

When morning came the boy found that all the able-bodied men in the village except his father had gone to the wreck and that all the women were out watching the sea. Presently his grandfather came to the house and was surprised to see that his father was still there. The senior Albury, although too old for the strenuous work of wrecking, owned a schooner that had been and still was the pride of his heart.

"You take the *Sophie,*" he told his son, "and go join the others. She'll be yours someday, anyway."

His son reminded him that there was no one left in the village to make up a crew.

"You go get ready, and get down to the wharf," the old man assured him. "I'll get you a crew."

And he did.

By the time Albury's father reached the *Sophie* with his arms full of extra clothing and all the cooked food in the house, his grandfather had made a trip through the town and rounded up a crew of his cronies, the old men who had been left behind by their stalwart sons and grandsons. Proudly the oldsters rose to the occasion and sailed the *Sophie* out into the turbulent sea.

"Nobody ever knew exactly where a wreck was," Albury explained. "My father used to say he could smell a wreck in the dark. No matter where a ship struck, there would be a half dozen wreckers clustered around her within a few hours."

This wreck proved to be a Spanish steamer, richly loaded with general cargo, foodstuffs and luxury items for the Havana market. It was late in the day when the *Sophie* approached her and found a circle of wreckers riding it out in the tossing sea, a respectful distance from the ship. The Spanish crew were holding them off with firearms, doubtless thinking they were protecting their ship from pirates.

"My father spoke Spanish pretty well," Albury continued. "He sailed the *Sophie* right through the ring of waiting wreckers and hove to beside the Spanish ship. He talked nice to the captain and soon was invited on board. Probably the Captain decided the boatload of old men wasn't too dangerous."

Albury's father was able to convince the Spaniard that the condition of his ship was serious, that assistance was at hand and that he had better take advantage of it and let them begin salvage operations. There was barely time to get the cargo off before the ship began to break up.

It was a field day for the 'Brilanders, who swarmed onto the sinking ship. In a few hours the streets of Dunmore Town were piled high with goods, dumped there hastily so that the schooners could return to the wreck again and again for more. Soon a kind of shuttle service was in operation, transporting the merchandise to Nassau. There was so much rice in the wreck that Nassau authorities sent word not to send any more to them, since they could not dispose of it.

"We had rice for breakfast, rice for dinner and rice for supper," Albury recalled, "and we sent quantities of it to all the neighbors. We children walked the beaches with the women and picked up cheeses, hairpins and rubber bands in small packages that floated ashore."

The ship itself was a total loss, and the Admiralty court at Nassau sold vessel and cargo at auction to local buyers. Salvage awards and government costs were paid out of the proceeds of the sale, and what was left went to the underwriters.

"A long time after that wreck," Albury added, smiling, "I was playing on board the *Sophie;* and in the after cabin, among some coils of rope, I found a big, shiny tin box. I tried to pull it out, but it was too heavy for me, so I pried off the lid. It was full of sugar plums—hard candy, you know. I stuffed all I could into my mouth and pockets and replaced the lid, intending to come back again for more. But my father saw me and asked what I was eating. I had to show him the box. He wasn't angry but heaved it up on his wide shoulder and took it home. The candy lasted all winter."

The next yarn the old man told may have referred to the same wreck. (I could not be sure and did not wish to interrupt him, for fear of breaking the flow of childhood reminiscence.)

"Near Harbour Island a ship named the *Vandano* or *Avondano* or something like that piled up on the reef, and about everybody in town got something for himself from the quantity of cargo brought ashore."

When the salvaged merchandise began arriving at Nassau, a rumor went around that city that the wrecked vessel carried a golden image of the Virgin Mary consigned to a church in South America. The image could not be found among the salvaged material, and nobody seemed to know anything about it. A few days after the wreck had broken up and gone down, a special constable from Nassau stepped off his sloop at Dunmore Town on Harbour Island with a search warrant and, to the dismay of the 'Brilanders, began a house-to-house search for the golden image.

There was consternation in town. Just about everybody had some bit of the merchandise or fittings of the doomed ship—plunder which, strictly speaking, had not been legally come

Freddie Maura, Nassau, Bahamas

Individuality has always had full play in the "out islands" of the Bahamas. For her grocery store on Harbour Island, Mae Sturrup devised an effective way of advertising merchandise.

by. Someone thought of taking what he had and hiding it in the tall grass out behind the town. The idea caught on, and; all who could do so followed suit. It was a good plan, except that a watching prankster learned where the things were hidden and, after dark, went out and hid them somewhere else. There was plenty of excitement next day, but nobody ever found the golden image or heard of it again.

"We finally decided that all the talk that went around was just some Nassau wrecker's idea of a practical joke on the Harbour Islanders," said the old man with a twinkle in his eye.

12

The City of Wreckers

With sea-borne trade on the increase, the power of Spain declining, piracy all but wiped out and the little ships of the 'Brilanders poking about the reefs, far-reaching changes were in the offing. Soon the wrecking grounds would pass into the hands of a vigorous, young nation, very conscious of its sovereignty. Spain had ceased to value her Florida properties and had traded them to Great Britain, which after a brief twenty years returned them in another territorial swap. This opened the way for the United States to consider their purchase from Spain.

The new nation was sea-minded and world-conscious. The old skill of the British shipwrights was flowering in its shipyards. Nathaniel Brown Palmer, John Griffiths and Donald McKay were turning out the finest and fastest sailing craft the world had ever seen. Every Atlantic port burgeoned with trade. Farm families in Maine were building their own ships after the crops were gathered, taking the cow, pig and chickens on board and trading up and down the seven seas. Gold had not yet been discovered in California, and the great rush westward that would draw men's hearts away from the sea had not begun. The sturdy colonies that had found their nationhood as a cluster of seaport towns were at the zenith of their brief, bright years of maritime glory.

In the welter of news brought home by returning mariners were accounts of both good and evil fortune. Mingled with the stories of success and high adventure were dire tales of shipping losses, of tropical storms through which no vessel could

Painting by Charles Robert Patterson

Glory of the Seas, Donald McKay's last clipper, was built in 1869, sailed until 1908, was a cold-storage bin for fish and finally junked. Patterson's painting has saved her for posterity.

live and of shipwrecks and rescues from reef, key and sandy shoal. Little was said about deliverance from these dangers. To the seagoing trader, his losses loomed large, and gratitude for his release from peril was often obscured by the bitter memory of the fat share of cargo he had had to pay for it.

Such a memory was often rendered more poignant by the conviction that the wrecker who had saved the ship was probably a scoundrel. Captains often complained that wreckers forced their way on board their vessels, removed cargo even when it was secure and demanded excessive pay for their services. Every shipwrecked captain was inclined to look upon professional salvors as human scavengers, fattening on the misfortunes of honest mariners. By the time he was safe at home with a sadly depleted cargo or profit, a skipper could see little skill in their methods and little justice in their claims. These opinions spread quickly, and by the time it was generally known that there were professional wreckers in the remote southern seas, it was believed that they should be more avoided than sought after. Tales of their conspiring with lighthouse keepers, hanging lanterns on the necks of wandering goats and inventing other fantastic deviltry to lure ships to the rocks were common, though there was no evidence to support them.

American empire building and industrial expansion were only beginning in 1821. Few roads as yet led back from the coast into the interior of the country. The only highway system was nature's network of rivers and streams. Farm produce, lumber and livestock from inland states were loaded on flatboats and carried down the rivers and streams to the Mississippi and then south to New Orleans. At that port everything was transferred to coastal sailing vessels, which carried cargoes across the Gulf of Mexico, around Florida and up the coast to the eastern seaboard cities — or even to Europe. Merchants along the Atlantic coast knew that losses were continually being sustained in the perilous bottleneck of the Florida Straits, and they were the first to recognize the growing importance of the wrecking trade based on the Bahama Islands. These merchants shared the law's opinion that wreckers were agents of rescue whose business was salvage, saving lives and merchandise and refloating damaged vessels which might otherwise be lost.

The first man to recognize frankly the need for an official wrecking station on the American side of the Straits was John Watson Simonton. Among men of stature developing in the United States at this period of national expansion, Simonton holds a unique position. His field was small compared with that of the empire builders who followed him a few years later, blazing the trails across the continent. But he developed responsibly and capably one of the most unusual communities in the lusty, new country — a city of mariners, settled for the avowed purpose of serving the shipwrecked at a profit. Simonton had business interests in gulf ports, Havana and New York, and made frequent voyages between these points and his home in New Jersey. He was thus able to see at first hand the need for a maritime rescue and salvage station in the approaches to the Gulf of

Mexico, and to foresee the opportunity of developing a community there equipped to do marine servicing and repairs.

In his many trips through the Florida Straits, Simonton had noted a logical place for such a settlement: the little island of Cayo Hueso (Bone Island), which lay athwart the reef at the very entrance to the Gulf of Mexico, ninety miles across the straits from Havana. Here the blue waters of the Gulf Stream circle out and begin their long course up the coast to Hatteras. The choice of Cayo Hueso was confirmed by one of Simonton's friends, who was shipwrecked nearby and taken there by his rescuers to ride out the storm. He described its convenient location close to the reefs and its accessible, protected harbor.

The island was a solid mass of limestone and coral about two miles wide and four miles long, lying far enough from the mainland to be thought safe from Indian attack. A ridge of rocky shore on the deep-water side was suitable for homes and wharves. It was uninhabited, since there was no natural supply of fresh water; but the abundant rainfall could be caught and stored without difficulty. The surrounding seas teemed with fish, and game was abundant in the thick woods.

In 1819, Florida — a refuge for marauding Indians, fugitive slaves and white renegades — was still Spanish territory. General Andrew Jackson, who was sent to restore order on the ill-defined border of the Louisiana Purchase, seized Pensacola and St. Marks on the Gulf of Mexico coast and placed that region under military control. The situation prodded Spain into signing a treaty on February 22, 1819, ceding all of Spanish Florida to the United States for a consideration of five million dollars. The treaty of cession was ratified in July 1821.

The following December, Simonton wrote to the secretary of war, Smith Thompson, calling his attention to Cayo Hueso: "It is the only eligible situation for a depot of wrecked property on the whole coast of Florida."[1] On January 19, 1822,[2] Simonton, then visiting in Havana, bought Cayo Hueso for $2,000 from Juan Pablo Salas, a resident of St. Augustine who was in Cuba for the Christmas holidays. News of the purchase spread quickly

Key West's waterfront still shows traces of its early days as a wrecking center. The great winds still blow and the commercial and sports fishing fleets still provide occasional casualties.

up and down the coast. Within a few weeks, Simonton had sold portions of the island to three businessmen, who became his partners in the enterprise.

On March 25, Lieutenant Galbraith Perry of the U. S. Schooner *Shark*, under orders from the Navy Department at Washington, landed at Cayo Hueso, raised a flag and took formal possession of the key and the neighboring islands in the name of the United States, as part of the territory ceded by Spain. This move was important in view of the offshore location of the key and the vague boundaries of much of the United States at that time. It could hardly have been a coincidence, however, that the ceremony took place so soon after Simonton's purchase, for two of his partners were present at the landing. In April, Simonton arrived with a shipload of building material and workmen.

But an unexpected complication quickly arose. Hardly had work begun on the first building when another party of men appeared, supported by the U. S. Schooner *Revenge*, and claimed the island as the property of John Geddes. They asserted that Salas, before selling the island to Simonton, had made a conditional sale of the same property to John B. Strong in return for a thirty-one-ton sloop, the *Leopard of Glastonbury*. Strong had transferred his claim to Geddes, and it was in support of this claim that the rival party had landed and was erecting a small building. Simonton immediately took the matter to court, where a compromise was effected: he received a clear title to the island, and Salas deeded 500 acres of land in east Florida to Strong to satisfy the Geddes claim.

Among the acts of Congress at this time were many measures regulating navigation in a determined effort to build up America's shipping industry and protect it from foreign competition. Simonton was astute enough to deal directly with the lawmakers in Washington and to anchor his colony firmly in federal statutes from the start. By the close of 1822, Congress and the President had declared Cayo Hueso a port of entry, with a deputy collector of customs as its first public official.[3] Already vessels from North

Atlantic ports were beginning to sail on wrecking voyages to the Florida Straits. Passing shipmasters, traders, commercial adventurers and fishermen soon began dropping in to look over the new settlement. These men could climb the rigging of their ships in the harbor and, with a spyglass, see the skeletons of old wrecks dotting the reefs offshore. To thrifty New Englanders, who could cut ice from a Connecticut pond and make a profit selling it at Havana, the new settlement at Key West (as they were soon pronouncing the unfamiliar name Cayo Hueso) looked like a gold strike. Here were a good harbor and high land for a town with what appeared to be an endless supply of shipwrecks at its very door. A smart man with imagination could picture a rugged and profitable life, and even the dullest could see the opportunity for shopkeepers, warehousemen, ship fitters, sailmakers and the like. Responsible merchants foresaw fortunes in buying and selling wrecked ships and cargoes. They all began to move in, and a self-sufficient, turbulent, frontier community quickly took shape.

Upstanding, durable and individualistic, these pioneers became contenders in a scramble for quick wealth as intense in its own way as the oil booms of a later date. Vessels from farther north began basing at Key West, and a company was formed at St. Augustine to send a schooner to the wrecking grounds during the storm season. Governor DuVal of Florida, petitioning Congress for a lighthouse, wrote in 1824: "Key West, a little village of hardy seamen, is undisturbedly reaping a rich harvest from the enormous losses of commerce on the reefs and the vast, unlighted coast." [4]

The first settlers to arrive here were able and intelligent men, but the riffraff were hard on their heels. Yankee shipmasters; merchants and speculators from Virginia, Carolina and the gulf states; traders and adventurers from New York — these shrewd adventurers mingled with fishermen, turtlers, shipwrecked crewmen and the drifters that gravitate to every waterfront town. Some of the settlers came ashore from wrecked vessels, saw teeming prosperity — heaps of salvaged merchandise piled on the shore and in the streets; bolts of lace and embroidery unrolled and strung on fences in the sun to dry — and decided to throw in their lot at the port of their rescue.

Everyone who came was water-borne. Some sailed down in their own schooners, as thousands of Florida-bound families today pack their furniture in trailers for the trip south. Often the settlers brought building materials with them; others lived in tents on the beach until they could build shelters from salvaged timbers and sheathing. The island soil was shallow and the coral rock so close to the surface that little gardening was possible. People lived on what they could take from the sea, or find in wrecked vessels on the reef, or fetch in a day's sail from Havana, the nearest settled community.

It was the do-as-you-please era — lusty, expanding, self-confident. Grogshops lined the waterfront. There was not an American magistrate, school, church or court of law nearer than Pensacola, 400 miles away. No news came from the outside world unless a passing ship dropped anchor in the harbor or someone made a trip to Havana or Charleston. Houses began to go up on the west shore, the deep-water side of the island, each with its shop and ways, as natural to it as a chicken coop to a farmhouse. Next came wharves and warehouses to receive and protect merchandise brought in from the sea. Prospects in the wrecking trade were bright, and if excessively good weather should interrupt the supply of distressed shipping, there still remained good profits in fishing, turtling and sponging. Adjacent waters teemed with fish: a hook and line might snag a 300-pound jewfish, or a one-pound grunt, or any of hundreds of varieties in between. With a ready market over at Havana, a man couldn't lose.

Yet with all its prosperity, Key West never lost its daring or its heart. There were no provisions for lifesaving south of the Carolinas until after the Civil War, but the wreckers accepted this responsibility as their natural duty. Rescued persons were taken to their homes and cared for as guests. At times every house in town sheltered one or more shipwreck victims, and tents were

Along the deep-water side of Key West, the sturdy stone warehouses of the wreckers still stand. Here rescued cargoes were protected pending action of the court. This one became a beer warehouse.

set up on the beach for the overflow. It is a remarkable and little-known fact that during the first eleven or twelve years of the Key West settlement — until the hurricane of 1835 — no life is known to have been lost in the surrounding seas because of shipwreck. The wreckers themselves took this lifesaving part of their work so much in stride that today it is all but forgotten.

About the time Simonton and his friends were arriving, a few third-rate pirates still skulked in the West Indies. They were small fry as pirates go, but their nuisance value was high and kept trade in a dither. Britain, France and the United States decided to take simultaneous steps against them. Commodore David Porter, who had commanded the American privateer *Essex* in the War of 1812 (and himself had been rated as a pirate by the British) was ordered south with a squadron of pirate chasers in 1823 as commander-in-chief. The commodore was the proud master of the first steam vessel in the American navy, an old New York ferryboat called the *Sea Gull.* With it as flagship and twenty-one oddly assorted small craft, including some twenty-oared barges named *Mosquito, Gnat, Galinipper, Midge* and *Sandfly,* the commodore sailed in Key West Harbor, established it as his base of operations and set up a naval depot and storehouse.

The accepted technique of pirate chasing in those days was to go after them in the biggest and best ships available. The pirates, wise in the ways of their shallow seas, used fast, light-draft vessels that could dodge into shallow bayous or river mouths and disappear, while the frustrated forces of law and order remained stuck in the mud outside. Commodore Porter developed a new technique, sold it to his superiors and, with his mosquito fleet, sailed southward to try it out.

Basing his craft in Key West Harbor he would steam out in the innocent-looking *Sea Gull,* towing a string of empty barges behind, and cruise slowly along near one of the pirates' known hangouts until he sighted a suspicious craft. As soon as identification could be made Porter would man the barges and go after the suspect with superior force and faster craft. His method paid off too well! Spain became uneasy and invoked an edict, signed in 1592 by Philip II, which forbade foreign vessels from entering the Gulf of Mexico.

Soon afterwards, when chasing a Spanish picaroon near Puerto Rico, the commodore saw his quarry land at Fajardo. He sent a naval lieutenant ashore in a small boat to continue the chase, but Spanish officials arrested the luckless lieutenant and locked him up. When the news reached the commodore, he stormed ashore, secured the release of his officer and demanded and received an apology. While this incident discouraged further piracy in the Caribbean, it also ended the career of the commodore in the United States Navy. Spain charged him with violation of Spanish territory, and he was offered up by his superiors as a sacrifice to international courtesy. Indignant at his suspension from duty for six months, he resigned his commission and joined the Mexican navy. Eventually he was officially forgiven and spent his last days as United States ambassador to Turkey.

13

The Do-As-You-Please Era

New World frontiers were often stabilized by courage and fair dealing long before organized society or legal processes got there. Along the fringes of the sea, it was much the same as in the settlements reaching westward out into the Great Plains. Many of the early settlers were equipped with the sturdy morality that makes human living possible out beyond the edge of things. Such people carried their own law with them. But there were others who had no such inward restraint, to whom the absence of legal processes meant an opportunity to do as they pleased. The new colony of Key West had its share of both. The wrecking captains and crews were free spirits of the Bahamian and the American coasts, British in background and often so alike in speech and character as to be indistinguishable one from another. The family tie, strained in two recent wars, had never been severed by bloodshed in that area.

During the do-as-you-please era, the figure of John Watson Simonton looms large. Simonton spent portions of his time in Key West, but did not make the island his home or abandon his wide interests elsewhere. His sponsorship was in the nature of a commercial venture: he held title to the island and divided it with three business associates — Pardon C. Greene, a shipmaster and trader from Rhode Island; John William Fleeming, a merchant of Mobile, Alabama; and John Whitehead, son of a New Jersey banker. The four men sold (or freely deeded) parcels of land to desirable families who arrived and thus exerted some control over the quality of settlers received into the community. Simonton could take the initiative when necessary but he preferred to remain in the background and let the settlement grow in its own way. What profit he made came through the mercantile business on the island of Pardon C. Greene.

Future students will have to assess Simonton's contribution to history; but in the introduction of law and order into lower Florida, there is no question that his example as leader and citizen, as well as his influence with the government in Washington, was invaluable. His settlement throve from the beginning. As fast as newcomers sailed into the harbor and got their bearings, they sailed out again; bound for the reefs. When not otherwise engaged, they began putting up houses for the families that would join them later.

The first real problem to face the new venture was competition. Bahamian wreckers, and occasionally Spanish wreckers from Cuba, continued to operate on the reefs as vigorously and successfully as if that area belonged to them. They continued to occupy stations at Cape Florida, Key West and Tavernier, just as they had always done. The third was a choice rendezvous convenient to Conch, Molasses, Elbo, French and Careysfort reefs, all of them hazardous to vessels on a lee shore. These wreckers would cruise up and down the coast by day, looking for shipping in trouble, and return to their anchorages at night. How to get rid of them was the problem.

Soon after Florida became an American possession, Andrew Jackson was appointed governor. He was assisted by a legislative council, which created the local law, such as it was. To attend early sessions of the council, a delegate from Key West had to sail up the coast to New York City, then ride successive stagecoaches back to Georgia and travel by horseback down to St. Joseph, on the gulf coast near Pensacola — or, later, to the new capital at Tallahassee. In the bustling new settlement of Key West, it was seldom that anybody had time to make such a trip, and the new legislative council could not have been very well posted on matters of wrecking. Nevertheless, its ire was soon stirred against the neighboring Bahamians, who, as always, were patrolling the reefs on the Florida shore. In 1822 the council called upon the national Congress to "provide some law upon the subject of wrecking at the Peninsular [*sic*] of Florida, which is now in the hands of foreigners . . . and is frequently made the pretext for piracy and smuggling."[1] Later the council addressed a memorial to the President, urging that the wrecking grounds on the Florida coast be closed to all but American vessels.

Bahamian wreckers took their casualties to Nassau and looked to the British Admiralty court at that city for their salvage awards. The Key Westers, in the absence of a court, practiced a crude sort of arbitration to determine their fees. Some enterprising well-wisher, one not overburdened with respect for legal processes, evidently gained the ear of the council members, for the memorial to Congress regarding Bahamian competition included a recommendation that the tariff on wrecked merchandise be reduced and some kind of machinery "less tedious and expensive than a court of law"[2] be authorized to deal with salvage claims. The eager council members did not wait for Congress to act on their request. On July 4, 1823, before the better element at Key West knew what was happening, they passed their own legislation setting up what became known as "wreckers' courts." This very convenient procedure, which could not be called either tedious or expensive, provided that a wrecker might present his claim for compensation to a justice of the peace or a notary. That official was empowered to summon a jury of five disinterested men who would determine the amount of compensation due the wrecker and whether it should be paid in kind or from the sale of the vessel or its cargo.

This legislation gave a semblance of legality to the determination of salvage fees while keeping such matters out of the hands of the regular courts. The act was promptly condemned by underwriters and the more responsible wreckers themselves, who realized that it gave a wrecker power to choose his own judge and jury and to plunder a wreck under the guise of legal action. For several years this uneven state of affairs rocked along amid lawsuits and legal wrangles over the validity of the wreckers' courts.

Meanwhile, the competition of the 'Brilanders continued to be brisk. The Bahamians saw no reason why they should give up their lucrative activity on the reefs. They had gotten there first and were most advanced in the knowledge of reef and current. The Key Westers forbade the "foreigners" to sail the reef and threatened to throw them off the keys if they continued their activities in American waters. The Bahamians' answer seems to have been "You and who else?" At this delicate point the records grow discreetly silent. It had only been six or eight years since Americans and Britons elsewhere had been at each other's throats, fighting a sea war and hurling worse than threats at one another. There is no record that actual violence broke out on the Florida reefs. But one does wonder.

Governor William P. DuVal of Florida wrote to Congress in 1831 describing the early years: "No violence was, it is believed, committed." He added that the Americans "avoided all amicable association with the foreigners, refused to furnish provisions or aid them in any manner, threw every possible obstacle in their way, enforced vigorously the revenue laws of the United States, relating to foreign vessels in our waters . . . and adopted many other expedients extremely vexacious to those against whom they operated."[3]

The Americans did hold a trump card: the reefs were on their side of the channel. As the tension mounted, Simonton turned the eyes of his boisterous colony to the only possible solution of its problem: the enactment into national law of some basic regulations to bring order into the wrecking business. One strongly suspects his deft hand in the act passed by Congress on March 3, 1825. No matter who was responsible for it, this excellent piece of legislation did service to all sides; it forestalled conflict and made Key West.

Entitled "An Act Concerning Wrecks on the Coast of Florida," the statute read:

Be it enacted by the Senate and House of Representatives of the United States of America, in Congress assembled, That, if any ship or vessel shall, after the passing of this act, be engaged or employed in carrying or transporting any property whatsoever, taken from any wreck, from the sea, or from any of the keys or shoals within the jurisdiction of the United States, on the coast of Florida, to any foreign port or place, every such ship or vessel, so engaged and employed, together with her tackle, apparel, and furniture, shall be wholly forfeited, and may be seized and condemned in any court of the United States or territories thereof, having competent jurisdiction.

Sec. 2. *And be it further enacted,* That all property, of every description whatsoever, which shall be taken from any wreck, from the sea, or from any of the keys and shoals, within the jurisdiction of the United States, on the coast of Florida, shall be brought to some port of entry within the jurisdiction aforesaid.

Sec. 3. *And be it further enacted,* That all and every forfeiture or forfeitures, which shall be incurred by virtue of the provisions of this act, shall accrue one moiety to the informer or informers, and the other to the United States, and may be mitigated or remitted, in manner prescribed by the act, entitled "An act to provide for mitigaing or remitting the forfeitures, penalties, and disabilities, accruing in certain cases therein mentioned," passed the third day of March, one thousand seven hundred and ninety-seven, and made perpetual by an act passed eleventh February, one thousand eight hundred.[4]

The 'Brilanders were good losers. One by one they boarded their vessels and set sail for Key West to look over the new town and get acquainted. Then they went back home; loaded the wife and children, the dog, goat and household goods (and sometimes the house itself, broken into sections of convenient size) onto the schooner, with a lighter or two in tow; waited for a favorable wind; and then set out on the 200-mile voyage down the keys.

Soon Bahama Cockney and Bahama Oxford accents were as common on the straggling new streets of Key West as Down East Yankee or the soft drawl of Alabama. The 'Brilanders did not all come at once but drifted in family by family through the years, until 1835, when the gradual elimination of slavery was completed throughout the Bahamas. Then the remaining Harbour Islanders, with one foot on the land and one on the sea, gave up the struggle to be planters and looked elsewhere for a livelihood. Where was it more promising than across the narrow seas in the thriving new settlement on the American side? In this way many new citizens were added to Key West — wreckers, divers, pilots, merchants, speculators in wrecked goods, ship chandlers — and among them one small boy named William Curry, who was to become the most renowned citizen of the wrecking world, Florida's first millionaire and last private banker.

The wreckers' courts sanctioned by the legislative council were duck soup to the unscrupulous. Many Key Westers would have none of them, but continued their own form of arbitration until something better could be devised. When the community was three years old, however, a flagrant case of fraud played unwittingly into the hands of law and order. Young Jacob Housman sailed into Key West Harbor from Staten Island, New York, and found it to his liking. In September 1825, unsatisfied with the Key West method of arbitration, he towed the wrecked brig *Revenge* 500 miles up the coast to St. Augustine. There he found a notary who gathered five "disinterested" men and formed a wreckers' court, which awarded Housman a neat 95 per cent of the value of the salvaged property, a very satisfactory deal.

The *Revenge* was of French registry, and the French consul happened to be visiting in St. Augustine at the time. Her master, outraged by the verdict of the wreckers' court, appealed to the consul to help him obtain a more just settlement. The consul became indignant at the palpable fraud and had the salvaged property libeled in the superior court. This brought the whole matter of wreckers' courts into litigation. The court's verdict favored the captain of the *Revenge,* and the judge ruled the wreckers' courts invalid. In 1826 the United States Congress confirmed this, voiding the Florida act that had created them.

For a time, arbitration was the only means of settling salvage claims at Key West. But arbitrators were notoriously on the side of the wreckers, and their decisions were often distasteful to underwriters and shipowners. Each award was paid with a portion of the wrecked ship's cargo, which was eventually sold at auction at Key West.

This state of affairs could not go on indefinitely. Simonton saw the growing danger and moved quickly to avert it. In conjunction with the more thoughtful Key Westers, he obtained the cooperation of the legislative council in a joint petition to Congress. This urged the creation of a federal court at Key West, to be charged with the unique duty of controlling and regulating wrecking in nearby coastal waters. When opposition to the plan developed in St. Augustine, which also hoped to attract the rich wrecking business, Simonton set out on a hurried trip to Washington. Some paragraphs of the memorial he presented to Congress make interesting reading:

In our list of grievances pressed against the mother country was the sending our citizens abroad for trial. . . . But in what constituted the difference, in the cases then complained of, and the present? To be sure, the distance was greater from America to England, than from Key West to the United States, yet in the principle there was no difference. . . .

The frequent wrecks which take place along the reef of Florida makes it matter [*sic*] of interest to the citizens of our commercial towns, who of course are in want of some tribunal competent and independent, which . . . may decide upon the amount of salvage, properly chargeable on the various shipwrecks that take place. The property when abandoned must in some way or other be disposed of. The wrecker, with a view to his own interest, will carry it to that point, where least hazard from the dangers of the sea will be encountered, and where on its arrival it may most speedily be decided on. . . .

Capital and capitalists will always go where profit is to be found; a law established then, which will recognize Key West as the point of resort for the various wrecks that take place along the coast, will so attract public attention, as that property will always bring its fair and proper value, and thus everything of suspected injustice to owners be avoided. Already considerable capital is centered on the island, in addition to which, merchants from Havana, only about nine hours sail, will, as they have usually done, resort there when sales are about to take place. . . .[5]

The lawmakers seem to have been impressed, for they passed the desired legislation on May 23, 1828, establishing a federal superior court at Key West, fixing its jurisdiction, naming its officers and providing

> That no vessel shall be employed as a wrecker, unless under the authority of the judge of said court; and that it shall not be lawful to employ on board such vessel, any wrecker who shall have made conditions with the captain or supercargo of any wrecked vessel, before or at the time of affording relief.[6]

When news of the creation of the new court reached Florida, it was duly announced in the small newspaper at Key West. The same issue carried a notice of the arrival of a ship with an assorted cargo of merchandise and a passenger list reading: "C. E. Arledge and lady and five lawyers." The do-as-you-please era was over.

Into the welter of unrestrained rivalries, jealousies, friendships, cliques and collusion came the law. Through the devotion of two able judges, James C. Webb and William Marvin, who used the powers granted them with wisdom and courage, the arbitrary disposal of wrecked property was to be transformed into an orderly and responsible activity, and a handful of oddly assorted adventurers were to become the founders of the richest United States city, per capita, of its time.

But neither legal processes nor human progress could lessen the violence or blunt the danger of the wrecker's calling—above all in those brief spaces between disaster and total destruction, when he and his men struggled to the limit of human endurance to cheat the sea of its immemorial prey.

14

Growing Pains

The coming of law to a frontier community accustomed to doing things its own way often brings turmoil. The pride of the big fellow whose word is law, and the apathy of the little man who accepts it, are both disturbed by the intrusion of a stricter code; they either ignore or resent it. The self-sufficient wrecking settlement at Key West was no exception. It would be pleasant to record that, upon the coming of a federal court, it settled down into a law-abiding and orderly community. But it did not. Its attitude toward law in general resembled its feeling about religion: everybody saw the need for it and welcomed it, until it interfered with his personal habits and desires. Then compliance tapered off — or stopped in its tracks.

In the first days, however, when the demands of an orderly and law-abiding way of life were just beginning to replace the do-as-you-please era, the following incident took place:

Samuel Otis was the keeper of the jail, which was a small frame building quite distant from the settled part of the town. A man by the name of Ayres, who was in the habit of getting drunk, had come to Key West. He was taken in custody by Captain Otis and carried to the residence of Col. Greene, who was one of the magistrates, who upon being told that Ayres was drunk again ordered him put in the lockup, after the following conversation had taken place:

"Well, Squire, Ayres has been drinking again! Shall I take him to jail?"

"You may do with him what you please, Capt. Otis," replied the justice, not well pleased at the moment with the interruption.

"Just as you say, Squire," was the answer of the obsequious

officer, and he forthwith announced to the gentleman in attendance that he must proceed to jail.

"Rot me if I do, Capt. Otis. Ain't I a free citizen of this here republic? I tell you I won't go unless I please, and I don't please unless I get my clothes."

"Well Ayres, where are your clothes?"

"Why they are down in the old shed by the water, and there they may stay for all [of] me, for I won't go to get 'em that's flat, Capt. Otis."

"Will you stay here, then, Ayres, while I go."

"No, I won't; how can you 'spect a man to stay here in this hot sun?"

"Well, Ayres, I don't want you to stay here, then; but while I go after your clothes, do you go to the jail, knock at the door, and Peter will let you in."

Peter, the jailer, was no less a person than one of three mutineers who had been sentenced by the Admiralty court to six months imprisonment, and had stayed there because the judge had commanded him to do so. He was the factotum of Capt. Otis, kept the keys and locked himself in after every necessary opening of the prison doors.

Ayres proceeded to the jail and knocked and when Peter asked who was there he replied "It's me — open the door! Otis says you must let me in, and though I don't like altogether to be shut up with such fellows as you be, I 'spose I must, for they say its law."

Upon that, the doors opened . . . and the prisoner within admitted the prisoner from without.

Jefferson B. Browne, himself an attorney, has preserved this bit of early law enforcement in his book *Key West: The Old and the New.*[1]

Another incident occurred a year or two later, in 1830, when the judge of the new court had become a respected and leading citizen of the town. A Key Wester was tried for murder. It was serious business and a test of the willingness of the community to go along with the new order of things:

Norman Sherwood very probably celebrated the Fourth of July blind drunk, for that appears to have been his normal state. He got into a fist fight the following day with a man named Jones. (Jones may not have been the baptismal name of his adversary, as it was common practice for a certain type of settler to select a new name for himself when he came to town.) Bystanders separated the two, but Sherwood went home to get his pistol and soon returned, telling the world he was going to kill Jones. Onlookers prevailed upon him to do a little target practice and then go away; but as soon as he remembered Jones, he came back and took up the search again, declaring he would shoot any man who tried to stop him.

He ran down his quarry in a grogshop, and the customers quickly scattered. It looked as if Jones was in for it until Sherwood's partner, John Wilson, came up behind him, laid a hand on his shoulder and remonstrated. Sherwood whirled and fired, perhaps before he knew who it was. The crowd overpowered and disarmed him. Jones was saved but the peacemaker died in a few minutes.

At the trial that followed, Sherwood frankly admitted regret at killing his friend but declared that the shooting was his partner's fault. He reminded the judge and jury that he had publicly stated his intention to shoot any man who tried to stop him from killing Jones. When somebody did interfere he did it at his own risk. But this defense did not avail, and Sherwood became the first man in Key West history to be sentenced to be hanged.

During the trial Sherwood was housed in jail, a small, dilapidated wooden structure that had started life as the caboose of a sailing vessel and had arrived at Key West via shipwreck on the reef. It was probably the same jail that Ayres had graced a year or so earlier. The lockup was far from secure, and it was common knowledge that Sherwood had more than one opportunity to make his escape. On the day of execution, as he was being led to the gallows, someone asked him why he had not fled when he could easily have done so.

"They want to hang somebody for a pattern," he muttered in reply, "and I guess I'll gratify 'em."

In his recognition that the new law must take its course, Norman Sherwood contributed about as much to the cause of justice as a rum-soaked derelict could under the circumstances.

The new court handled civil and criminal cases when necessary, but its main purpose was the regulation of wrecking. Its first wrecking decision, rendered on November 3, 1828, involved a cotton carrier named *Nanna.* Wreckers had taken off 450 bales of cotton and refloated the vessel. She was valued at $60,000, and the judge fixed the salvage fee at $10,000. Each crewman's share was $110; boys half this amount, officers more.

The first federal judge, James C. Webb, soon retired to become secretary of state of the new Republic of Texas. His successor, William Marvin, a man of towering character and abilty, was the author of *A Treatise on the Law of Wreck and Salvage,* which has been authoritative in both the United States and the nearby British colonies to our own day. Judge Marvin's knowledge of maritime law, tempered with an understanding of the wrecker's needs and temptations, enabled him to maintain a position as veritable czar over salvage matters for nearly a quarter of a century. The Board of Underwriters of the Port of New York, in its report for 1850, paid tribute to Judge Marvin's evenhanded justice and urged that his service be recognized by a more adequate salary.

The judge's chief means for maintaining authority over the wreckers was his power to grant, withhold and revoke their licenses. The United States revenue cutter stationed at Key West kept watch to see that only licensed vessels and captains worked the wrecking grounds. A license could be revoked for embezzlement of wrecked goods, for grounding a vessel under pretense of piloting her, or for colluding with or corrupting the master of a distressed ship by unlawful presents or promises.

A case notable for its verdict in the interest of fair play was that of the ship *Amos Watchitt,* wrecked near Key West in 1830. The wrecking schooner *Trident* was running along the reef nearby, and her captain saw the other vessel heading directly for the reef. But he gave no warning. After the *Amos Watchitt* struck and went on the rocks, it was floated free and taken to Key West by the *Trident*'s crew, who then claimed a salvage fee for their work. Judge Marvin's ruling denied any payment whatever to the wreckers and took away the captain's license.

The judge's power over the amount of compensation to be awarded for a salvage job was absolute. He used this power consistently to raise the standard of the services performed and the ethics of the business. Typical of his method was a case in which a bark carrying a few passengers was stranded and bilged. Fearing that the vessel would break up under the bumping and buffeting of the waves, the passengers and some of the crew took to the boat and rowed in the general direction of land. When the first wrecker arrived and learned the situation, he left the wreck and went to seek the missing boatload of men. The second wrecker to arrive also sailed on to find the endangered passengers and crew. The third wrecker went to work transferring the cargo to his own ship. When the case came before the court for settlement of salvage, the three wreckers received equal amounts for their services.

A licensed wrecker was required to carry adequate equipment for pulling a stranded vessel into deep water. If the equipment broke or if he failed to get the ship off at the first high tide, he received a lower amount of compensation. A wrecker was held liable for damage to goods, occasioned by any faulty condition of his own craft, while transporting them from the wrecked ship to a warehouse. The judge ruled that regardless of the labor involved, the salvage awarded for saving a vessel intact would necessarily be greater than that allowed when the ship itself was lost and only its cargo saved.

From the legal point of view, the payment of salvage was as much a reward for intangibles as a compensation for services performed. Judge Marvin, commenting upon the immaterial factors that influenced his decisions placed first in importance the degree of enterprise exercised by the wrecker. The fact that he put to sea in tempestuous weather, risking his own life and property to lend aid to others, rated high with the judge. Next he considered the degree of danger from which property had been saved. The third factor was the amount of labor and skill brought into play. When divers risked their eyesight, for example, by working in submerged holds where dyestuffs, chemicals and even poisons were loose in the water, the awards were more liberal than when dry merchandise was merely transferred from one vessel to another and brought safely to port. Lastly, the judge considered the value of the merchandise itself.

A salvage award represented services actually and voluntarily performed. A mere attempt to help, no matter how dangerous, carried no reward. "Whatever of personal gallantry, or of laborious exertion, or of severe sacrifices, may have been already borne," says a legal ruling, "it comes to nothing unless the property is actually saved by the asserted salvors."[2] The wrecker received no compensation whatever unless he brought vessel or cargo safely to port. Should the master of a wrecked vessel agree to pay the wrecker a certain sum, regardless of the success or failure of the salvage effort, that agreement would void any claim the wrecker might make for salvage. If the salvaged ship and cargo were small and the wrecker's services great — as often happened — adequate pay was just not possible.

The court's concern was not entirely in behalf of shipowners or masters. Sometimes the rights of the wreckers had to be defended. One such case involved a ship that was grounded and bilged. Its master and crew took the lifeboat and went for help. A wrecker coming upon the scene took possession of the abandoned craft and began transferring the cargo to his own ship. Before he had completed the work, the missing captain returned with a tug and demanded that the salvor surrender possession of the cargo and vessel. The wrecker refused, declaring he was legally in possession. Soon the owner's agent arrived and demanded possession. He too was refused. The wrecker engaged all the men willing to assist him and continued his work.

The captain and agent, unfamiliar with the law and probably convinced that they were being robbed, returned to Key West and swore out a warrant for the arrest of the wrecker, claiming he had committed larceny. This forced his removal from the distressed ship, and possession of it passed into the hands of the agent, who made no effort to prove the larceny charge. The salvor, however, took the case to court, where the judge ruled that he had been in lawful possession, since the vessel had been abandoned and was in peril of total destruction. A salvor under those circumstances had the right to retain the ship until its salvage was complete, and to receive a just reward for his services.

In the case of the bark *Byron,* the court's decision went the other way. Salvors had carried an anchor ahead of the stranded craft, planting it so as to hold the vessel on the rocks, rather than pull her off as they should. The judge ruled that this action was not the result of ignorance, but an effort to keep the ship on the reef so that the salvors could build up their services and collect more salvage money. They forfeited any payment whatever for their pains.

Whoever presented a claim for salvage had to come into court with clean hands. Such a plea required a basis of honest service and a clear understanding that the wrecker had placed before the court all the property he had saved. Property found derelict or abandoned at sea had likewise to be placed in the custody of the court, and the finder had to make a formal claim against it for salvage. The practice in Key West was to sell the property, pay the salvage award and hold the remainder of the proceeds for a year and a day. If at that time no owner had appeared, the balance was paid to the finder or salvor.

No award was ever asked or expected for saving human life. At times the homes of the little community were overflowing with persons rescued from the sea. Full hospitality seems to have been the custom: the victims either were accepted aboard some outgoing craft or remained and became citizens of the town.

Only once does salvage remuneration seem to have been paid for lifesaving. This exception concerned a brig bound from Havana to a European port with a cargo of sugar and four or five passengers. The vessel went hopelessly aground on a reef eastward of Key West. Only one of its lifeboats was in seaworthy condition, and that one could not hold all the passengers and crew. The officers and men labored desperately to build a raft and were finally able to launch it, dividing the survivors between it and the lifeboat. But seas were heavy and the wind contrary. In order to save anybody at all, the raft had to be cut adrift and left to fend for itself.

The lifeboat was well on its way to Key West when it met a wrecking schooner, whose master was soon informed of the plight of the disabled ship and of the people adrift on the raft. The lifeboat was sent on its way to Key West, and the wrecker set off at once to find the raft. The search took two days and two nights, but the wreckers did find it and took its despairing occupants safely to Key West, where they rejoined the other survivors.

Only then did the wreckers return to the stranded brig. They found it so badly broken up during its two days on the reef that it was impossible to save much more than the rigging, sails, chains and other fittings. "In this case," wrote Judge Webb, who presided, "I awarded to the salvor all the avails of the articles saved, in value not over three or four hundred dollars, as a just though inadequate compensation for efforts in saving human life. And this was the first and only instance in which I ever gave an award for such an object."

15

When the Women Came

In the beginning, Key West was an all-male community with plenty of money to spend. The first women to arrive were predatory visitors from the Havana waterfront cafés. But these girls were not interested in taking on the responsibilities of frontier life, and soon returned to Havana. The first woman settler came in 1823, when the town was about a year old.

Irish-born Ellen Russell Mallory, with her sick husband and two small sons, came not in search of wealth or adventure but to find a healthful climate. The Mallorys were presented with a building lot and there put up a large house, which after her husband's death, Mrs. Mallory turned into a boardinghouse. For several years she was the only woman on the island. Her house became the home of some of the town's leading citizens and was always hospitably open to the sick and the injured. In time it became known up and down the coast as a haven; anyone needing care might be brought ashore there from passing ships and would find a ready welcome.

The next women to arrive were two German sisters, who came to town by way of a shipwreck and decided to remain rather than face further travel by windjammer. At that time the settlement was a rare assortment of masculinity: not only wreckers, divers and pilots, but also ship carpenters, spongers, fishermen, turtlers, gentlemen speculators in salvaged merchandise, gamblers, ship chandlers, sailmakers and riggers, grogshop operators, shipwrecked mariners and the inevitable riffraff.

As money began to flow, houses went up, and married men made quick trips north for their wives and families. Single men sailed away on romantic voyages to Nassau and Havana, to return with brides. The wreckers did not build rude log cabins for their womenfolk in the manner of mainland settlements. Many put up spacious, well-proportioned houses of comfort and even luxury. The material in some instances was salvaged mahogany and cedar, put together by ship carpenters. They did not use nails, but employed mortise and tenon joints, secured by pegs or trenails. Because of the frequent and savage hurricanes, each house was anchored to the underlying rock, which was too solid to permit cellars or basements. Their timbers were four-by-fours or eight-by-eights; no flimsy two-by-fours were used in the old town. Often an observation platform or widow's walk was placed on the roof, where a member of the family might sit with a spyglass and keep an eye on approaching ships skirting the reefs of the Sambos and passing the lighthouse into the harbor. Some of these staunch old houses are standing today, having weathered the hurricanes of more than a hundred years.

Incoming families often brought furniture and household goods with them. Others began housekeeping with odds and ends taken from wrecked vessels or found among salvaged cargoes. The latter might include luxury items, such as Chinese bric-a-brac, oriental rugs, tapestries, silver or china, which had been consigned to Havana or the South American markets. One housewife bought an iron bed at an auction of wrecked merchandise; her small son, unscrewing the brass balls at the top of the hollow bedposts, discovered a cache of smuggled silverware. The descendants of Captain John Lowe still tell the story of a cargo of square pianos that ended its voyage on the reef. The pianos were rescued and brought in to be placed on sale at an auction. Immediately every family in town developed a taste for music; if the house was too small, the baby's crib was hoisted on top of the new piano. In time every household owned a set of monogrammed table silver, though the initials did not necessarily match the name of the present owner. A salvaged shipment of velvet is said to have supplied material for men's vests for forty years.

Larry Karns Studio, Key West, Fla.

From the "mirador," or widow's walk, of the Caroline Lowe home at Key West, wreckers or other members of the family often watched the reefs through a spyglass for signs of trouble.

Living was of the raw, frontier sort; but the abundance of luxury items to be seen in every house, and the presence of genteel and well-dressed persons on the streets, gave the place an air of refinement it did not wholly deserve. Newcomers were puzzled to find an isolated community many miles at sea displaying such a high degree of culture. As time went by and prosperity increased, both men and women dressed in the mode of the day. Girls wore clothing from England and France — white ribbed silk stockings, prunella boots and kid gloves — obtained perhaps through shops in Charleston or Havana. Lace fans, gauze scarves and rice straw hats were not uncommon, nor were dresses of *moiré* silk or jaconet. A wreck sometimes yielded water-soaked cottons, linen, laces, embroidery or mosquito netting. All the little girls in town had dresses cut from the same bolt of calico or gingham. The men wore high beaver hats, closefitting gray trousers with a strap under the foot, and high rolling stocks. At sea they exchanged this elegance for jerseys and wide, short pants — or a pair of old trousers rolled up over their knees.

A small newspaper began to appear at irregular intervals, and Simonton sent down files of New York City papers to help the editor keep in step with the outside world.

Little by little the vicissitudes of island living were softened. A Cuban came to town with two or three cows and drove them daily from house to house, milking from the cow for each customer. A Negro fisherman sang his mullets, grunts or groupers through the streets and cleaned them at the kitchen door. Each family kept a goat, whose duty it was to eat the garbage. Cuban families kept a milk goat for each new baby. Tough native beef cattle were shipped occasionally from Punta Rassa on the Florida mainland, where there had been herds from the earliest days of settlement. By 1829 two boats were bringing fresh meat once a week from St. Marks, at the head of the Gulf of Mexico. Pigs were introduced and soon were running wild. Somebody tried raising sheep, but they lost their wool in the heat.

Flower and vegetable seeds were brought from many localities and planted in the shallow earth. Tropical blooms and a few sweet potatoes and melons began to relieve the white coral bareness of the settlement. Somebody discovered that a coconut, thrust into a crack made in the limestone with a crowbar, would take root and grow lustily. Soon young coconut trees were showering their fruit into the streets. About this time, civic pride began to sprout. The town council passed an ordinance forbidding bathing in public in front of the town. White offenders were to be fined $5 and slaves punished with stripes not to exceed twelve.

No experienced mariner wished to sail the reefs in an easterly gale. Key West Harbor soon became known as a convenient refuge in which to wait a change of wind, and maritime visitors began dropping in. Should a vessel fail to make the harbor entrance, all hands knew that the watchers on the housetops would see their plight and send them help. As early as 1829 the small packet *Postboy* brought mail from Charleston once a month, unless her unpredictable master decided to hunt sea turtles or go a-wrecking on the way. Mail packet night was an important event. Everybody stayed up until the *Postboy* arrived, no matter how late. The usual nine-thirty curfew, or "bell-ring," for slaves to be indoors was omitted. Children stayed up. There were lights in every house, and little groups of neighbors gathered to drink coffee and eat sweets.

In ten years the community was booming. Its main and only industry involved many related services — diving, lightering, warehousing, storage — and a long list of banking and legal affairs, such as arrangements for exchange and banking in foreign ports, mortgages on cargoes, ship clearances and inventories. Then, too, there were the auction sales.

Only less exciting than the stampede to a shipwreck were the auctions of salvaged merchandise held by order of the court as the only means of disposing of wrecked vessels and their cargoes. Frequent auctions provided the town with entertainment and most of its food and supplies. First a notice was posted in a public place saying that the marshal would cry the goods of the

Larry Karns Studio, Key West, Fla.

Bahama House, Key West, is one of many brought from Harbour Island by schooner or lighter. Some claim it made the journey in one piece; others, that it was broken into convenient sections.

ship So-and-so, beginning on a given date. Cargoes were displayed on the open wharf where buyers could examine them. If necessary, goods were stored in stone warehouses built along the waterfront convenient to the wharves.

Quantities of wrecked merchandisie were turned in this way. There were northbound cargoes of cotton from the gulf states; mahogany and cedar from Cuba; cochineal from Campeche; sugar, molasses and coffee from Mexico. Southbound vessels carried general merchandise, provisions, dress goods, shoes, wines and luxury items. In the decade from 1848 to 1857, 499 vessels were disposed of by libel at Key West, valued at over 16 million dollars. These did not include the vast number of total wrecks. Speculators came by ship from Charleston, Mobile, Havana and sometimes even New York to bid on important wrecks. They joined the local merchants, wreckers and owners of seaworthy vessels, who soon learned to buy shrewdly and transship merchandise to other ports, where they could sell it at a profit.

On auction day a bell was rung on the agent's wharf about nine o'clock in the morning, and the whole town turned out to watch the fun. Sales took place on the wharf, with the auctioneer standing on an upturned hogshead. Near him were his helpers — lumpers to heave out the goods for inspection by prospective customers; a bookkeeper to write down buyers' names, bids and purchases; a checker to count packages and quantities; and a collector to take cash money, although most buyers did not carry funds with them, but came to pay up a day or two later. When everything on the wharf had been sold, the auctioneer led the way into a warehouse. There lanterns were lighted in the gloom, and the sales continued.

Sometimes a coasting vessel calling at Key West with bananas, carrots, limes, tomatoes or other garden truck would place its cargo on a wharf to be auctioned. The master would send a man in a horse-drawn vehicle through the streets, ringing a dinner bell and calling housewives and grocers to the coming auction. The grocery advertisements in the little newspaper heralded the arrival only of such routine items as "flour, rum, lard and dried peas," and one can imagine the housewives' excitement at the unexpected auction of fresh foodstuffs.

Whichever type of sale was one, families would gather at the scene early in the day, often bringing their lunch, and would stay until sundown. All sorts of objects might be offered for sale; a boy might go home at night carrying a new pair of shoes many sizes too large for him, a mattress and pillow for his bunk, or a whole stem of ripe bananas. One of the boys in the Lowe family paid fifteen cents for his stem of bananas and promptly ate all he could hold. That night his parents were called on for some vigorous doctoring. Through the remainder of a long life, he never ate another banana — or even looked at one, if he could avoid it.

As more women and children joined their menfolk, the bare wooden houses took on the characteristics of homes, and the instability of the town's all-male society yielded to a feeling of permanence. One by one, the graces of community living began

Beside a barroom stood the Key West branch of the New York Stock Exchange. It was replaced by a modern building in 1957. The blackboards by the door listed current market quotations.

to appear as the influence of the women increased. With several hundred families on the island enjoying a high degree of prosperity, and with the steadying hand of the new court keeping order, a time came when the lack of religious and educational facilities began to trouble the serious-minded. A mass meeting was called on March 9, 1831, to discuss the subject. Those who attended agreed that Sunday meetings in the courthouse and home instruction of the children were not enough. They decided to look for an unemployed preacher of some Protestant denomination who would come and start a real church, and who would also conduct a day school for the children.

This worthy resolution met with little response from the mainland clergy. Public opinion, when it was aware of Key West at all, had written off the island as both disease-plagued and beyond the pale of respectability. For two years no minister of any faith could be found who showed any interest in the town's spiritual welfare. A committee made up of the postmaster, two judges, the collector of customs, the United States marshal and the surgeon of the local army post tried to find a preacher willing to live on the island — and to keep him there once he had arrived. Five ministers came and went in rapid succession. Among them a small wooden church was put up and dedicated, quite logically, to the great victim of shipwreck, St. Paul.

The sixth applicant for the pastorate had just been approached when a hurricane totally destroyed the church and most of the other buildings in the community. Preacher number six sailed into the harbor with instructions from his superiors to "ascertain the character of the parish and if you find it as being unworthy an effort to rebuild . . . abandon it." He did not abandon it. On the contrary, the Reverend C. C. Adams planted the Protestant Episcopal faith firmly on the island, and started classes for the children on the three R's and navigation.

In the forties Key West was a wide-open frontier town, proud, boisterous and successful —a tough spot for any religious denomination. The 'Brilanders were arriving from the Bahamas in ever-increasing numbers, and they were determined churchgoers. Just as Mr. Adams was getting well started, they brought in a Wesleyan Methodist preacher, but he was soon run out of town by an element of the population who decided that too much religion might be bad for business. His successor, young simon Peter Richardson, was as engaging a personality as ever stepped off a windjammer into a brawling, lusty seaport.

"I resolved that I would wipe up the earth with the first man that insulted me," wrote young Simon Peter some years later. There were thirty-two grogshops in town, and their proprietors did not relish further encroachments of organized religion. The whiskey men had attempted to "wash" the former preacher—that is, to tie a rope around his waist and shoulders and toss him off a wharf into deep water, then haul him in and repeat the treatment. "It is a terrible ordeal to put a man through," wrote Simon Peter. "He eluded their grasp by taking refuge on the boat that brought him over. He suffered many other indignities that were heaped upon him during the year . . . and the more I thought over the treatment he had received, the more indignant I became . . . until I felt that if I ever heard of any attempt to 'wash' me they would smell fire and brimstone."

To his surprise the young preacher was cordially greeted upon his arrival. He lodged with a friendly family and soon began to cool down. His letter continues:

In a few days the judge, lawyers, doctors and prominent citizens called to see me, a reception I never had before nor have had since. I was invited to the Masonic lodge and chapter, and made chaplain of both. My little chapel was soon filled with the women, the men standing around outside. . . . I collected about four thousand dollars, and from the rock of the island put up and paid for a large stone building; but it was not covered in when that ever-to-be-remembered storm [of 1846] came and prostrated all to the ground. . . .

This was the condition of affairs in October. I took the lumber and what I could bring from the wreck of the stone church and put up a small building to preach in, and large enough for my Sunday school.

I was married in 1847. I had been married only a few weeks when the Catholic priest and the Episcopal and Baptist preachers came to the Island, and all determined to go to the mainland and collect money to build churches, because of the storm. This was one of the trials of my life. I had the island largely under my control. Many of the best families had joined the church but had nothing left after the storm. They were utterly helpless to build, and if those preachers succeeded in building the people would have to go to their churches, having nowhere else to go. . . . I saw that all was lost, in that still formative state, unless I had a church large enough to hold my congregation together. . . . I did not consult feeling nor the relations of my young wife. I simply informed her that I would have to leave her with her good mother for a time until I could get money to build a new church.

Richardson canvassed cities throughout the South, raised over $3,000 and bought lumber for a new church.

I had the lumber sawed at the mills [in Charleston] and engaged a sloop to take it to Key West. I never believed in spirit-rappings or any other superstitions, but I had a distinct presentiment that that vessel was going to be wrecked. So strong was my impression that I left a duplicate of the bill at the mill. I went to the insurance office and proposed to insure. The agent dissuaded me, declaring there was no danger on the coast at that season of the year. The captain said he would be glad if he could get wind enough to carry his vessel to Key West. But with all this, I insured. . . . On July fifth I left Charleston, with thirty-two hundred dollars in gold, on a United States propeller for Key West. . . . I immediately employed workmen to commence the building, but my vessel failed to put in her appearance. Finally I saw a large yawl coming into port with flag up. It was the captain of the sloop. . . . His vessel was wrecked on the Florida reef, and was a total loss. I soon had the bill duplicated and sent forward and collected my insurance. I had the church built storm-proof, and by October it was finished, paid for, and I was in it and preaching.[1]

Not all the women of the early town were timid and feminine. Bathsheba Greene Dixon, for example, was a different kind of a girl. She inherited energy, fortitude and a degree of independence from her Rhode Island ancestors. Widowed early in life, Bathsheba ran a coaling station and entered into contracts with the United States Navy to coal its steam-propelled vessels. She had a crew of men employees, who came loyally at her call whenever a ship arrived to be coaled. She was very brave and, after her husband died, lived alone down near the waterfront. Whenever it became necessary, day or night, she would hitch up her horse to the buggy and start out alone to waken or round up her crew.

Once a deputy sheriff tried to arrest Bathsheba for some minor offense. She indignantly pushed him out of the house and barred her doors. The deputy had the bad judgment to return later with a posse; they broke in her front door and cornered her upstairs. She fought the whole crowd, using her fists like a man and pulling handfuls of the deputy's whiskers like a woman. Chairs were broken and the house upset. But Bathsheba won: the deputy withdrew and called off his men, and the charge against her was dropped.

Yellow fever struck the settlement year after year during the long summers, but there is no record that the community was unduly dismayed. Some died of the fever, but others nursed them to the end and bravely carried on. The military surgeon at the little army post served as doctor to all. The womenfolk cared for friend, foe and stranger, leaving their own homes when necessary to give aid elsewhere. Mrs. Mallory's boardinghouse was sometimes overflowing with patients brought in from passing ships.

The best "yellow jack" nurse in town, though, was the owner of the Gem Saloon. He was a bulky British sailor, completely illiterate but with a heart as big as his body. His real name was George Alderslade, but he was known as Captain Jack. He could always be depended upon to give his services freely when a fellow man was in need. On one occasion, as he sat solemnly by a bedside peering at some pictures on an illustrated paper he was holding upside down, he was heard to mutter, "There's been a hell of a hurricane someplace. Five ships capsized!"

By 1850 — less than thirty years after it was founded — Key West was the richest community, per capita, in the entire United States. It boasted 650 houses, and there were nearly fifty vessels in its wrecking fleet, which was the only source of its prosperity, its notoriety and its buoyant self-satisfaction.

Edwin Levick Coll., Courtesy The Mariners Museum, Newport News, Va.
The pilot boat, or Baltimore clipper, used by most nineteenth-century wreckers, was originally developed as a privateer. It was also in great demand by smugglers, slavers, even pirates.

16

Business Is Business

It is seldom remembered that wrecking was ever a legitimate business and that beneath its romantic and adventurous surface were orderly principles of method and procedure. Many of these principles have carried over into our time and are operative in the ocean salvage industry, whose crewmen are still known as wreckers.

In the early nineteenth century, the vessel most in demand for salvage work was the pilot boat or Baltimore Clipper, a rakish topsail schooner. This light, fast craft, inexpensive to build and easy to maneuver, was designed on lines far in advance of its time. With only a small crew, it could take any kind of weather and outsail just about anything on the seas. It drew from eight to ten feet of water, while a large coaster of the same period drew about eighteen feet.

There is some difference of opinion as to the origin of the pilot boat, but all authorities agree that it was developed in the shipyards of Chesapeake Bay, where it was fitted with the schooner rig between 1730 and 1750. It first came into use in the United States as a "Virginia built" privateering vessel and was widely used for this purpose in the Revolutionary War and the War of 1812. With the coming of peace, it appeared in the West Indies trade and gradually acquired the name Baltimore Clipper, although it was never a true clipper.

The pilot boat had long, easy, convex water lines; a low freeboard; and raking masts, stern and sternpost, with a great dead rise amidships and slack bilges. It was built for hard work and stability, with wide clear decks, a beam rather great for its length, and a great deal of drag to the keel aft. Because of these characteristics, the Baltimore Clipper was also sought after by illegal traders, smugglers, slavers and even pirates. Some persons believe it was adapted from the French lugger, which it resembled; others claim it was developed from Swedish fishing craft seen in Chesapeake Bay in very early times. But it was more likely a product of the New World.

A cocky little ship called the Jamaica Sloop was developed by the early buccaneers in the West Indies. It had wide use there before 1725 and also became popular with the pirates. Even the British Royal Navy had a few in the eighteenth century. The Jamaica Sloop was built all over the West Indies and eventually in Bermuda, where it became known as the Bermuda Sloop. There was much interchange of trade between Virginia and Bermuda in colonial times, and the famed Baltimore Clipper was probably an American version of the Jamaica (alias Bermuda) Sloop. It still influences our yachts and fishing schooners.

In the *Maryland Journal and Baltimore Advertiser* of June 17, 1795, appeared an advertisement of "A New Vessel for Sale. . . . Burthen 136 tons, of pilot boat construction, built at Baltimore and launched the latter part of last month. She is built with liveoak and cedar, nailed and finished after the French

Courtesy The Mariners Museum, Newport News, Va.

An early lithograph of the Boston wrecking company, Wells & Gowen, shows the efforts of that firm to refloat the U.S. Frigate *Missouri* after she burned and sank at Gibraltar in 1843.

manner, being calculated for extraordinary sailing."[1] Even today these small, sharp schooners are being built in the more remote islands of the West Indies.

An interesting eyewitness description of a wrecking vessel and its officers has been left by John James Audubon, in his *Journal.* While in Key West in 1832, he visited on board several such ships and recorded his impressions:

> As we approached the largest schooner, I admired her form, so well adapted to her occupation, her great breadth of beam, her light draught, the correctness of her water-line, the neatness of her painted sides, the smoothness of her well-greased masts, and the beauty of her rigging. . . . Silence and order prevailed on her decks. The commander and the second officer let us into a spacious cabin, well lighted, and furnished with every convenience for fifteen or more passengers. . . . These rovers were both from down east, were stout active men, cleanly and smart in their attire.[2]

It is a far cry from such a craft to the average man's conception of a wrecking vessel. But wrecking and salvage have always been rated as less than respectable, and the professional salvor is only now beginning to come into an honored place in the seafaring community.

In northern waters the wrecker did not put to sea until he was called for, but in the southern seas this was not the case. Sometimes the casualty was able to send out a lifeboat to seek help, but more often the wrecker, on his own initiative, found the unfortunate craft. No one has ever been able to explain satisfactorily how the early wreckers, with no means of communication, were able to locate the vessels. "We can smell a wreck in the dark" was a characteristic reply.

Apart from instinct, there were a number of ways to locate a distressed ship. The wrecker knew the dangerous localities and could judge where the currents, tides and weather were most likely to drive helpless ships. Some wreckers patrolled the reefs daily. The Bahamians often outfitted their vessels for a cruise and remained weeks or even months in the vicinity of the wrecking grounds, until their provisions ran out or they found a wreck. Many a Key West gallant did his courting on his sweetheart's housetop lookout platform as she sat, spyglass in hand, helping her father get more business. And some wrecking captains paid fishermen and beachcombers to watch the sea and bring them word of a ship in trouble.

Everybody watched shipping as it sailed north or south along the channel, the only highway of communication. On the Bahamian side of the channel, families lived on some of the islands; after the Seminole wars, settlers began to appear on the American mainland. With these familes on the alert, the 'Brilanders patrolling the reefs, the housetop watchers posted at Key West and the fishermen, spongers, turtlers and occasional lighthouse keepers scanning the sea, there were not many areas where a vessel could long remain out of sight of some human eye. Stephen R. Mallory, Key West's first United States senator and the brilliant son of Widow Mallory, who ran the boardinghouse, declared in a speech before the Senate: "There is scarcely a day . . . that you may not see in the business season, from one hundred to one hundred and fifty square-rigged vessels entering and clearing from the Gulf."[3]

A few items of "Marine Intelligence" from the first issue of the weekly *Key West Gazette* (March 28, 1831) show the bustling activity of the wrecking station during February and March:

Feb. 2 Brig *Mount-Hope,* [Capt.] Crocker, Providence, Salt, furniture &c. — [Agent] P. C. Greene (the *Mount-Hope* was bound to St. Marks, and arrived here in distress, having run upon the Double-headed Shot Keys, and sustained considerable damage.

Feb 18 Schr. *Toison,* [Capt.] Cobb, New York, dry goods, furniture, jerked beef, &c. [Agent] P. C. Greene (The *Toison* was brought in a wreck, having run upon the Florida Reef, when on a voyage to Mantanzas.)

March 22 Sloop *Splendid,* [Capt.] Smith, Florida Reef, goods from ship *Amulet* — [Agent] J. Whitehead. (Ship *Amulet,* [Capt.] Winsor, from Boston, bound to New-Orleans, with a cargo of dry goods, furniture, shoes, fish, &c, was wrecked on the Reef — vessel totally lost — great part of the cargo, crew & passengers saved. . . .

Schooner *Thistle,* [Capt.] Wheedon, Florida Reef — goods from wreck ship *Amulet* — [Agent] J. Whitehead.

Schr. *William Ross,* [Capt.] Barker, cotton, from wreck, British Brig *Marcella* — [Agent] O. O'Hara (The Brig *Marcella,* bound from New-Orleans, to Greenock with a cargo of Cotton, was wrecked near Cape Florida, on the 15th February — Vessel totally lost — crew, and cargo (in a damaged state) saved.

March 24 Schooner *Henry,* [Capt.] Emery, Boston, building materials — [Agent] J. Whitehead — (The schooner *Henry* from Boston, bound to Mobile, with a cargo of materials for building a light-house at Cat-Island, ran upon the Florida Reef, on the morning of the 23rd March and having been got off with the assistance of the wreckers, was brought into this Port — Cargo all saved, with the exception of some bbls lime thrown overboard — The Court awarded $400 salvage. . . .

Mar. 27 Schr. *Florida,* [Capt.] Rooke, Florida Reef, sugar, &c. [Agent] F. A. Browne (The *Florida* is from the wreck of the schooner *Waverly,* [Capt.] Sellers, of and for New-York, from New-Iberia, and last from this port, whence she sailed on the 13th March, and ran ashore on the Florida Reef, near Cape Florida Light — Vessel entirely lost, crew and cargo saved.[4]

A blast blown on a conch shell announcd a shipwreck to the early Bahamian wreckers. A bell mounted on the Key West wharf rang out the alarm to that community; in later years, a whistle on the ice plant roused the town. Always the summons was followed by the cry "Wreck asho-o-re!" echoing through the streets, and the pounding of running feet as the menfolk sprinted to their vessels and took off in the traditional race to the wreck. The alarm sometimes caught men painfully unaware.

Captain Amos Sauls, a New Englander, came to Key West in 1830. He sailed a smart wrecking schooner and lived alone in a small cabin down near the waterfront. The captain was a

God-fearing man and went to church on Sundays, dressed in his best shore-going clothes. Occasionally after church he was the guest of some hospitable family for dinner. It may have been in this way that he acquired a taste for guava duff, a delectable dessert, served hot with sugar and brandy sauce. So irresistible was the pudding that he learned to make it for himself. Each Sunday, when not invited out, he would return to his house, change his shore clothes for seafaring garb and whip up a guava duff, letting it boil several hours on his charcoal-burning cook-stove.

One Sunday (runs the tale in Marie Cappick's *The Key West Story*) the guava duff had just begun to boil on the captain's stove when the cry of "Wreck asho-o-re!" rang down the street. Key West did not tolerate fishing or sponging on the Sabbath, but a shipwreck couldn't very well be put off till the next day. Captain Sauls hesitated. It was not so much his religious convictions that bothered him; it was the guava duff. He paced the floor in shameful indecision as his cronies trotted down the street to the wharf. A few minutes later, as the alarm died away, neighbors watching the race from their porches on Front Street rubbed their eyes and looked again. Among the running men headed for the waterfront was a figure staggering along with a burden almost too heavy for him to carry. It was Captain Sauls, both arms clasped around the lower portion of a sheet-iron stove in which a fire burned brightly — and on top of which a pot of guava duff sat steaming merrily, on its way to the wreck.[5]

Maritime law had always provided that awards of money or merchandise should be paid to volunteer salvors, and in practice the awards had always been larger than for comparable services on land. The wrecker's risk and daring were taken into consideration, as well as his labor and skill.

As time went on, these liberal awards brought about the recognized legal principle of *excessive compensation.* This principle relating to ocean salvage came to America directly from seventeenth-century England, as did the whole theory and structure of wrecking. It seems to have grown from the belief that human nature is selfish and that men need a special incentive if they are to help others at their own peril. More especially, excessive compensation was a means of persuading the masters of insured vessels to go to each other's aid on the high seas. Insurance regulations permitted a ship to turn aside from its course to save human life, but not merely to save merchandise. A skipper needed strong inducements to risk voiding his ship's insurance by assisting a vessel in distress.

When wrecking became a commercial enterprise, the principle of excessive compensation was seen to be its very foundation. The wrecker risked his ship and his life — and the speculator risked his fortune — on the probability of serving profitable shipwrecks. This was the sum and substance of American wrecking.

Salvage awards in most cases were determined by the court. It was legal for a wrecker to make his own agreement with a shipmaster for salvage services if he wished, but the court was not bound by such an agreement if it proved to be unjust or if the wrecker had taken advantage of the situation. There was also the possibility that the wrecker could not properly estimate the damage in advance and might have to use more men and vessels than he at first supposed. He could therefore refuse to make any financial agreement on the spot and leave the salvage decision to the court.

The wrecker's duty required that he refloat the damaged vessel in deep water, or else tow it to port to be placed in custody of the court. If the ship was too badly damaged to be saved, he was to transfer crew, passengers and cargo to his own or other vessels and take them to port. His rights to an award were based on his services in having kept near lost or abandoned property with all the means at his command to preserve it. A wrecker did not acquire the right of possession; the shipmaster remained legally in charge. But by his services, the wrecker acquired an interest in the property. If the master, after being relieved by wreckers, attempted to sail away to a distant port against their consent and without settling their demands, they had the right to take control of the ship, sail it to a convenient port and place it in custody of the law. It is easy to see how an irate master describing such an occurrence could make it sound very much like piracy.

When a crippled vessel had been brought into port, her master was required to go immediately before a notary and "Note and extend a Protest" in which his crew joined. The "Protest" described the experience they had just come through, the state of the weather, the ship's course, the accident which imperiled it, the conduct of its officers through the emergency, the loss of sails and rigging, the injuries to vessel and cargo, and any agreements the captain might have made with wreckers at sea or in port.

Next the wreck master presented his "Libel in Rem" against the property for compensation or salvage. He stated the value of the ship and cargo, described the exertions to which his men had gone to rescue the property and petitioned the court for what he considered a fair award of compensation.

The vessel's master then presented an answer to the salvage claim, often demanding a reduction of the amount. An open hearing at the courthouse followed. The court examined all the factors involved, and fixed both the compensation to be paid the wrecker and the final disposition of the balance of the salvaged property. Sometimes salvage was paid in kind — that is, in merchandise from the vessel's cargo. At other times, vessel and cargo were ordered sold at auction, and a specified percentage of the proceeds was given to the wrecker, with the remainder going to the underwriters. A typical notice of such an auction read:

U. S. MARSHAL'S SALE

By virtue of an order of sale from the Hon. William Marvin, judge of the Admiralty Court for the Southern District of Florida, I will sell at Public Auction on the 15th inst., from the Ware House of F. A. Browne, Esq., all the cargo then unredeemed by the payment of Salvage and expenses of the ship TELUMAH, lately wrecked on her voyage from Liverpool to Havana, Consisting of Iron in bars, crates of Crockery, Hard Ware, Sugar boilers, castings of Machinery, etc. Terms of sale — Cash on delivery — ten days to be allowed the purchaser to pay for and receive his goods — Consignees in Havana may have their goods delivered them at any time before the day of sale, by the payment of Salvage and expenses.

J. B. BROWNE, *U. S. Marshal*

KEY WEST, December 4, 1845

When a vessel was of thirty tons or more, the salvage payment was divided into shares: three to the master, two to the mate, one-and-a-quarter to the cook, one each to the crewmen and a half-share to boys under eighteen years of age. Divers shared according to the actual service each performed on the job.

In the earlier days, the underwriters sent an agent to Key West whenever a major shipwreck occurred. Travel conditions being what they were, the agent usually got there long after the ship and cargo had been disposed of. This resulted in charges of indecent haste in closing out a case. Eventually the Board of Underwriters of the Port of New York stationed a permanent agent at Key West. The board even went so far at one time as to enter the wrecking game itself. It outfitted a vessel, which was stationed at Key West. The underwriters' crew, however, were paid regular wages and remained in port waiting to be called for (as wreckers did in New York), while the Key Westers were out in all weather hunting up business. The experiment was soon abandoned.

If the court considered the condition of a damaged vessel at all doubtful, it appointed a board of survey — a ship's carpenter, a shipmaster and a merchant — to examine her and determine whether she might proceed, or should be held for repairs, or should be sold as unseaworthy. Before 1835 this meant that ropes were fastened to the top of the vessel's masts and run through heavy blocks on a wharf. A strain was then hove to the tackles and the vessel careened until one side of her bottom was out of water — a dangerous business on a squally day.

The law required a shipmaster to notify his owners if possible in the event of trouble, then sit tight and await instructions. A careful master would also try to communicate with the nearest agent of Lloyd's before taking action. If the emergency was acute, the master might act as the owner's agent and make repairs, or take part in court action involving ship and cargo. He could borrow money on the credit of the owner and, in extreme need, might sell the ship and cargo outright.

The captain's authority in emergency equaled the emergency itself and went no further. Only if impending peril might soon destroy a vessel was he free to sell. "Good faith and necessity for the sale must both be present," ruled Judge Marvin, "or nothing on earth will make it legal." Nor could a master legally give away wrecked cargo: he was required to consign it to someone at the port of distress who would act as his business agent. Usually the agent was a merchant who had adequate warehouse facilities. If the cargo was perishable, or would become worthless if continued to its destination, the master might then sell it for the best price he could get.

Wrecking was heavy, perilous work. It had to be done at breakneck speed without waiting for bad weather to abate. Incoming sea water could play havoc with a cargo, and the ship might at any moment become a victim of the sea. "You have to be wiser than the people in trouble, who often don't realize the gravity of the situation," wrote Klaas Toxopeus in *The Flying Storm*. The average shipmaster disdained the services of a wrecker. Few yielded to the situation without a struggle, and sometimes stubbornness caused fatal delays. While captain and crew were frantically trying to work their ship toward deep water, the wreckers would draw off and sit in a circle, sometimes forbidden to take hold at a moment when help would have been effective.

Even after a ship went to the bottom a good wrecker could, with judicous use of divers and gear, relieve her of her cargo, rigging and fittings. By the very nature of his work, a wrecker was forced to develop remarkable skill. With only wind for power and the simplest of equipment, he was able to do salvage jobs that today seem incredible. "There is a lot in knowing what you have at hand," commented a Key Wester, after he had detached the bronze propeller of a sunken steamship with dynamite and made tackle fast to haul it aboard his own small schooner. Another, with only a small sailing vessel, floated and towed to port a steamer loaded with coal and with eighteen feet of water in her forepeak. A dozen Negro skin divers from the Bahamas, working together to strip the sheathing from the bottom of a vessel underwater, could release a sheet of copper in about three minutes. Then they would rise to the surface, lie gasping on deck for about five minutes and be ready to go down again, keeping this up for five or six hours.

When all this was done and the empty hull lay abandoned on the sea bottom, a clever diver could still go through her in a leisurely, methodical way and find valuable articles — hidden money, jewelry, secret lockers or unopened sea chests. The possibilities were endless.

17

Colorful Fragments

The details of long-forgotten shipwrecks are elusive, apart from the dry dust of public records; but now and again the memory of some oldster yields the timeworn tatters of a happening so colorful and intriguing that, with a little patience, they can be darned into a first-rate tale. These stories may have an embroidering of fancy, but they are not made out of whole cloth. Here are a few:

According to some historians, approximatey one-eighth of all the gold the world has ever possessed has been lost in the sea. By far the greatest portion of it went down in the Caribbean Sea. Of all the plunder lost by the Spanish in their conquest of the Americas, the fabulous sunken treasure of Key Largo is probably the costliest. (Yet fiction writers have doubtless realized more wealth from writing of this lost gold than have all the treasure expeditions that sought to retrieve it.)

It was customary for treasure-carrying vessels to rendezvous at Havana and form a *flota,* or convoy, which proceeded through the Florida Straits to the Gulf Stream, which it rode northward to Cape Hatteras. Then it would alter its course and ride the prevailing westerlies back to Spain. An entire year's take went down the drain several times, but the disaster of 1715 seems to have been the worst. The loss that year included the cargoes of fourteen Spanish galleons — loaded with gold, silver and gems taken from Peru, Mexico and Spanish America — that were sunk in a hurricane along Careysfort Reef and the upper keys.

When news of the loss reached Spain, the first attempt at underwater salvage in the New World was organized. Wreckers, divers and special equipment were rushed across the Atlantic. With the help of survivors of the wrecked fleet, the salvors were able to locate at least one of the sunken galleons; and after weeks of diving, the expedition brought up a quantity of gold and silver. The amount was unknown, but the startling news of the sunken plate fleet quickly made its way around the West Indian area. Many heads wagged, and many eyes glittered, but one man — Captain Henry Jennings, then at Port Royal — did something about it. Hurriedly gathering a squadron of two ships and three sloops, he sailed with 300 fighting men to Key Largo.

Jennings seems to have been a British privateer at the time, a man of good standing and intelligence; but it is hard to be sure about him. The family appears to have rated very well. His kinsman, John Jennings of Bermuda, was master of a successful privateer, speaker of the House of Assembly and a justice of the peace. Another member of the family was chief judge of admiralty in Bermuda. But things being as they were in the eighteenth century, it is a bit difficult to place Henry accurately in the social scale. Some historians write him off as a pirate, who followed on the heels of the buccaneers and set the course of much of the indiscriminate piracy that followed.

Jennings' fleet arrived off Key Largo at dawn one morning, too late to intercept several million pieces of eight, which were well on their way to Havana. But he attacked and drove off the Spanish salvors and took what treasure was left on shore, about 350,000 silver dollars. On his way back to Jamaica, Jennings encountered a Spanish vessel carrying 60,000 pieces of eight and a cargo of cochineal and indigo. He added that to his bag.

Back at Kingston he had to step softly, for his raids had been conducted at a time of ostensible peace between Spain and England. Yet the treaties of Utrecht, signed in 1713, had not made much difference in the attitude of Spanish ships of war toward British craft in the West Indies. Asserting their claim to a monopoly on transportation of Spanish coins, cocoa and hides, the Spanish continued to seize any vessel they saw fit. This highhandedness may have impelled the Jennings raid. Some believe that, incensed at the Spanish attitude and avid to even the score, he refitted his ship, returned to the sunken fleet and did further salvaging of the Spanish hoard. Others claim that for a short period he sailed in open piracy.

Three years later, when the king's pardon was offered at Nassau to all pirates willing to surrender and quit the business, history shows that Jennings was among those present. He then returned to Bermuda and settled down with his kinsmen in a life of respectability.

While quantities of Spanish gold were lost through ignorance of seasonal weather patterns or accidents in navigation, no little amount went to pirates, privateers and buccaneers. These, in turn, had their misfortunes up and down the coast, and sometimes the sea swallowed the captured treasure along with their broken ships. There is no doubt that some of this missing gold eventually came into the hands of wreckers.

A Harbour Islander tells a story of a boyhood neighbor who made his living gathering sponges in the Bahamas. He was a diver and worked in shallow water over the sponge beds. This man would occasionally take a single golden doubloon to a shop at Nassau and ask the proprietor to change it into Bahamian coins. The shopkeeper told friends about it, and soon it was being noised about town that the sponger had found a treasure. This he denied stoutly. When some of his cronies tried plying him with rum to loosen his tongue, he always cooperated to a certain point; but when pressed for information about his doubloons, he would reply, "Give me another drink, and maybe I'll remember." He never did.

As time went by and the sponger continued to produce his single gold coins, he was finally called before a magistrate, who sternly questioned him as to the source of his wealth.

"Can't I have a doubloon as well as anybody else?" he demanded.

"Well, yes, of course."

"Has anybody in town lost any?"

"Not that I know of."

"Then what do you want mine for?"

The inquisition was abandoned as hopeless.

For years the man was watched, but nobody ever discovered where his doubloons came from. Then, one summer, a severe hurricane lashed the islands. It sank and scattered shipping, leveled houses and church steeples, and drove great waves up into the Nassau streets. The sponger came into the devastated town a few days later with greatly chastened demeanor and announced that he was ready to tell his story.

Years before, when diving for sponges in comparatively shallow water on the outer edge of the reef, he had come upon a pocket in the coral in which rested some wreckage. Prowling among the remains of a vessel, he turned up a rotted sea chest in which lay a heap of gold doubloons, almost invisible under the coral cement that encrusted them.

He removed as many of the coins as he could carry and rose to the surface. In his small sponge boat, safe from observation on the empty sea, he pounded and rubbed the coins until they came clean and recognizable. He knew he would have to bring up the remainder of the treasure and find a scure hiding place for it. The money was safe for the moment where it was, so he carefully noted the spot and rowed home to think over the problem. Cautiously, he changed his first doubloon into Bahamian money and had no trouble. The more he thought about it, the more he feared to move the gold to any place that would be accessible from his home. Then it occurred to him simply to leave the gold where it was. It had been safe there for a hundred years or so, and he could draw on it any time he wished.

Year after year, the arrangement had worked out to his satisfaction. Then came the recent hurricane. When he returned to the reef after the storm and dived on his treasure, a strange panorama unfolded in the dim green light. The whole contour of the sea bottom was changed. Sections of the reef had broken off under the pounding of the seas, and mountains of clean white sand had washed in, filling the coral pocket and drifting over the reef. The broken treasure chest and its contents had completely vanished. Frantically the sponger dug and scratched and scooped. But never again was he able to find a trace of the vanished gold.

From several sources came portions of the story of the *San Jacinto,* a Union gunboat that kept watch on Southern waters during the Civil War.

By the 1860s, persons living on both sides of the Bahama Channel had moved back and forth, married and intermarried, until they were of one stock. The national boundary that ran between them was all but meaningless. It would have been strange if the sympathies of those on the Bahama side had not rested with their Confederate neighbors across the channel. There was also, of course, the little matter of profit. Nassau was reaping a rich harvest supplying provisions and war materials to Confederate blockade runners. It was enjoying a prosperity the port had not known since the bad old days of the pirates.

A lot of excitement was stirred up on both sides of the Gulf Stream when the *San Jacinto* intercepted the British steamship *Trent* on the high seas somewhere off the Carolina coast and took from her, as prisoners of war, two representatives of the Confederacy who were en route to England to negotiate a loan. Great Britain protested the seizure vigorously, and for a time open hostilities between the countries seemed ominously near.

Soon afterwards the commander of the *San Jacinto,* no doubt still jittery from the near catastrophe, was cruising discreetly off the Bahama Islands near Eleuthera, watching for unidentified sail that might be running supplies from the British colony to the American coast. Late one afternoon he sighted a suspicious craft hugging the shore on the inside of a line of cays.

The strange vessel showed every indication of flight, and the *San Jacinto* promptly gave chase, running along the outside — that is, seaward of the cays. As the two vessels were in this position, night descended, and visibility dropped to zero. Running without lights, pursuer and pursued came abreast of Green Turtle Cay, the *San Jacinto* on the outside and the blockade runner on the inside. The stranger was racing to reach Whale Cay Channel ahead of the gunboat, for that was the only place it could reach the open sea and make its escape.

On Green Turtle Cay lived a justice of the peace whose house fronted the sea on a slight ridge, the highest point on the flat, sandy cay. The justice liked to sit up at night and read, with the heavy jalousies at his window closed to keep out mosquitoes and gnats. On the night of the chase, unaware of the battle threatening outside, the justice closed his book and swung open the shutters for a breath of fresh air. The feeble light of his lamp reached out across the dark beach, beyond the line of breakers, to the *San Jacinto,* which was then exactly offshore. Presently a shout came from his neighbor, "Shut the window, you fool!" It roused the ire of the old man, and he leaned out the window and roared an impolite reply.

On board the *San Jacinto,* eyes straining across the low island for a glimpse of the white sail of the blockade runner discerned a faint glimmer of light, just about where the fleeing vessel ought to be. There was a quick summons of all hands on deck; guns were run out; powder and shot were brought up from below and made ready. Every man was on edge to turn in a substantial prize after the embarrassing *Trent* affair. So absorbed were they in the job at hand that for a time no one gave much thought to the safety of their own vessel. With guns ready and trained on the speck of light, at the very moment of the command which might have blown the unoffending justice of the peace to bits and precipitated still more embarrassing international complications, the *San Jacinto* struck the reef head-on with a sickening jar.

It was a calm night. The startled crew swarmed overside and found the gunboat firmly grounded and bilged, beyond hope of refloating. The commander ordered his men to land on nearby No Name Cay, and they set to work in the dark, stripping everything movable from the *San Jacinto.* By morning a ring of wreckers from Abaco and other close islands had gathered near the bilged ship, ready to give aid. But the Yankee crew was armed, and warned the wreckers to keep away. Realizing that the gunboat was in immediate danger of being swept off the reef and sunk, the wreckers attempted to go on board anyhow. But they were driven off by musket fire from the beach. At that point, the Harbour Islanders began to arrive on the scene. They lived farther away, and it had taken longer for them to hear the news and make the run.

One of these men, a wrecker named Albury (the same who, as a boy, got a whipping for talking to the neighbors about his father's "brass dollars") now becomes the hero of the tale. He had grown to manhood and the command of his own wrecking schooner. When he learned that the officers of the *San Jacinto* would not talk salvage with any of his competitors (probably taking them for friends and allies of the blockade runner, who by this time had gotten safely away), he bathed and shaved and put on a fine blue suit, which he kept on board his schooner for special occasions. Then he launched the ship's boat, ran up the British ensign at its stern and had his men row him in dignity to No Name Cay.

The Yankee captain, in no mood to fire a second time on the British flag, permitted the enterprising wrecker to land on the cay and received him courteously. After a short conference, the Bahamian was able to convince the harassed officer of the wreckers' good faith. Arrangements were entered into for the salvage of the gunboat's stores and fittings and the transportation of her men to Nassau.

Tradition has it that several of the Yankee crewmen swam over to Green Turtle Cay and liked it so well that they stayed.

And as recently as the economic depression of the 1930s, men from Green Turtle Cay had a go at retrieving the brasswork and metals of the seventy-year-old wreck.

His Catholic Majesty's brig *Curreo No. 1,* bound for Spain under the command of Captain Qureau, was wrecked on Careysfort Reef in April 1829. She carried passengers and crew numbering forty-five men, and a cargo of gold and silver. The following morning, as the American wrecking sloops *Native* (under Captain Grover) and *Splendid* (under Captain C. M. Johnson) were patrolling the reef, they met two small boats from the *Curreo No. 1,* carrying Captain Qureau and eighteen men, who had set out to secure help for the distressed vessel. All then proceeded to the wreck, where they learned that twenty-three of the passengers had sailed away on a raft to try to reach land. The *Splendid* proceeded immediately to search for the raft and came up with it in the Gulf of Mexico, about twenty miles to the north, where it had drifted between the keys. Captain Johnson took the castaways on board and returned to the wreck of the Spanish brig. There every effort was made to save the cargo, which was placed on board the two wrecking vessels. At three o'clock in the morning, it became necessary to depart for Key West, with all the *Curreo*'s passengers and crew and whatever cargo had been saved.

On the way, Captain Qureau informed the Key Westers that his men were about to mutiny, seize the two sloops and sail to the Spanish port of Mantanzas. He requested arms and offered to help the wrecker head off the mutiny. Captain Grover gave him a pistol and immediately hoisted his flag union down, denoting distress. Soon they were joined by three small wrecking sloops, who convoyed them to Key Rodriguez and stood guard all night. The next morning, two more wreckers arrived and escorted them to Indian Key. There a well-armed sloop took over guard duty and continued with them to Key West, where all arrived safely the fourth day after the wreck. Evidently the court then took over, as there seems to have been no international dust raised over the case.[1]

At about the same period a large vessel, the *Mississippi*, struck Loo Key Reef at almost the spot where the famous British frigate *Loo* was lost on February 5, 1744. The *Mississippi* with her cargo was valued at $100,000, quite a rich ship for that time. Three wrecking craft got to her about four o'clock in the afternoon. Their combined crews, comprising thirty-nine men, worked at fever heat until six o'clock the next morning, lightening the ship so that they could pull her off the reef on the morning tide. They transshipped thirty tons of cargo and jettisoned sixty tons of ballast. The strategy worked, and the *Mississippi* was freed. For this massive effort, the salvage award was only $14,699. Each wrecker's share was $188.

A glimpse of the dark, or at least shady, side of wrecking is revealed by a story about a Bahamian wrecking captain who went on a voyage to the South American coast in the mid-nineteenth century. On their way home, the wreckers came upon a stranded cargo ship that had broken her back on a submerged rock and was going to pieces so rapidly that she could not last many more hours. The men tried to board the wreck, but were fired upon by her crew, who had taken refuge on a nearby island. Unwilling to forgo such an opportunity for loot, the wreckers waited until dark and went on board in the night. They found the ship in two pieces, and the gap between them was opening and closing with the waves. Some of the men dived into the hold while the gap was open, remained inside while it closed then came out when it opened again. They took what they could hastily collect, including some Spanish doubloons, and did not bother to report the wreck when they returned home. It was indulgence in this sort of thing by a handful of wreckers that sometimes brought the charge of piracy against them all.

A shipload of ice might be supposed to have little attraction for anybody after it had been wrecked in tropical seas. But there is a story of an enterprising wrecker from Abaco who carefully protected the sawdust-covered cakes of ice he recovered from a stranded vessel and hurried them to Nassau, at a time when ice was little more than something people read about in books. The court acted quickly, and the ice was sold at auction to a local grocer. For a few days there was a great rush of the curious to buy. Parties broke out all over town. Then the sale of ice began to fall off and soon stopped dead.

The disappointed merchant began questioning his customers: Wasn't the ice good? Didn't they enjoy their cold drinks and iced puddings?

Replies were prompt and hearty: they did.

Then why, asked the merchant, had everybody stopped buying it?

"Well," explained a satisfied customer, "We liked it fine when it was fresh. But by now it must be no end stale."

At Nassau they tell of a consignment of tombstones which the United States Army was sending to mark the last resting place of some fighting men in Cuba. The vessel ran into trouble and was towed into port by wreckers. The cargo was surrendered to the court and eventually sold at public auction. Many of the stones were bought "good cheap" by local people and may be seen today in Bahamian cemeteries, lying face down on the ground. On the underside of each stone, next to the earth, is the name and date of death of an American soldier. On the top side, visible to all, are similar details of the Bahamian citizen who lies buried beneath. Some declare that the unsold stones were used to pave the criminal courtroom in the local police headquarters.

Some of the old tales are tragic and full of the mystery of the sea.

Captain Benjamin Carey of Key West was the well-liked master of a fine wrecking schooner, a skillful and capable man, with a long record of rescues and salvage behind him. Although he was a son of Bahamian parents, the glamor of Spain had always attracted him, and for years he had planned to visit that country when he could spare the time. At last, soon after the turn of the century, the opportunity came. He set out on board a Spanish steamer from Havana as a passenger and arranged to come back on the same vessel on its return trip, then cross the straits from Havana to Key West on whatever craft was available.

All went as planned, and Captain Carey completed his visit. He was almost back home when the steamer ran into a hurricane. Havana pilots did not go to sea in so violent a storm, and the steamer's master had to fend for himself without hope of aid from shore. Unable to enter Havana Harbor, he could only turn and make a run for the Gulf of Mexico, hoping to escape the worst of the blow. He passed Key West safely; but having no information as to the course of the storm, he sailed straight into the heart of it. Fifty or sixty miles inside the gulf, his ship was swept onto the barrier reef near Dry Tortugas.

Ben Carey's cronies among the divers and wreckers of Key West learned of the missing steamer, knew their friend was on board and set out to hunt for her. They visited every likely spot, but to no avail. When it seemed reasonable, they dived. At last, after days of fruitless searching, they found the steamer lying on the bottom of the gulf — a total wreck. They located their friend on board, with the dead crew and the passengers still in their cabins, and took his body home to Key West, sorrowing as would other men for a neighbor and friend lost to the sea.

But a few days later, business considerations overcame their grief. The wreckers returned to the Spanish steamer to salvage what they could of the cargo, the fittings and the personal effects on board. The first diver to go down returned to the surface puzzled: the Spanish steamer was not there. Another went down, and another, but they could not find the ship. All day long, they dived and surfaced and dived again. But she was gone. The quicksand bar off Dry Tortugas had swallowed her, and no trace of the sunken vessel was ever seen again.

18

Shenanigans

After the royal pardon of pirates at Nassau in 1718, a number of shady characters settled in the Bahamas. Each man received an allotment of government rations; when this had been used up, he lived a meager, hand-to-mouth existence. The reformed pirates' only source of livelihood were the sea and the soil; and some of the half-starved ruffians, accustomed to excesses of food and drink, reverted to their former trade. It is reasonable to assume that others joined the older settlers and learned to go out to the wrecks, for here was a calling to which they were well suited by temperament and experience. What such men brought to the wrecking trade in the way of methods and ethics is not recorded. One can only surmise.

Anglican missionaries traveling through the Bahamas in behalf of the Society for the Propagation of the Gospel left reports that intentional wrecking was practiced to some extent there. Dr. A. Deans Peggs, headmaster of the government high school at Nassau, observed in his *Short History of the Bahamas*:

> The population was still far from being a model of rectitude. While piracy itself was all but suppressed, piratical instincts were by no means dead. Their previous outlet being denied, they were diverted into a respectable form of depredation, which was tolerated under the law. Deliberate wrecking received fresh impetus as by it the fruits of piracy could be reaped without committing the sin.

While tales of false lights and criminal lightkeepers are surely untrue, there were other, less sensational ways of bringing about shipwrecks — or of improving upon those that were

Courtesy Yachting

The steamship *Alicia*, en route from Spain to Havana in 1906, ran aground on Ajax Reef in the Bahamas during a nasty blow. She lay on the reef hopelessly bilged as wreckers gathered round.

not sufficienty serious. Bahamian and Floridian wreckers were not professional pilots, but they were usually qualified to pilot a vessel to or from the gulf when it sailed inside the reef. Wreckers, acting as pilots, have been known to run ships aground. They knew places where they could drive a vessel over a sharp pinnacle of coral, bilge it and yet maintain apparent innocence by taking soundings which showed a safe depth of water over the side. Wreckers have also been known to mishandle a distressed vessel while floating it so as to bring about more severe damage to ship and cargo, thus increasing their services and fees.

But the most fruitful kind of hocus-pocus all down the years has been the collusion of shipmaster and wrecker after a mishap has taken place and while the vessel is in distress. Schemes to defraud owners and underwriters usually follow the pattern of a large-scale demand for salvage by the wrecker on the scene of misfortune, the subsequent approval and payment of the claim by the shipmaster and then a split of the award between the two. "No ship was ever lost," runs an old saying, "without its master profiting from the disaster" — an adage which suggests that the shady business was not all on one side.

In a slight variant on this procedure, a ship's master might agree to settle the question of salvage by arbitration, rather than by a libel in court. The arbitrators, friends of the wrecker and well-schooled in their duties, would meet and agree on a large fee. The master, having an assurance from the wreckers that a portion of the fee would be returned to him, would then agree to the specified sum in the name of the owners of the vessel, and it would be paid over.

There are even reported instances of a captain wrecking his own ship in exchange for a definite sum to be paid him by the wreckers, who would take over the ship immediately and carry the innocent crew to port. Returning to the casualty, the wreckers would land a portion of its cargo in a safe hiding place for their own future profit. The broken vessel or the remainder of its merchandise would then be taken to port and turned over to the court, with all hands declaring that nothing else had been saved.

In the confusion of unloading a wreck, it was seldom possible to get every bit of its cargo ashore. Portions were often jettisoned by the master in an effort to float his vessel before wreckers appeared on the scene. A bilged hull often broke up before all the cargo had been transferred. Thus it was usually impossible to check the manifest papers against the salvaged cargo with much accuracy. There is no doubt that goods were sometimes pilfered en route from the place of distress to the warehouse of the United States marshal, where they were turned over to the court. Occasionally, however, a ship that had been partially unloaded was pulled off and taken to port. It was then possible to check her cargo lists with what the wreckers brought in, and there could be trouble if complete honesty had not prevailed.

An amusing yarn is told on the Key West waterfront of some members of a wrecking crew who secretly filched a wooden case of merchandise from the goods they were bringing to port. They left their booty on a lonely bit of shore. When they returned and opened the case, they found themselves in illegal possession of twelve dozen Spanish prayer books. When their sense of humor overtook their chagrin, they confessed their theft to shipmates who had been on the same job. To their delight, they found that their friends had also engaged in some private pilfering — and had gotten prayer books for their pains.

On the other hand, a master and his owners at times conspired to "sell her to the underwriters": the ship was insured to the hilt and then deliberately run aground. Many old windjammers are said to have come to this end when steam propulsion arrived on the seas. Another form of owner-master conspiracy was to issue a manifest insuring a cargo well above its actual value and then sink the vessel where divers could not get at it to check its cargo.

Another shady trick that survives in legend was based on a prior agreement between a criminal captain and a complacent wrecker. According to the agreement, a wrecker would just happen to come sailing by at the exact place and time that a ship was in peril. The wrecker would take off the crew and become wreck master with a day's lead over his competitors, a privilege worth a substantial sum. This scheme seems a bit unrealistic, however, for prior communication between captain and wrecker would have been extremely difficult. Such tales were quite possibly cooked up by the competitors of a lucky wrecker who happened to be near the scene of wreck when it took place.

"My daddy used to tell of a ship that piled up bad on Abaco Reef," recalled an old man in Nassau, the same who told the story of the *Sophie* and her elderly crew. The shipmaster, wishing to wreck his vessel for reasons of his own, had used the excessively bad judgment of running her on a reef head-on, in good weather and broad daylight, and in plain sight of a wrecker who lived on Abaco, just opposite the scene of his misconduct. The wrecker, supposing the mishap to be genuine, crossed the bay and hove to beside the grounded vessel with such alacrity that its captain did not have time to abandon ship and get away with his men. In fact, he showed little enthusiasm at the quick arrival of succor. He demanded that the wrecker carry him and his crew to Nassau before doing anything about saving the cargo of the bilged and hopelessly stranded ship.

There was no profit in rescuing seamen; a wrecker did that for free. But any damaged craft full of merchandise had its possibilities. Ignoring the captain's wishes, the wrecker and his men swarmed aboard the listing craft, tore off the hatch covers and got to the cargo, breaking out huge hogsheads of sugar onto the slanting deck. They worked fast and thoroughly, transferring the casks to their own schooner before the rising water in the hold could get to them.

All went merrily until somebody made a pot of coffee. Unaccustomed to such an abundance of sugar as there was on the wreck, one of the wreckers seized an axe and exuberantly smashed open a cask. Red earth flowed out of the jagged hole. There was a sudden hush and a knowing exchange of glances from man to man. Every wrecker able to lay hold of a tool dropped into the waterlogged hold and broke into the hogsheads. Every cask was filled with red clay.

Of course, said the old man, nobody but the men who were there that day ever knew exactly what took place. There was no doubt the ship's captain had a sum of money in his possession belonging to the owners and that they had commissioned him to purchase sugar in Jamaica. Certainly the ship had called at a little-known port, and its crew had brought aboard a full complement of heavy sugar casks. It was a fact that the vessel now lay a total wreck in the bright afternoon sunlight as it shone on the smooth, lime-green sea.

The captain and the wrecker had a long wrangle in the captain's cabin, after which they came up together carrying a small chest. Together they rowed ashore with it to the wrecker's cottage, where the captain remained overnight. After dark, they buried something near the Conch Rocks, in a spot plainly visible through the window of the wrecker's cottage. By the following day the sea had claimed the luckless vessel, and the captain and his men were taken to Nassau as shipwrecked mariners.

"My daddy knew most of those wreckers," the old man said thoughtfully, "and often heard them talking about it." They had been willing to keep what they knew to themselves, for a price. That price was supposed to have been half the money in the captain's chest, distributed equally among them. The other half was stashed safely away in the ground near the Conch Rocks, awaiting the captain's return.

In a few weeks the Abaco wrecker and his family left those parts and never returned. He probably went across the Channel to join the Harbour Islanders who were settling down in such numbers in Key West. The crooked skipper did not come back to Abaco Island to claim his share of the ill-gotten money, and nobody ever heard of him again.

"Where did the money go?" The old man smiled. "Your guess is as good as mine. But there didn't any of us boys think it worthwhile to go over to Abaco and dig around, hunting for the captain's share."

Even with legal supervision of wrecking in the Bahamas and on the American coast, owners and underwriters suffered many a loss from the sharp practices of some of the wrecking fraternity. Many were petty tricks, but others were more serious, ranging from exaggerations of tonnage of the wrecking craft in order to earn higher salvage fees all the way to outright embezzlement of cargo.

It was a punishable offense for a wrecker to take any merchandise at all from a vessel he was rescuing. A common trick was to hide a case or two on some small island when sailing to or from the distressed ship. The wrecker could return for it at his leisure. At Harbour Island they still tell of a neighbor, a well-liked and respectable citizen, who had been away on a wrecking voyage. After a long separation from his family, he returned home, proudly carrying as a gift a huge packing case he had been able to scrounge from a wreck. It was big enough to hold almost anything. When the first board was ripped away, the mother gave a little cry of delight. The gleam of the lamplight flickered along the smooth surface of china. With excessive care, the wrecker lifted the top boards and pulled away the packing material. The family stared down into the huge case in dead silence. A dazzling assortment of chamber pots of various sizes and varieties met their startled gaze.

Looting from the hold of a wrecked vessel was also held criminal business. So careful was the court in this regard, and so untiring was the Key West agent of the underwriters in ferreting out abuses, that there is a case on record in which a wrecker was penalized for feeding the crew of a salvaged vessel with food from the ship's own stores. The judge ruled that it was the duty of a wrecker to feed rescued seamen out of his own supplies and to leave the cargo and stores of the wrecked vessel intact. However, wreckers on duty were eventually permitted to take food and drink for themselves from the galley or icebox of a distressed ship.

A good story illustrating this point is told about one of the last great shipwrecks in the Key West area. In 1906 the S.S. *Alicia,* en route from Spain to Havana and full to her hatches of general merchandise, piled up near Ajax Reef in a nasty blow. A passing ship took off her crew and landed them at Havana. News of the wreck was telegraphed to Key West, and seven schooners set out that night in spite of the storm. Twelve hours later, they reached the Bahamas. After many more hours they located the *Alicia* in a particularly difficult spot; but the gale was still severe and they were obliged to run to nearby Saw Key for shelter until the seas subsided.

Once on board the *Alicia,* the Key Westers found her abandoned and a most valuable wreck. There were linens and laces, silks and wines, household furniture, provisions and pianos in her ample holds. The wreckers knew that it would not be long before the Bahamian Black Fleet would show up and claim a share of the prize. To forestall this, a dozen Key Westers took up positions on the *Alicia*, pretending to be members of her regular crew, while the others set to work busily removing cargo. When the Black Fleet arrived, their spokesman offered to salvage the cargo for a share of one-third of its value. The offer was refused, but the Bahamians soon realized the trick that had been played on them, and a fight started.

The Key West wreck master did some fast thinking. He knew the Black Fleet would get help or reinforcements from Nassau much quicker than he could from Key West, so it behooved him to wade into the melee and stop the fight. He promised to repay the Bahamians for a boat of theirs that was smashed in the fracas, and proposed that the two parties of wreckers divide the job evenly between them. To emphasize the point, he painted a red line down the center of the *Alicia's* deck. The Key Westers fell to on one side of the line and the Bahamians on the other. By the time the customs inspector, the underwriters' surveyor and a British gunboat arrived on the scene, all were working side by side in obvious good will.

But the underwriters' surveyor, on the alert to protect property of the insurers, turned up evidence indicating the theft of certain items of cargo by the wreckers. The steamer lay on her side in shallow water. Examining her position, the surveyor found she was resting on something that appeared to be a bed of ale bottles. The *Alicia* had carried a goodly consignment of ale, much of which seemed to be missing. The underwriters' agent and the wreck master had been good-natured antagonists in many a prior encounter. When the latter was asked how he would explain the presence of all those bottles in the sea, he solemnly explained that the vessel had a hole in her bottom and that the bottles had evidently washed out during the storm. "Strange," declared the surveyor. "Not a single bottle has a cork in it!"

When the libel case for salvage came up in court, the question of the empty ale bottles was presented, probably without much hope of proving embezzlement. Wreckers were notoriously keen at sailing one point windward of the law. Their lawyer reminded the court that, although looting from the hold of a wreck is criminal, taking food or drink from a vessel's icebox is not. The wreckers declared under oath that they had taken nothing but food and drink, and that every case of ale they consumed had come out of the ship's icebox. This was literally true, for every case of ale had been placed in the icebox first, then removed and consumed.

Harper's New Monthly Magazine, April 1859
This wood engraving of the period shows Indian Key, the wreckers' rendezvous, lying well at sea near the most dangerous portion of the Florida reefs.

19

The Uninhibited Career of Jacob Housman

Jacob Housman lived and died a wrecker who threw out the rules and played the game his own way. There is no more colorful chapter in the annals of American wrecking than the story of this arrogant and lawless Staten Islander and the settlement he built on Indian Key. The tale has elements of opera: the virile barytone, the noble and martryred tenor, the beautiful soprano and the chorus of Indians and wreckers, with the thunder of doom for a finale.

Young Housman was an ambitious lad who found hauling freight around New York Harbor in his father's windjammers too tame for his talents. In the early 1820s he made off with a schooner — without bothering to tell the elder Housman of his plans — and set a course for the West Indies, hoping that conditions there might be more congenial. He had almost reached the Caribbean when he ran afoul of the Florida reef and limped into Key West for repairs. In that brash new town he saw fortunes being made by men with no more equipment and experience than he possessed. It looked good, and he decided to remain.

From his arrival in the settlement, Housman showed intolerance of advice or restraint. He plunged vigorously into the wrecking business and, with his early maritime training and his keen appetite for the profits of the game, was soon a daring and successful wrecker. But the price he paid for this success was the respect and good will of the community. From the start he was at outs with the men around him. Key West was a raw and boisterous place; its ideas of justice and integrity were as varied as the maritime fortune hunters who made up its citizenry. Yet it did have a few definite opinions about what a wrecker should and should not do during his working hours. Housman's methods with the luckless craft that fell into his hands outraged even Key West's pliant sense of respectability.

The amount of salvage awarded him by local boards of arbitration for servicing shipwrecks was seldom to his liking, and he found it impossible to bring the arbitrators around to his way of thinking. So he began to consider better ways to make this business pay. There were innumerable islands along the Florida coast. Perhaps, on one of these, he could develop a settlement of his own, where his talents would have freer play and receive the rewards they deserved. Housman was young and his ambitions somewhat extravagant. He dreamed of building his town around a central square in which there would be grass and flowers, not the white coral dust of Key West. There would be cottages for his crews and a big house for himself — all standing along straight streets, not higgledy-piggledy as in most frontier settlements. He would have warehouses and wharves and a general store with all the merchandise required by wreckers and their families. He would build a hotel, too, where men away from home could spend a merry evening. He may even have dreamed of a post office, a customs collector and a courthouse, all with county officials of his own choosing. Certainly he dreamed of a woman, a beautiful one, to share his kingdom.

All of this would require money, and lots of it. But quick

profits were the order of the day, and Housman managed to acquire a goodly share. By 1825 he owned and operated three wrecking schooners and was recognized as an outstanding figure in wrecking circles.

By this time, also, the territorial legislature had enacted a law which authorized wreckers' courts as a means of fixing salvage claims. In Key West the new system was not popular; there the old way of arbitration was continued. In September 1825, however, Housman — disregarding custom, precedent and legal opinion — towed a wrecked vessel, the brig *Revenge,* 500 miles up the coast to St. Augustine. There he found men who set up a wreckers' court and awarded him a profit in keeping with his own ideas — namely, 95 per cent of the total value of the vessel and cargo. Had he deliberately sought to outrage the feelings of Key Westers, he could not have found a better way. When this maneuver became known, public indignation boiled. He was accused of having robbed the brig and defied civil and military authority. As has already been related, this incident provoked the French consul and eventually led to the outlawing of wreckers' courts in Florida.

This fracas may have been the spark that lighted Housman's resolve to separate himself from Key West and start his own town. Before the year was over, he had found the location he needed, Indian Key, and bought out two squatters who were living there. The island was well out to sea, near the most dangerous portion of the reefs. It had a small, snug harbor, which was already in occasional use as an overnight anchorage for wreckers patrolling the reefs. It had been the location of a trading post during the days of Spanish control, and mainland Indians had paddled out to trade skins of otter and raccoon for firearms and whiskey. Housman decided that he, too, might do a little trading. He moved in building material, tools and slave labor and went to work. He hewed cisterns in the solid rock and hacked out streets from the mangrove scrub. He brought in some good earth and planted flowers on what would be the central square. Little by little his dream took substance, until eventually it was all there — no longer just a dream, but an actual fact.

Housman's village was more than a crude pioneering effort; it was Florida's first real estate development. There were wharves and warehouses for wrecked merchandise, the big house for the master, small cottages for his crews and his slaves, a store where the more friendly Indians began to trade and a row of cannon to protect the town. But the climax of it all — the crowning glory of Indian Key — was the Tropical Hotel, a large frame building which provided, in addition to sleeping accommodations, a bar and the unheard-of sophistication of a billiard room and a bowling alley.

By 1833, Indian Key was a thriving community of forty or more men, women and children. Wreckers tied up at the wharf at night to spend a pleasant evening at the hotel, rather than sail the distance to their homes at Key West. The store was booming: Housman claimed that it netted him $30,000 the first year. Everything he earned through it and his wrecking activities went into improving the new town. He was its king; and one day, after an unexplained absence, he sailed grandly into the little harbor with a beautiful woman he had brought from Charleston to share the kingdom with him. Her name was Elizabeth Ann.

Soon penniless derelicts, fishermen and beachcombers who lived among the keys were seeking Housman's favors, especially credit at his store. By judicious extensions of credit, he soon had a group of hangers-on who served him as spies and lookouts, bringing him exclusive information of vessels in trouble. He allowed each man a share in the profit from such a wreck. Sometimes he used these men as "disinterested ship captains" to sit on the boards of arbitration which awarded salvage payments. Eventually they became his county officials.

When a lookout discovered a ship in distress, he often had to travel thirty or forty miles to report it to Housman. Of course, he ignored any wreckers he met on the way and thus left the imperiled vessel at the mercy of the sea longer than necessary. Housman, in turn, did not hurry to its aid, but often lingered at

Courtesy The Miami Herald, Miami, Fla.

Two bodies lie buried on lonely Indian Key. Jacob Housman's grave is shielded by a broken headstone; the bones of Dr. Henry Perrine, hastily interred after the raid, have never been found.

home until after dark, when his competitors had come ashore to relax for the evening at his hotel. Then he would steal away to the wreck without being observed or followed. Under the law, a wrecker who did not proceed at once to a vessel in distress would forfeit his license; but Housman's word was the law at Indian Key, and he arranged matters to suit his own convenience.

Or almost so, for his word was not quite the whole law. Indian Key lay within Monroe County, which embraced all of south Florida, and the county seat was Key West. After 1828, whenever Housman was so careless as to allow matters to become issues of law, they were referred to the new court at Key West, with its fearless and incorruptible judges. His very license to engage in wrecking was issued by that court.

It is interesting to compare the rival communities and the men who founded them: Key West with its law-seeking, public-spirited John Watson Simonton; and Indian Key with its Jacob Housman — able, but lawless and grasping. In equally sharp contrast was the ultimate fate of the two towns. Key West was to grow into an orderly, thriving, attractive city; Indian Key was to sink back into the wilderness through blood and fire.

With the establishment of the court, Housman was very soon in trouble at Key West. First one charge, then another was brought against him by shipmasters whom he served. But he always had a string of witnesses who swore that his conduct had been exemplary, and time after time he slipped through the toils of the law. Once, realizing that charges of collusion with the captain of a wrecked vessel were about to be made against him, he towed the vessel out of the territory and all the way to Charleston, South Carolina, for adjudication of his salvage claim. In another case, the master of a ship he was aiding committed suicide during the salvage operations.

When possible, Housman organized his own boards of arbitration, or wreckers' courts, at Indian Key. One such board awarded him 35 per cent of the cargo of a cotton carrier that he successfully refloated. The captain turned over one-third of his cargo and signed a statement that he was satisfied with the arrangement. But the consignees were not and brought suit for the return of the cotton. Investigation revealed that there had been no imminent danger to the vessel, nor had the wrecker encountered any peril in transferring about a hundred bales from her to his own craft. The weather was good, and the relieved ship had floated easily and continued on her way without repairs. It would have been less costly if her master had simply tossed the hundred bales of cotton overboard. The court found that fraud had been committed and awarded the full value of the cargo to the owners of the vessel, declaring all salvage fees forfeited. Housman returned the fees — and had one more score to chalk up against Key West.

On July 1, 1828, Daniel C. Mellus, who claimed to be entirely dependent upon Housman's bounty, discovered the brig *Vigilant* aground and abandoned on Rachel's Key. Her French captain and crew had reached a nearby island. Instead of notifying Housman of the wreck, Mellus evidently tried to pull a fast one. He took the captain to a friend who acted as interpreter and learned that the *Vigilant* carried a cargo of silver specie, dyewood, fustic and sarsaparilla. With the help of his friend and the crew of the *Vigilant,* Mellus floated the vessel and started with it to Key West.

In some way Housman got wind of the incident. He overtook the ships en route and demanded that Mellus divide the salvage award with him. When Mellus refused, Housman threatened to take over the wrecked brig, making such a convincing show of force with muskets and other weapons that the overawed Mellus yielded. Housman promptly made an illegal agreement with the *Vigilant*'s captain to deliver the vessel to Key West for a payment of 75 per cent of the value of vessel and cargo, including the silver. Part of this amount he would return personally to the captain in recognition of his cooperation. Housman's settlement with his henchman was typical: he handed Mellus a receipt for $3,000 *to sign,* declaring that this would completely balance his unpaid account at the store.

At first Housman swore to Mellus that he received nothing for saving the silver on board the *Vigilant.* Later, in an expansive mood, he boasted that the total salvage paid him had been $30,000. This was too much for the wretched underling. Mellus boarded his craft and sailed down to Key West to tell his troubles to the judge. Soon afterward he brought suit against the *Vigilant,* claiming $6,000 salvage fees for his services in refloating the ship. The captain, unwilling to appear in court, left that amount of money with his agent at Key West and sailed with Housman to Charleston. Housman was placed under $10,000 bond pending trial. Just how he got out of this scrape is not recorded.

Housman and Mellus evidently reconciled their differences, for the *Key West Register* of August 20, 1829, reported Mellus at Indian Key and again unlucky, this time in what appeared to be an effort to bring Housman some business. An article over the signature "A Passenger" asserted that Mellus had acted as pilot on a vessel on which the writer had been traveling. While on deck and in full control of the vessel, Mellus had permitted it to drive ashore near the mouth of Newfound River. The ship was not damaged, but the captain, enraged by the pilot's carelessness, had sailed immediately to Indian Key to put him ashore. But about a mile offshore the ship stranded on a bed of rocks and sand, this time seriously. The captain lowered sails and hoisted the ensign half-mast with the union down — a sign of distress — and waited for the Indian Key wreckers to come and get him. When nobody came, the mate rowed ashore, but he found the hotel empty and all the wreckers at sea. He rowed on to Key Tavernier and there found Capt. John Watson, whom he declared to be "very polite and attentive." Watson, with the *Thistle,* lightened and floated the vessel, and in thirty-four hours had her safely at Key West.

For years there had been Indian trouble on the mainland. South Florida was the hunting ground of a number of tribal remnants which, at different times in history, had fled from enemies farther north and found refuge there. Settlers pushing deeper and deeper into the Indians' lands called on the government to send troops to protect them and to drive out the redskins, whom they feared. The situation was inflamed by forays of slave hunters, who raided the Indian villages and carried away Negroes who had found refuge there — and even their children who had been born in the villages. Conditions grew worse: treaties were signed and then broken as more and more settlers poured into the Indians' lands.

Finally, Washington ordered the regular army to rid Florida of its native inhabitants and to take them, by force if necessary, to areas in the West not considered desirable for white settlement. At this, the Indians rose in battle. Then followed the long horror of the Seminole wars.

Refugees on their way down the coast to Key West sometimes stopped at Indian Key and told of Indian atrocities, such as the murder of the keeper of Careysfort lightship and the burning of the Cape Florida lighthouse. Key West lay far enough from the mainland to be considered safe from Indian attack, and Simonton had seen to it that it had a small army garrison for its defense. Housman tried to get a similar garrison for his island but failed — and blamed the failure on political influence exerted from Key West. He did spend thousands of dollars of his own money arming and drilling his settlers, in the vain expectation that he would be reimbursed by Congress.

At this point he again ran afoul of the law. This time he was charged at Key West with stealing goods from a large wreck on Careysfort Reef. Some of the cargo he had turned over to the court, but a considerable portion had been diverted to his warehouse on Indian Key. He was caught red-handed, and witnesses swore that his vessels had stopped repeatedly with choice bits of merchandise while en route from the wreck to Key West. The judge found him guilty and gave him everything in the book. All his claims for salvage were voided, and his license as a wrecker was revoked.

Stung by this indignity, Housman determined to remove himself from the last vestige of Key West jurisdiction. By the end of 1835 he had become widely known as a successful wrecker and promoter. With ready wit and self-assurance, he traveled to the territorial capital at Tallahassee and brought all his influence to bear on the legislative council. That immature body, impressed by his evident importance in the rich wrecking trade, obligingly took his advice and on February 4, 1836, divided Monroe County into two counties. Key West would remain the seat of Monroe County; Indian Key would be the seat of the other. As Housman returned triumphantly to his domain, the news of an Indian massacre of an entire company of United States troops near Tampa was echoing up and down the keys. Housman named his new county Dade in honor of the gallant major who had commanded that ill-fated expedition. Then he set to work building a courthouse at his own expense and organizing his county.

About three years later, on Christmas Day, 1838, a distinguished visitor came to Indian Key with his family, occupying a large house that had been built by the postmaster and deputy collector of customs, Charles Howe. The visitor was Dr. Henry Perrine, former United States counsel at Campeche, Mexico, whom the federal government had granted a township of land on Biscayne Bay, so that he might carry on experiments in adapting tropical plants to Florida soil. Perrine planned to start agricultural communities in Florida to raise the fruits and vegetables he would introduce. He even talked of reclaiming the Everglades.

Dr. Perrine's friends urged him, in view of the Indian troubles, to begin his work on the offshore islands, where he would be safer than on the mainland. When offered the house on Indian Key, he accepted gratefully and began setting out his nurseries on several nearby keys. He soon discovered what sort of men his neighbors were, and history records that he and his family did not indulge in social intercourse except with his host and friend, Charles Howe.

In 1836 the *America* had been shipwrecked off Dry Tortugas. Among the passengers was one Thomas Jefferson Smith, a lawyer. Smith lingered in Florida and soon became associated with Jacob Housman; in time he was handling Housman's not exactly legal affairs. Housman made Smith his first county judge and his lobbyist at Washington. Smith's legal ethics were wide open to criticism, but there were only about fifteen voters in the county, and all were Housman's men. Housman appointed the other county officials from among his cronies, keeping out of office himself. His freedom now seemed complete.

Heady with success, Housman soon began to overreach himself. Questionable methods of trade were making his store unpopular. His profits dropped away. Carrying on a semblance of local government, he made more enemies by putting into the stocks Indians who displeased him and by imprisoning unruly seamen. He lived in constant fear of Indian attack and kept a sloop ready for an escape day and night. As his finances went from bad to worse, Housman made a grandiose gesture to the governor of Florida, the Congress and the President of the United States. He proposed that he be empowered to catch or kill every Indian in the territory of Florida for the sum of $200 a head. There was no taker of this outrageous proposal; but the Indians themselves soon learned of it, and the gesture sealed his doom.

The new county seat, meanwhile, seemed to be running into trouble with the federal authorities. Housman made another amazing proposal: he asked for a grant of land in south Florida near Cape Sable where he might form a settlement "with the rights of the people of said settlement of self-government within the circle of three miles radius from the centre thereof, with an exception from all control of all officers and all laws of the revenue, navy and military departments of the government of the United States." The petition had hardly been made when retribution struck.

In the stifling, pre-dawn heat of August 7, 1840, James Glass, a wrecker living at Indian Key, was unable to sleep. Glancing out of his window, he saw massed war canoes drawn up on the shore. Quickly he wakened George F. Beiglet who shared the house with him, and the two attempted to reach Housman's home, where they knew they could get guns and ammunition for the settlement. But they ran into Indians in the darkness and could only shout, rouse the neighborhood and run for cover. As the village wakened, the Indians attacked from two sides, shooting and screaming as they came. Housman and his lady ran out the back door of their home and into the water, their two dogs racing and barking beside them. Housman drowned the dogs to silence them, then swam around to his dock and got a skiff. In it he and Elizabeth Ann escaped to the sloop *Medium*, which was at anchor offshore.

Men, women and children hid in cisterns, under wharves and beneath houses. Those who were found were shot or beaten to death. Dr. Perrine at first courageously faced the redskins from the front porch of his house, reminding them that he was the white medicine man, their friend, who would continue to help them. The Indians halted and listened and even turned back, for it was Housman they were after. But soon the whiskey and gin they looted from the storehouse turned them into shrieking savages. Baffled in their search for Housman, they returned to the Perrine home, broke in, beat the doctor to death and set fire to the house. Perrine's wife and children first hid in a swimming pool (called a bathing cellar) under the house. From there they were driven by heat and smoke into a tunnel, originally built to conceal an escape boat, which was being used as a pen for sea turtles. From the tunnel they crawled between pilings under an adjoining wharf. Burning cordwood over their heads was about to fall through when they struggled out into the water. When the looting was over, the Indians — a war party under Chief Chekika himself — set fire to everything on the island and sailed away through the smoke.

The following day Housman and his lady returned to the smoldering ruins. Everything but one small house was gone. They found two or three of their slaves alive, but could retrieve little of their former possessions. In desperation they sailed down to Key West, where Houseman auctioned off his remaining personal property. He was broke.

Setting aside old enmities, the Key Westers took him in and gave him work on a wrecking vessel. But the transition was too great. Housman's career had touched its zenith and could only slide off to oblivion. A few months after the disaster at Indian Key, he died as he had lived: fast and violently. On May 1, 1841, while working on a wrecked vessel on a reef in bad weather and a high sea, his foot slipped as he stepped from one craft to the other. He fell between the heaving ships and was crushed.

The old Key West cemetery was swept away in a hurricane a few years later, and the bones of the early wreckers drifted out on the stormy sea they knew so well. But Jacob Housman, in death as in life, was not with the men of Key West. On a small, forgotten island, lying seaward of the cluster of keys (which today are linked by the bridges and causeways of the great Overseas Highway) there is a single, lonely grave. Around and over it clamber strange tropical plants, which have spread wild

The Charles Howe house on Indian Key was occupied by Dr. Henry Perrine and his family, 1838-1841. It was built over a "bathing cellar" from which an escape tunnel led out under the wharf.

from the experimental gardens of the horticulturist, Henry Perrine, who died nearby. The broken headstone which lies across the grave has been washed by the storms of a hundred years, yet the words are still legible:

HERE
LIETH THE BODY OF
Capt. JACOB HOUSMAN
. . .
PROPRIETOR OF THIS ISLAND
WHO DIED BY ACCIDENT
MAY 1ST 1841
AGED 41 YEARS AND 11 MONTHS
To his Friends he was sincere
To his Enemies he was kind
To all Men faithful

Elizabeth Ann, before sailing back to the outer world from which she had come, had taken her lord home to rest in his desolate kingdom on Indian Key.

20

Some Famous Wreckers

It was 1906 when the *Alicia* drove on Ajax Reef. Bilged and waterlogged, she lay on the edge of the coral with almost no visible evidence of damage. A fleet of wrecking vessels hovered around her while two shifts of fifty men each manned the tackles, bringing up her cargo. The resourceful wreck master in charge of the salvage operation — and of many others like it — was Brandish W. Johnson, one of Key West's last and greatest wreckers.

"Hog" Johnson — so nicknamed because he invariably won the race to every wreck he helped salvage — was a huge man with a powerful physique and exceptional skill. The son of a gentleman yachtsman of an old and wealthy Long Island family, he was educated at the United States Naval Academy at Annapolis, but resigned before graduation and went to sea in the coasting trade with a sickly brother. After several strenuous years — during which, among other exploits, he carried arms shipments to the Mexican dictator, Porfirio Díaz (and was well rewarded) — he visited Key West, liked it and settled down to become a wrecker.

Johnson brought with him technical training, wide experience, a zest for taking chances and just enough recklessness to make him a leader in wrecking circles. He was law-abiding up to a certain point, but usually followed his own code of ethics and did not hesitate to ignore laws of which he did not approve. His robust audacity and drive made him popular, and his backlog of skill and ability made him an outstanding figure, not only in Key West but up and down the Atlantic seaboard.

Johnson built his own thirty-five-ton schooner, named it the *Irene* after the Bahamian girl he made his wife and sailed it for thirty-five years. It is said that he and Irene (the woman) broke up and were divorced several times. But always he returned, wooed and won her again, and went through another marriage ceremony. In curious contrast to his lusty, seafaring personality, his life on shore was that of a good citizen and a cultured gentleman. He loved music and literature, dressed well and surrounded himself with beautiful things gathered from around the world. A collection of figureheads from wrecked vessels, which he preserved in his boatyard, was far-famed.

Witty and clever, Johnson would use any trick to outwit his fellow wreckers, but he knew no ill will or malice, His firm was at one time employed to pump out a large lighter that had filled with water and then return it to its owners at Jacksonville. Johnson put in his pumps and went to work; but no matter how fast he pumped, sea water continued to run in. He finally reported that the lighter was ruined, as sea worms had eaten out its bottom. He offered its owners $200 for the wood and materials, and they gladly accepted. Johnson then replaced a missing board in the bottom, pumped out the water and took possession of a perfectly good lighter worth around $5,000. When the former owner saw it and expressed his surprise, Johnson replied nonchalantly, "Oh, it wasn't as bad as I thought." And the laugh was on the owner, for the wreckers' code resembled the old horse-trading code of New England: it was not exactly dishonest, but it allowed no small degree of guile, exaggeration and buffoonery.

In money matters Johnson took the line of "come easy, go easy" and put off his creditors from wreck to wreck when necessary. He was a bundle of energy; and in dull seasons, when other wreckers were enjoying a comfortable relaxation, he was off in several directions at once. On one such occasion he loaded the *Irene* with pineapples, which some of his friends grew on a neighboring island where the soil was good. Taking advantage of a fresh southwesterly wind, he arrived in New York Harbor on the sixth day. He sold the pineapples and loaded on coal, which he delivered in Maine. He then brought ice from Maine back to New York, and sailed from there with a general cargo for Key West. It took him thirty-two days against unfavorable winds to reach home, but he had earned more money than all the other wreckers in town had made during the same period.

Johnson's skill was illustrated when the propeller of his vessel was bent on a rock twelve feet under water, a serious mishap. He loosened the screw with a small charge of dynamite and keyed on another propeller underwater — accomplishing, with only the help of his own crew, a repair that would ordinarily have required a long tow, a period in dry dock and heavy service charges.

Throughout the century the Key Westers, being what they were, gave their full sympathy to the cause of liberation in Cuba. Long before the outbreak of the Spanish-American War, they provided safe and convenient headquarters for the patriots and offered them every kind of assistance, including no small amounts of money. The far-famed gunrunner *Three Friends* often loaded war materials for the Cubans at sea, taking them from wrecking schooners that sailed innocently up and down the reef.

When a Mexican gunboat ran aground on the Hen and Chickens shoal, Hog Johnson was commissioned to salvage her. Johnson brought several barges, moored them beside the wreck and began in a very leisurely manner to load them with coal from the gunboats' ample bunkers. He neglected, however, to move the coal to Key West. Instead, he left it on the barges month after month; and by a strange coincidence, the master of the *Three Friends* kept drifting in on dark nights to refill his bunkers. This happenstance saved the *Three Friends* many hours of steaming back up the coast for fuel.

Johnson never lost his zest for life, never knew caution and never recognized his limitations of years or strength. He died in the sea, a stout old man, heaving and pulling a damaged schooner up the ways.

The exploits of the *Three Friends* have been told and retold

A hurricane finally ended the colorful career of the *Three Friends,* thus defeating the valiant efforts of Mrs. Dorcas Drake, her builder's granddaughter, to save her for posterity.

for over half a century. She was a powerful and beautifully designed deep-sea tugboat, built on the St. Johns River near Jacksonville in 1896, for wrecking and towing on the Florida reefs. With the growth of the Cuban insurrection against Spain, the *Three Friends* became the most noted gunrunner of her day. The man who designed her, who headed the group that raised the $40,000 to build her and who served as her master on some of her most adventurous voyages was Napoleon Bonaparte Broward. Broward was a romantic and colorful figure — riverboat captain, politician, wrecker, sheriff of Duval County for many terms and, eventually, governor of Florida. Broward never belittled his experience as a wrecker. In an autobiographical sketch written during his gubernatorial campaign, he declared: "During the years 1902 and 1903, I was engaged in the wrecking business at Key West, my family and I having spent a part of that time very happily among the hospitable people of that island city. At present time I am in the towing and wrecking business between Jacksonville and Key West — and sometimes Tampa."[1]

Many other colorful characters tread their way down through the brief hundred years when American wrecking flourished. There was Captain John H. Geiger, who first went to Key West as a pilot with Commodore Porter's pirate-chasing squadron. He was a portly man with big, blue eyes and thin, white hair, a grip like a vise and a heart as tender as a child's. Geiger loved flowers, and the yard around his large, square house was a tropical garden of strange and exotic blooms. He was an exceptionally skilled pilot and master wrecker. Advancing years drove him to the cupola of his house, where he sat out the remainder of his life, spyglass in hand, watching the ships pass in and out of the Gulf.

"Old Man" Jaycox, another seaman and wrecker of Key West, vaunted his great strength. He boasted his ability to walk the length of his schooner's deck with a full-grown man seated on each of his outstretched hands.

"Bull" Weatherford was a barebacked diver — one who went down without a helmet or diving dress. He was noted for his ability to make great, curving dives under a vessel and to stop a leak or cut out damaged parts of the keel and bolt on new pieces under water.

Ben Baker, king of the wreckers during the 1870s, was tall, gaunt and shrill of voice, with sharp eyes and a hooked nose. He was supplanted by a man of very different aspect, Sylvanus Pinder, a robust and handsome 'Brilander. Pinder was high-spirited, jolly, and somewhat of a gentleman.

Still another type was George "Rabbit" Demerritt, a small man of tremendous vitality. He first came into public notice when he outfought three brothers in turn, all larger than himself. Demerritt started out as a ship carpenter and boatman. Later he became the outstanding wrecker of his day — and sheriff of Monroe County.

On February 18, 1907, one of the most noted master wreckers of the northern coast died in his home in New London, Connecticut. Captain Thomas A. Scott was born in Snowhill, Maryland, in the 1820s. He was a deep-water sailor at the age of fifteen, and master and owner of the schooner *Thomas Page* soon after. Following his marriage, he left the sea, but he was not successful on shore.

While Scott was living at Fort Lee, New Jersey, an incident occurred that influenced his whole career and brought him back to the sea. He was riding the ferryboat *Union* across the North River to New York City when she was run down by a harbor tug. The tug quickly backed away, leaving a hole in the side of the ferryboat through which water came rushing. Realizing that the clumsy craft would sink with all on board long before she could make shore, Scott thrust himself into the opening and, with his own body, checked the inrush of water until the boat was in its slip and the passengers safely ashore. It was a deed of courage and selflessness, and brought Scott considerable public acclaim, plus a check for $100 from the ferry company, with which to replace his ruined clothing and pay hospital bills for some broken ribs.

While Scott was still at Fort Lee, a steamer burned and sank nearby, and he contracted to raise her cargo. This was the beginning of his career as a wrecker. In time the T. A. Scott Wrecking Company came into being; it removed to the Thames River at New London, Connecticut, and became known up and down the coast for its able handling of salvage jobs. Soon it was doing underwater engineering and construction work. The underwater foundations of the Brooklyn Bridge and the Race Rock Light were among its outstanding achievements.

The tragedy of Scott's life was the loss of his only son, who was knocked overboard by a boom during work on a submerged vessel. The boy must have been knocked unconscious by the blow, for he did not reappear. Scott went down at once in his diving rig and vainly searched the bottom until his men forcibly brought him to the surface, fearing that he would sacrifice his own life in the effort.

In commenting on the passing of Captain Scott, the *New London Day* declared: "Captain Scott was a type of rugged, honest manhood of the highest order. . . . Not only was he a capable, hardworking and efficient wrecking master, but he was of unquestioned integrity and sterling loyalty to fundamental principles. . . . There is no maritime company on the Atlantic seaboard that has not had cause to bless Captain Scott and his intrepid crew of wreckers."[2]

Captain John Lowe and his wife, Bianca Kemp, descendants of the Eleutherian Adventurers, left their home on Green Turtle Cay in the Bahamas to join the growing colony of 'Brilanders at Key West. Captain Lowe was a deep-sea skipper and a churchgoing wrecker. When his daughter Euphemia married the millionaire-to-be William Curry, Lowe became a partner in Curry's mercantile business and brought his fine wrecking schooner, the *Lavina* into the firm. He was a large and powerful man who was once brought back to life after it was thought he had drowned; he lived to the ripe age of eighty-nine.

John Lowe, Jr., after six months' schooling, went to sea with his father. At thirteen he was a licensed skipper, and soon rose to a prominent position in the growing city of Key West. He combined wrecking and mercantile interests, operating a fleet of fifteen sponge boats. Like his father, he lived well beyond his eightieth birthday.

Caroline, another member of the Lowe Family, distinguished herself during the Civil War by mounting daily to the widow's walk on top of her big white house and flaunting a Confederate flag, à la Barbara Frietchie, as Yankee patrols marched past the house. They forbade further demonstrations and even searched the house, but they never found her flag. Nearly a hundred years later, when the beautiful old house was being renovated for use as a night club, workmen tearing away the rotted railing of the widow's walk discovered a faded Confederate flag in a hollow railing, where Captain Lowe had probably kept his spyglass many years before the Civil War.

Rupert Knowles of Key West still remembers the last of the master wreckers of that locality, Alfred Acheson, nicknamed "Bub Smart." As early as 1898, when he was just eleven, Acheson would listen for the whistle on the Key West ice plant to blow the signal which broadcast the news of a wreck on the reef. He would follow the pounding feet to the waterfront, and often some good-natured wrecker would take him along as cabinboy, giving him a quarter-share of whatever the men made on the trip. The wreckers of that day all stepped back and let Acheson take charge, willingly following his leadership.

Acheson, Knowles avers, was clever and a great seaman, though without formal education. Public-spirited in his own way, he was known, when salvage money from a good wreck was being divided, to add to the list of those who had worked on the job the names of sick or destitute men who had not been there at all. It was a kind of primitive social security: the money came out of the sum earned by all who did the job, and they were willing to accept less than their rightful shares so that comrades who had fallen on evil days might have a little help.

Larry Karns Studio, Key West, Fla.

The Key West lighthouse, erected in 1846, replaced a former light destroyed in a hurricane. It is 102 feet high and shines through white sectors over deep water, through red sectors over reefs.

21

In Defense of Lighthouses

Lighthouses seem always to have been associated with wreckers. As with many traditional beliefs, there is probably a glimmer of reason for this one. But to track it down, one must search further back than the frontier lighthouse of the American shore. The tale of piratical lightkeepers who dimmed or extinguished their lights to lure vessels to destruction was probably first told of the sixteenth-century lighthouse on the Cornish coast of England. Whether it was true even then is doubtful.

The Romans, sailing around Iberia and across the English Channel, erected towers along the coasts as seamarks to guide their vessels. In the fourth century there was a huge lighted Roman beacon at Boulogne, said to have been 192 feet high, and a lesser one across the channel near Dover. But the early Britons were not sea-minded, and as the Romans departed from the British Isles, their lights and marks gradually disappeared. What sailing vessels were left in Britain fell to pieces from disuse. By the fifth century, shipbuilding was a forgotten craft.

It took the emotional stresses of the Crusades to rouse the English people to the need for ships. The church, as a religious duty, began setting out lights at dangerous localities as a warning to seafaring pilgrims. Before the Reformation, church towers near the sea were sometimes topped with these beacon lights. At Hull a monk who tended such a beacon had a new idea: to raise money to maintain his light, he secured the king's permission to levy a toll on each ship using the harbor. His idea caught on, and soon private landowners up and down the coast were putting up lights and levying tolls on shipping. In time, private lighthouses became quite a business. But these lights were fitful and burned only at their sponsors' pleasure.

It was Henry VIII who, after destroying the monasteries and ending their efforts to guide shipping, took the next bold step. In 1536 he chartered the Guild of the Blessed Trinity, whose duties included erecting towers and maintaining lights in them which would burn every night. The lords of the seaside manors, however, demanded the right to put up private lights along the coast — and to tax shipping for their maintenance — as a money-making project. This competition of private and public utilities led to confusion and ill will, which persisted until the government bought the private lights.

In the reign of Elizabeth I, the pilots and mariners formed a new organization, the Brotherhood of the Most Gracious and Undividable Trinity (later known as the Corporation of Trinity

House). The brethren were granted wide powers, including the right to levy taxes on shipping; to erect and maintain buoys, beacons and seamarks; to supply pilots, design and build ships, and supply personnel for the Royal Navy; to arbitrate disputes arising in these areas; and to oversee salvage matters.

The ill-famed lighthouse at St. Agnes in the Scilly Isles was erected in 1680. From the beginning it was unpopular with the people, who saw it as an unreasonable interference with the Lord's provision for them of supplies and luxuries which they could not buy for themselves. For a hundred years the St. Agnes light was a source of public outcry. Sometimes it shone brightly; at other times it could not be seen a few miles away; and occasionally it was completely extinguished. The keeper's relatives were wreckers, and the charge was made — and stoutly maintained — that the light was used to bring about shipwrecks rather than to prevent them. History inclines toward this view, accepting this as the only known instance of deliberately contrived shipwrecks on the coasts of England. Yet the early English lights were only a chandelier of tallow candles, or a fire of coals held in an iron lantern with a funnel at the top. At best they could not have been visible very far out to sea.

The first lighthouse in America was lighted on September 14, 1716, in Boston Harbor. It burned sperm oil, as did all the earliest American lights. In 1746 the people of Nantucket Island raised money privately for a lighthouse on Brant Point. Until it was built, the Nantucketers showed strong lights in their windows whenever a ship was expected.

The merchants and shipowners of New York began efforts for a lighthouse in 1761. The New York Assembly authorized a lottery to raise funds to build it. As the necessary amount was not forthcoming, a second lottery was held; and a tonnage tax was placed on shipping, as in England, to pay running expenses. In this way the light at Sandy Hook was built. It was first lighted on June 11, 1764, and remains the oldest original lighthouse in America.

With the coming of national independence, the new Congress of the United States — as its ninth act — set up the United States Lighthouse Service, under the Treasury Department, on August 7, 1789. (The service was passed from one governmental department to another until July 1, 1939, when it became a part of the United States Coast Guard.) The first lighthouse was authorized by the new nation in 1791; it was built at Cape Henry, Virginia, at the entrance to Chesapeake Bay. George Washington signed the order for a light at Montauk Point in 1796. Two years later the Cape Hatteras light, said to have been the highest brick tower in the world at that time, was erected; it was followed in 1799 by the light at Gay Head on Martha's Vineyard. All the early lightkeepers rendered aid to the shipwrecked as a matter of course.

Only a few weak lights stood along the Bahama Channel and the Florida Straits at the beginning of the nineteenth century. They suffered their share of suspicion, as did many bigger and finer lights in other parts of the world. Their proximity to the wreckers' settlement at Key West was no doubt considered reason enough for careful skippers to mistrust them. It was not uncommon to hear mariners, as they came ashore from incoming vessels, make the charge that one light or another had not been burning when they passed by. If, on a murky night, they had not sighted the lighthouse at the place they expected it to be, it was very easy for them to believe the lightkeeper a villain.

On the American side of the channel, the lighthouse program began in 1823, soon after the acquisition of Florida from Spain. Except for an old Spanish watchtower at St. Augustine, the entire coast was without a beacon of any kind until the first three lights were completed in 1826 — one at Key West, another at Sand Key (marking the main ship channel around Key West and into the Gulf of Mexico) and a third at Cape Florida, near present-day Miami. A single lightship, the *Florida,* was built at the same time to warn shipping off Careysfort Reef, the most dangerous spot on the coast.

Judge James Webb, who exercised the first legal control over

Key West wrecking, discouraged the early lightkeepers from leaving their stations to aid vessels in distress and awarded them only scanty fees for any wrecking they did. He maintained that the keepers' first duty was to their lights and that they should not be drawn away from them by other considerations. In 1831 the American navy adopted the same policy: its men were forbidden to participate in salvage awards for rescue work. Soon thereafter it was ruled that all government employees should refrain from making claims for salvage when rendering aid to those in distress at sea, unless their services actually exceeded the just limits of their official duty.

The frontier lighthouses and their keepers had a rough time of it. The early towers were often built by inexperienced hands, and even expert builders had not yet developed means for raising strong, well-situated lighthouses. The towers usually stood close beside the water near some particularly hazardous rocks or shoal. They were seldom over seventy feet high and were powered by oil lanterns visible for about twelve miles on a dark night. The lanterns were so easily obscured by fog, thick weather or even bright moonlight that a passing mariner could not accurately gauge his distance from the light. Often there were more shipwrecks near the lighthouses than elsewhere. The keepers and their families lived in the tower rooms or in small cottages at the foot of the lights, without protection from storm or from Indian attack. Some of them perished gallantly, their lights burning to the end.

Far from opposing lighthouses, the Key West wreckers took them in stride. They forbore to sabotage the lighthouse program even when a golden opportunity fell into their hands. The *Florida* had been completed and was being sailed by its builders' representatives to its station on Careysfort Reef. As it came southward down the coast, it ran into an easterly gale at a moment when it must have been hugging the edge of the Gulf Stream. The clumsy craft was swept ashore north of Key Largo. As soon as the weather cleared, the crew abandoned her and betook themselves in a lifeboat down the coast to report the mishap.

When the news reached Key West, several wrecking schooners set out to find the *Florida,* as they would have gone to any other ship in distress. In a few days they located and refloated the lightship and towed her down to Key West. There they handed her over to the court and merrily collected their pay for her safe return, quite as content to make money on a lightship as any thing else.

For twenty-four years, until the Cape Canaveral light was established in 1847, the *Florida* bore the only light between Cape Florida and Key West, 200 miles of seaway with all the hazards a ship could face. Hurricanes blew her off station several times, and the storm of 1835 stove in her lanterns and blew away her boats.

During her long lifetime the *Florida* was more than once accused of crooked business. One such charge was made at Key West in 1834 by an incoming shipmaster, but a letter of protest was published in the *Key West Enquirer* (as it was called during 1834) of December 6:

TO THE EDITOR:

A report was circulated here a few days ago that on Thursday night, the 27th ult. there was no light at the lightship on Careysfort Reef, — which is not true. I saw the light at twelve miles distant that night, and ran through the shoals from Caesar's Creek to the lightship, and stayed on board that night, during which I was on deck several times and saw a good light. After daylight I saw the lanterns lowered and the lights extinguished.

Captain Thompson, who made the report, was convinced by me that his chart (Blunt's 1832) was wrong, very far wrong, and that his vessel was near forty miles south of the lightship when he thought himself opposite to her. I make this communication in justice to Captain Walton, and request you to publish the same.

R. FITZPATRICK

Captain Walton lost his life about two years later when, after sending his family to Key West for safety, he refused to leave his post of duty on the lightship at the approach of hostile Indians. A passing ship sighted a canoe full of Indians approaching the lightship and hurried to Key West with the news. A revenue cutter sent to investigate found Captain Walton shot and scalped.

The lighthouse at Key West, completed in 1825, saw only a brief period of service. It was swept into the sea in a hurricane in 1846, carrying down with it the keeper and thirteen other persons, including his entire family. A survey for a new lighthouse was made promptly after the disaster, but due to the Seminole uprising and the long period of hostilities, actual rebuilding had to wait until 1848.

The Sand Key Light, standing on a small island 400 yards in circumference, was the best of the three lighthouses built along the Florida Straits. It was kept for a while by two women, Mrs. Rachel Flaherty and her sister, who lived on the island. It too went down in the great storm of 1846 and was not rebuilt until the close of hostilities, but there is no evidence that the plucky sisters shared the fate of the keepers of the Key West light. Until July 20, 1853, only a small, weak, floating light was maintained at Sand Key.

The Cape Florida light, completed in 1827, had a tragic and exciting finish. It survived several Indian scares in 1836: "The Cape Florida light is still kept up, although there is scarcely a day passes without Indians being seen in the vicinity," announced the *Key West Inquirer* on June 18 of that year. The long expected attack came in force on July 23. There are several versions of the story, but most of them agree that the keeper, John W. B. Thompson, and a Negro assistant keeper ran to the lighthouse and took refuge in the tower. The Indians, after looting and setting fire to the dwelling houses, saw the men in the tower and, unable to break in the door, set it afire. The flames spread through bullet holes to the oil in a storage tank inside and from there shot up the spiral stairway. When the heat became unbearable, Thompson tossed down a small keg of gunpowder, thinking to bring about a quick end to his torment. But the powder temporarily damped the fire; the burning stairs fell through; and he was marooned with his now dead companion on the platform at the top of the lighthouse. The Indians loaded everything they could into Thompson's sloop and departed.

The fire died out in the night, and the next day Thompson succeeded in attracting the attention of a passing vessel. Her master was unable to help him, but hastened to Key West and reported the disaster to the revenue cutter *Flint*. That vessel rushed to Cape Florida, and its crew fired a length of twine, attached to a musket ramrod, up the tower. With the twine Thompson hauled up a tail block and rope. Two men were then hoisted up to Thompson; they took him gently down and rushed him to Key West for medical attention. The light was rebuilt in 1847; it was damaged in the Civil War but served until 1878, when it was replaced by a better situated light on the nearby Fowey Rocks.

On the Bahamian side of the channel, efforts began as early as 1834 to find a builder who could put up two lighthouses, one on Great Abaco Island, the other at Hole in the Wall near Gun Cay. A Bostonian named Lewis finally took the contract and built the lights.

The much maligned light at Dry Tortugas, just inside the entrance to the Gulf of Mexico, was the last of the early lights on the sea frontier. Right from the start there had been something amiss about the Tortugas light. It was built about 1838 on Garden Key, one of a cluster of small islets surrounded by miles of half-hidden rocks, quicksand and shoals of sticky, white marl. Unnumbered vessels ended their voyage on these very rocks. Anguished skippers sometimes blamed the lightkeeper, accusing him of dimming or extinguishing the light. In view of the common distrust of lightkeepers, it was probably natural for a shipmaster, when he misjudged the distance from a light and felt his craft crunch helplessly on the rocks, to believe he had been victimized by a lightkeeper in cahoots with wreckers. If at such a moment a wrecking vessel put out from the landing stage of the lighthouse to aid him, nothing on earth would shake the captain's conviction that he was a victim of skullduggery.

One such incident took place in 1836, when the square-rigger *America,* of the packet line of E. D. Hurlbut & Company of New York, carrying a general cargo and thirty passengers, piled up on the shoals at Dry Tortugas. This was one of the most notable shipwrecks of the period. The *America*'s captain, a veteran of the line, had come out of retirement for this one voyage as a favor to his former employers. The ship was bound for Mobile en route to a European port, and the voyage had been smooth and pleasant. The passengers had bade each other good night about the time the light at Dry Tortugas was sighted. One of them, writing anonymously in *Harper's* magazine of April 1859, twenty-three years after the wreck, declared:

It was a calm, starlight, [*sic*] gently-breezing night, and our gallant bark . . . was making easy progress, when suddenly she brought up all standing and hard aground.

In a moment all were startled from their berths. . . . Soundings were made forward, aft, and in all directions around the ship, and our position was ascertained upon a sunken reef. Sails were backed, and all possible efforts made to clear the reef, but in vain. . . .

Soon a small fishing-smack came near, and from it a rough specimen of humanity, who said he was master of the smack, boarded us. He held also a wrecker's license. He was, therefore, not regarded very favorably by our company. . . . A stout, burly, red-faced, sunburned sailor, whose only clothing consisted of a Guernsey shirt, pantaloons rolled up to his knees, and a slouched, weather-beaten hat. . . ."[1]

The wrecker's offer of assistance was refused. The *America*'s master was a competent seaman and believed, as did many other masters under like circumstances, that he could refloat his ship by his own efforts with anchors and sail. In addition, the captain distrusted the wrecker and rebelled at the price he set upon his services.

The ship was snared within the reef. Her captain did

refloat her, but she only struck again, driving farther onto the rocks than before. But he would not give up. and the struggle to save her went on for another day. Eventually a half-gale set in; the anchor dragged, and the ship was caught in the sands of a lee shore. The unwelcome wrecker returned, and this time was permitted to take off the passengers and their luggage and put them ashore at the lighthouse. The crew soon followed.

The eyewitness account continues:

> Now, according to the rules of professional wrecking, the voyage was ended; the wreck belonged to the underwriters; the wrecker who "first came" must be "first served" with the opportunity of saving property, ostensibly for the underwriters, but quite as much for the wrecker's own benefit. Our wrecker, with his crew of two or three fishermen, among whom the deputy light-keeper figured familiarly, had obtained complete possession of his prize.

For three days the party remained the guests of the light-keeper. The captain, seeing that the rising water in the hold of the ship was hourly lowering the value of the cargo, urged the wrecker to send for more assistance. On the fourth day, a few of the *America*'s passengers started out in a small boat on the fifty-mile sail to Key West, with the deputy lightkeeper as guide. But they returned to the lighthouse at dusk, convinced that the trip was too dangerous.

During the night, the eyewitness and the captain, who were both quartered on the ground floor of the overcrowded light-house, heard the deputy and the wrecker up in the light chamber, talking over the events of the day. Their voices carried clearly down the winding staircase. With considerable glee, the deputy told the wrecker how he had played upon the fears of the men in the small boat, warning them of the dangers often encountered on such a trip and prevailing upon them to return to the light-house. Now there would be no other wreckers coming to disturb their salvage work or to share in the rich harvest they would glean from the wreck.

Indignant at what he had heard, the *America*'s elderly captain took the boat himself the next morning and, with the eyewitness and a boy from the lighthouse, set out to summon aid. Oddly enough, all the dangers predicted by the wrecker for the previous journey were actually encountered on the way, but the captain finally made Key West in a howling norther. The lighthouse boat was recognized before he landed, and an excited crowd was on the wharf in spite of the storm, calling out "A wreck? Where?" Even before the visitors had left the wharf, wreckers were hurriedly preparing to put to sea. One smack just in from Havana unceremoniously dumped its deckload of oranges on shore and in the water, so impatient was its skipper to get away to the wreck. The *America*'s captain engaged a vessel to pick up his passengers at the lighthouse and take them to Mobile.

Back at Dry Tortugas the first wreckers had removed most of the dry and undamaged cargo before their unwelcome reinforcements arrived. But the job was too big for them to handle alone. The other wreckers assisted in the more difficult task of breaking out cargo from the lower hold, where water rose and fell at the ebb and flood of the tide. The last and hardest task of all was that of the divers. Deep in the *America*'s submerged hold they made fast to huge boxes and bales of merchandise, working courageously in water made nauseous by dyestuffs, drugs and even poisons. They did not cease their unpleasant but profitable activity until conditions became absolutely unbearable. After the wet goods had been dried as far as possible by exposure to the sun on a neighboring key, all the cargo was put aboard the wrecking vessels and taken to Key West. There it was surrendered to the court, under whose supervision the public sale took place.

Then came the suit for a salvage award. The court set a figure of $47,471 — said to be the largest amount ever decreed at Key West — to be divided among the participating wrecking craft. The share of each vessel was divided among owner and crew, with extra shares for the officers. The first wrecker, who would normally have been entitled to a higher rate than the others, forfeited this by his interference with the appeals for additional assistance from Key West.

The eyewitness account concludes: ". . . the wrecking system . . . is wise, humane, economical, and effective; but there is an obvious necessity that it be narrowly watched and faithfully guarded."[2]

Shortly after the wreck of the *America,* the *Key West Inquirer* carried an interview with Captain Thompson, keeper of the lighthouse at Dry Tortugas, in which he called attention to the unsatisfactory functioning of the light. He maintained that, because of the many miles of shoals on either side of the lighthouse, a shipmaster could not be sure in squally weather — or even in bright moonshine — just how far he was from the light. Thus he could easily run his vessel aground. He proposed that two lights, one at either end of the shoals, be set up in place of the present single tower. The *Inquirer* added:

> Recent events fully prove the inefficiency of the present light and we are informed that the Keeper has made frequent representations on the subject, and submitted plans for its improvement finally, however, recommending its suppression and the substitution of the two lights previously referred to.[3]

Captain John C. Hoyt, the Key West agent of the Board of Underwriters of the Port of New York, observed in his report for 1850 that the Dry Tortugas light had been somewhat improved, but that it still needed alterations, for mariners continued to misjudge their distance from it at night. Commenting on other nearby lights, Capt. Hoyt wrote:

> The three lightships on the coast are faithfully kept, but the power of their lights is by no means what it ought to be. The lightship stationed at Sand Key is old, and the light they attempt to show is miserable. Several vessels have been lost, and much valuable cargo, by the neglect of the Government to build a lighthouse at Sand Key to replace the one destroyed by the hurricane of 1846. The lights at Cape Florida and Key West are both very good.

At mid-century, thanks to the Key Westers, a new kind of warning light was installed at the Florida reef. In 1849 the wreckers' senator, Stephen R. Mallory, initiated in Congress the first survey of the reef, which in turn led to a system of lights positioned on the reef itself. This system was begun in 1850 and was continually improved, until the whole outer line of reefs was marked by a chain of lights, one or more of which was always in sight to any vessel passing through the Florida Straits.

Today it would be absurd to question the good faith and loyal performance of the keepers and crews of the lights on the closely settled American shores. But, strangely, we find it much less unreasonable to doubt the honor and faithfulness of their predecessors along a less settled coast. This skepticism is not based on any culpable conduct of the early lighthouse keepers, for there is no record that criminal actions ever took place. Perhaps it is only a sneaking fondness for romance and deviltry in the heart of every man that makes him cling to the outmoded villainy of another era, cherish it as fact and pass it along to snarl the lines and confound the compasses of future historians.

Larry Karns Studio, Key West, Fla.

Key West's waterfront was the site of the headquarters of Florida's first millionaire. Here William Curry dealt in ship chandlery, directed his wrecking vessels and financial interests.

22

High Tide

The clerks at Mr. Tiffany's jewelry store in New York, in the sophisticated year of 1880, fancied that they had seen about everything. But there was something about the stocky, elegantly dressed stranger, as he strolled from the private office in deep conversation with the manager, that froze them into attitudes of elaborate unconcern. They strained to catch a word or two of the talk as the men strolled down the center aisle to the big, brass-trimmed front door. The stranger had a strong, pleasant, smooth-shaven face, and spoke with what seemed to be a slight British accent. When the two had shaken hands, the stranger replaced his tall beaver hat and stepped out onto the crowded sidewalk of lower Broadway. The manager closed the door and turned to the staff, his eyes shining and his face flushed with excitement.

"Gentlemen," he anounced, "I'm not at all sure they have such a thing at Buckingham Palace, or even at Versailles, but the customer who just went out that door has left us an order for a solid gold dinner service of twenty-four place settings. In my office is a draft on his bank for one hundred thousand dollars that says he isn't fooling."

The staff caught its collective breath.

"You mean he wants knives and forks, don't you, not a whole dinner service?" the cashier inquired cautiously.

"I mean knives, forks, spoons, plates, cups and saucers, dishes, coffee service, tea set — *everything!*"

There was a moment of awe-struck silence.

"Who is he?" murmured the girl at table silver.

"William Curry, a ship chandler, from down South. Lives on an island, I believe. Only gets up this way once a year. Seems to have plenty of money to spend."

"Are you sure that's what he is?" asked the worldly-wise clerk at the diamond counter. "Ship chandlers around New York don't buy gold dinner sets, so far as I've noticed."

"What island does he live on?" asked another.

"I don't remember," the manager admitted. "It's one of the Florida Keys, those little islands down between our coast and Cuba."

"Isn't that where the pirates come from?" cried table silver.

"There aren't any more pirates," remonstrated wedding rings, in bored sophistication.

"Of course, it is!" said diamonds. "That's the place, only they call them wreckers now. It's the same thing. I have a cousin at Charleston, in Carolina, who's seen them come off the mail packet. They go up to Charleston and buy out the town. There's a whole settlement of them somewhere off the coast. They force ships to run on the rocks and then go out and plunder them."

"Do you suppose Mr. Curry is a — a *wrecker*?" asked wedding rings in a throaty whisper.

The manager frowned. "Mr. Curry is a gentleman. Didn't you notice his beautiful speech and the quiet dignity of his clothes? He is a member of the New York Stock Exchange and a man of great wealth. Don't let me hear any more talk about pirates and wreckers!"

With that he marched back to his office and firmly closed the door.

Something like this conversation must have taken place that summer morning in 1880 when William Curry, dressed in the acme of good taste, arrived in New York on the steam packet from Charleston. After engaging a suite of rooms at the Colonader Hotel, he stepped over to Mr. Tiffany's jewelry store to leave an order for some gold dishes for the wife and children. Really, it had been his idea, not theirs. He just wanted to eat his food off of gold — he always had — and now there was no reason in the world why he should not try it.

The unprecedented order was completed in a few months, and Tiffany's could not resist the temptation to show it off in its window for a few days. For a week New York was agog with questions and surmises about Key West and the Curry family. John Jacob Astor heard about the display and went to look at it himself. He took one glance at the exquisitely hand-wrought articles and ordered a set for his own family.

In time the gold dishes arrived at Key West and went into the Curry's corner cupboard without ceremony. There they reposed between meals, winter and summer, in the big house that never knew a locked door. The eight young Currys ate from them daily until after their marriages, when they left the parental rooftree and put up much grander mansions of their own. The servants merrily doused the gold dishes in the kitchen sink and accidentally tossed out a spoon or two in the garbage, just as they had done with the old silver ones. At first Mrs. Curry patiently fished them out, but eventually she issued an edict that no servant should dump out the garbage until the gold had been counted.

The set cost Curry $100,000 to start with. (There were twenty-four of most pieces and forty-eight of some.) Later, replacements and additions upped the total. At the Martello Gallery of the Key West Art and Historical Society are some yellowed invoices from Tiffany's, dated in the eighties and nineties, billing an eighteen-inch gold "waiter" at $1,825, a tea kettle at $1,100 and a dozen table forks at $839.50, or nearly $70 each. Persons living today who in their youth ate from the set — and Curry heirs who still have a few pieces of the fabulous gold service — declare that the workmanship was exquisite.

When William Curry died, Tiffany's, to help settle the estate, bought back any pieces of the gold service the heirs wished to convert into money. Since Tiffany's paid the current market value of the gold actually in each piece, it gave a higher price for the returned articles than it had received for them when they were new.

The spectacle of a modest man sitting down in an unpretentious house to a table set with regal splendor might seem bizarre in most places; but in Key West, where contradictions were the order of the day, it was taken in stride. There a man might sing sentimental ballads and play a Spanish guitar under his girl's balcony at night, and in the morning be up to his eyebrows in seawater, hauling the bucking, straining hull of a dismasted vessel through gale-lashed seas.

In William Curry, American wrecking reached its ultimate. He was a product of the sea frontier, warp and woof of his times — self-educated and self-made. His native ability and drive were combined with an innate gentleness and good taste which frontier living seemed to heighten rather than dull. Above all, he possessed a genius in financial matters and stock market maneuvers that nothing on earth could explain.

The Curry family came to America from Scotland and forged a chain of trade with the mother country. In time they became wealthy Carolina planters and were among the British loyalists forced to abandon their property during the Revolution. They went to Florida, then joined the influx of Tory refugees into the Bahamas and settled near Harbour Island.

When William was born in 1821 on Green Turtle Cay, the family boasted a Methodist preacher, a justice of the peace and several planters. But the struggling plantations died out with the eliminaton of slavery in the 1830s, and means of livelihood were meager. Young William, with only a wholesome family background and a common school education, heard tall tales of the riches to be had at Key West, the new town across the Bahama Channel. When he was sixteen years old, he seized an opportunity to try his fortunes there.

At Key West, Curry did not rush to join the crew of a wrecking schooner in search of quick profits. Even as a youngster he had little interest in a gamble, and his retiring nature saw little satisfaction in a seafaring life. On the contrary, his success appears to have resulted from a conviction that every move he made should be progressive, orderly and understood. Then its effect would be certainty and not chance.

He started as a clerk in the mercantile establishment of Weever and Baldwin, at a wage of one dollar a week plus a little room of his own over the store and meals at the owner's house. In later life Curry enjoyed telling about the first purchase he made out of his earnings. He saw a small pocket compass he wanted very much, impulsively paid a dollar for it and took it up to his room. But there he had no reason to use it. For a while he carried the compass around in his pocket and took it out occasionally to look at it. But it told him nothing he did not already know. Slowly it was borne upon him that the compass for which he had spent his hard-earned dollar was worthless to him, because he had no need of it. When he saw this unpleasant truth clearly, he took the compass out to the end of a wharf and threw it as far as he could into the sea. Forever afterward he took as a basic tenet of his career the fact that nothing really has value to a man unless he has use for it.

Curry served in subordinate positions for about ten years, always watching for opportunities to increase his small capital. Like Dick Whittington of London, he placed objects or small quantities of merchandise in the hands of friendly sea captains, who would trade the goods for him or sell them at a profit in the West Indies or Central America. Eventually he accumulated enough capital to open a small mercantile business, in partnership with a friend, dealing in vessel supplies and family stores for those connected with wrecking. His business increased from the beginning.

Curry never actually went to sea; he might be described as a wrecker once removed. He began by servicing the men who salvaged the shipwrecks; soon he was outfitting and provisioning wrecking vessels, as well as selling ship chandlery, marine hardware, furniture and foodstuffs. He married Euphemia Lowe, daughter of the wrecking captain John Lowe, who became a third partner in his business and brought into it a fine wrecking schooner, the *Lavinia.*

Both the marriage and the business arrangements were happy. The business expanded until it was operating a fleet of wrecking schooners and sloops, including the only clipper ship ever built in Florida, the *Stephen R. Mallory.* She was named for Curry's good friend, the wreckers' senator, and carried a life-sized figurehead of him. In later years Curry set up an ice plant, brought in the first two steam tugboats Key West had ever seen and was Florida's last private banker.

But by far the most remarkable achievements of this quiet, unassuming man were his operations in the stock market. Having at first no means of communication with New York other than letters carried on coastwise packet ships, Curry dealt brilliantly in stocks and bonds. His transactions amounted to sheer genius as the telegraph reached farther and farther down the coast. His judgment was accurate, his touch deft and sure. He was a prudent man, slow to decide and quick to act, free from vaunting ambition, pride or ostentation. The gold dinner service was no more to him than a little indulgence in the beauty he always loved and craved.

The Currys lived in a square house with a ground floor of stone and two upper floors of wood, Bahama-style. The front steps led up to the main entrance on the second floor, and there were ample porches around the lower stories. The house was white inside and out, except for the dining room, where the walls were painted light green. It was a comfortable, spacious house, yet no better than those of his neighbors. "Miz' Euphemie" became stout in her later days, so a small elevator was built into the house for her special use.

Curry's sympathies were with the federal government in the War Between the States, but he was able to carry on his business throughout the period of hostilities in a community of intense Southern sympathies. He avoided the use of Confederate money and took no chances with his growing capital, but exchanged what he could for British pounds sterling, which he kept safely in England. It returned to him after the war not only intact but also greatly increased in value by the soaring rate of exchange.

William Curry died in 1896, the richest man in Florida. He was no longer rated simply a "stout conch" (a Bahamian-Key Wester) but one of America's earliest millionaires. Curry was a keen student of men, quiet, methodical, firm — a born merchant prince.

The span of William Curry's long life was the measure of the great days of Key West. He saw the wreckers' city ride the incoming tide and grow from a small village of seafaring men to the richest city per capita in North America. Seething with its own interests, it rested its brief hour on the flood tide — rich, lusty, churchgoing, self-reliant, free and easy. Then the wind changed; the light faded; and the remorseless ebb set in at last.

23

The Remorseless Ebb

It was no fault of the wreckers that the lush and exciting trade they followed began to wane. The nineteenth century was a period of expansion: progress was on the march, and change was in the wind. The New World had broken with the past and was striding forward, rough-hewing its destiny as it went. Steam was inexorably supplanting the sailing vessel. Coastal lights and beacons were going up, and an international system of reporting wind and currents was being adopted. The Gulf Stream was being explored. Charts were becoming reliable and instruments more refined. Trained navigators were more numerous, and the electric telegraph was spreading along the coast. All these added up to fewer shipwrecks and increased safety at sea. But the basic causes for the decline of wrecking were taking place on land: the revolutionary change in the nation's transportation system and the discovery of gold in California.

In the mid-nineteenth century, domestic travel and freight traffic turned away from the sea and went inland. The opening of the Erie Canal in 1825 was the making of a number of new cities, but it did much to unmake the wrecking business. The long, expensive haul from the inland states to the eastern markets — by flatboat down the rivers of the interior and the Mississippi to New Orleans and Mobile, thence by coasting vessels across the Gulf of Mexico and up the Atlantic seaboard — had passed forever. Farmers and growers began to send their produce north to the Great Lakes and through the canal to New York and the seaboard cities. Chicago, Detroit and Cleveland were born. No longer would the lightkeeper at Dry Tortugas sight 150 sail passing in and out of the gulf in a single day.

About mid-century, gold was found in California, and the discovery triggered the great trek to the gold fields. With the surge of population westward, roads opened into the interior, and in a few years railroads were creeping slowly across the land. Growing boys ceased to dream of going to sea and making a fortune in strange lands. There was too much good land in their own country waiting to be developed, and too many other opportunities for enterprising, ambitious and adventurous spirits. Men's minds and hearts were filled with the magic of gold, silver, copper, wide lands, new towns, cattle, wheat. . . .

American clipper ships, which had startled the maritime world by their beauty and speed, sailed from New York around Cape Horn loaded with gold-seekers. At San Francisco they were often abandoned and left to rot in the harbor, while every man on board rushed away to the diggings. The isolationism that was to grip the nation for generations began to appear.

By the end of the nineteenth century, progress and technology had all but done away with the perils of the sea. There remained only the dangers associated with storms, machinery failure, fog or ice — and, of course, the unpredictable human element. With the improvement of communications and weather forecasting, shipmasters were able to dodge severe storms or remain in port until danger was over. The public began to feel safe at sea, and the overseas tourist business came into being.

In a few years the independent wrecker would pass into oblivion, along with America's brief period of maritime ascendancy. His services to the shipping of his day would be forgotten, and even his name would slip from memory. Only an ugly shadow would linger in the public thought or flit through outmoded fiction to tell that he had ever passed this way.

In 1847 the United States Congress — prodded no doubt by the benevolent societies and humane societies in Boston, New York and Philadelphia — made its first appropriation of $5,000 for lifesaving apparatus. The following year it set aside another $10,000. The first surfboats, life cars, blue flares and mortars (for shooting lifelines from shore to ship) were placed in small boathouses along the New Jersey shore between Sandy Hook and Little Egg Harbor in 1849; soon after, a few were placed on Long Island. But with no one responsible for the equipment, it was soon scattered and lost. In 1850, Congress set aside $20,000—half for lifesaving facilities on Long Island and the Rhode Island shore, and half for North and South Carolina. In 1854 captains were appointed at $200 a year to take charge of the lifeboats; but the crews were still volunteers until 1871, when the chief

The New York waterfront bristled with masts in the late 1880s. Clippers and full-riggers from all oceans berthed along South Street until well after the turn of the twentieth century.

Painting by Charles Robert Patterson

of the United States Revenue Cutter Service — almost single-handedly — set up the first lifesaving stations with trained and fully equipped personnel.

But these early stirrings of the public conscience in behalf of shipwrecked persons took little or no notice of property or cargoes lost at sea.

Early in the century, the Board of Underwriters of the Port of New York was uncomfortably aware of the number of ships being wrecked along the northeastern coast, of the tragic loss of life in some localities and of the value of the cargoes destroyed. As a first step to ease the situation, it took over the operation of whaleboats, which the New York Benevolent Society had placed at intervals along the New York and New Jersey shore. The board continued to provide for them until the government's modest lifesaving service began in 1854. But the lifeboat crews could do little more than save a few lives; and the underwriters soon realized that something more had to be done if they were to cut their losses. Help must be available swiftly if a vessel faced an emergency as it came in from the sea.

The problem was of major proportions, and the pressure on the underwriters was intense. Between 1844 and 1858, according to official figures, 60,292 ships put into North Atlantic harbors from southern ports alone. None of these vessels could expect help if it was wrecked, unless some passer-by on land happened to notice its distress signal or came upon it, a helpless, overturned hulk in the surf.

The New York insurance men reasoned somewhat as the wreckers of the Bahamas had done: if prompt assistance could be given by capable men, many casualties could be aided before they foundered or were driven to disaster on the shore. But the underwriters approached the problem from a different angle. They had no vessels with which to patrol the coastal danger points; but they did have agents, many of them farmers and fishermen, located at frequent intervals up and down the seaboard. It was a simple matter to organize these men into a seaside alarm system and instruct them to keep vigilant watch on passing ships in their area. Any agent who sighted a vessel in trouble was to mount his horse instantly and gallop to the nearest point of relief. He was to spare no effort and, if necessary, ride the horse to death. What was the life of a horse when the safety of a ship full of passengers and merchandise was at stake!

When horse and rider reached the local underwriter's office, the office would immediately communicate with a commercial wrecker and authorize him to go out to the casualty. He was to do everything necessary to aid it and save its people and cargo; the underwriters would foot the bill. From this point on, the wrecking companies dealt directly with either the shipowner or the underwriters. An owner might prefer to have his ship refloated at his own expense if it was not too badly damaged. Or he might take the insurance settlement, in which case the wrecked vessel would belong to the underwriters, who might decide to have it raised, refitted and sold in order to lessen their loss. If neither the owner nor the underwriter claimed the wreck, the wrecker was free to refloat it himself as a speculation.

The man to whom the underwriters turned in emergencies was Captain Israel J. Merritt, a skilled and responsible wrecking captain who had been doing salvage work since 1835, when, at the age of fifteen, he had found work aboard a wrecking vessel operating off Long Island and Manhattan. From 1853 to 1860, Merritt served as the board's salvage agent with a blanket commission to go to the assistance of every distressed vessel that his ship, a converted Gloucester mackerel schooner, could reach. If Captain Merritt could not give aid to a stricken ship, it was written off as a total loss.

In May 1860 the underwriters took a major step toward organizing their salvage operations on a businesslike basis. They created a new organization, the Coast Wrecking Company, and with unanimous agreement set Merritt at its head. The company prospered quickly, and increased its prosperity throughout the 1860s and 1870s. In 1880, Merritt was able to buy it outright;

he did so — and rechristened it the Merritt Wrecking Organization.

The coming of steam navigation did not put the Merritt company out of business, as it did so many other wreckers who clung to the age of sail. When steam-propelled craft appeared, Merritt added two tugboats to his fleet of windjammers and kept pace with the times. By 1885 his company had a second base at Norfolk. In 1897 it consolidated with its principal rival, the Chapman Derrick & Wrecking Company of Brooklyn, and in 1922 with the T. A. Scott Company of New London, Connecticut. The result was the Merritt-Chapman & Scott Corporation, which by 1958 had diversified its operations and reached a net worth of 142 million dollars. It is probably the oldest salvage firm extant in the United States, and certainly has done more than any other firm to bring the methods and skill of the early wreckers directly into the modern world.

In 1921, Key West was the scene of a unique celebration. On the one-hundredth anniversary of the founding of the city, the Wrecking Register at the United States Courthouse was officially closed amid a flourish of nostalgic oratory. Thereafter, no more licenses were issued to boatmen or shipmasters to go a-wrecking. The sons and grandsons of the old wreckers pulled in their belts and turned elsewhere for a livelihood. Wrecking, they were convinced, was dead. Soon the very word dropped out of use.

But the forward thrust of progress had not completely bypassed the wreckers' city. During the previous year, Merritt-Chapman & Scott had bought out the last of the local wreckers and stationed its powerful ocean salvage vessel *Relief* at that strategic port. The big bully of a steam tug was not welcomed with much cordiality by the Key Westers. They threatened its crew members with mayhem if they came ashore, and promised to burn the ship. Before they got around to it, however, the master of the *Relief* decided it would be smart to anchor offshore when she was "on station," until the local zealots cooled down. Today the feud is past, and descendants of the early Bahamians and Key Westers are crew members of the big, new tug which crouches on constant alert at the mole in front of the city, ready to dash anywhere from the Delaware capes to Tampico on a mission of relief.

Small wrecking schooners no longer patrol the reefs in search of business, nor do straining horses race the beaches to bring word of disaster at sea. The rescue vessel receives its call by radio directly from the distressed ship, or by radiophone from its metropolitan headquarters. With a few quick blasts of its whistle, it calls its crew and puts to sea.

The straining eyes of men waiting and hoping on the canted deck of many a crippled ship have lighted with relief as the big tug came tearing out of storm or fog with its house flag — a galloping black horse on a white background — whipping in the gale. The flag is a deserved tribute to the gallant ponies of another day, who died that ships might have aid in time. But what tribute has ever been paid to the men who answered the calls for help and put to sea, in storm or calm, without support, with few tools, with little thanks and often no pay at all — the wreckers, the only agents of deep-sea rescue of their day?

A sloop is always useful. This one was among the equipment of a modern salvage firm engaged in 1957 in raising a sunken cargo of ore in the Gulf of Mexico, about fifty miles from Key West.

24

The Word Is Salvage

Despite all our vaunted progress, the sea remains as elemental and unchanged today as when the ape man first rode his tree trunk out a river mouth and felt the pull of its swinging tides. We may have learned to travel under it, and on its troubled surface, and through the sky above it; but all our learning has not changed an atom or an element of it.

Ships still run aground occasionally in spite of all safeguards. They still collide at sea; have machinery breakdowns, fires and explosions; and encounter storms that cripple them disastrously. For as long as great waters remain, there will be ships in danger and men to go to their aid.

An era did end with the passing of sail. But wrecking, which is as old as the seven seas, did not go out with the windjammer. It only changed its dress and its name to keep pace with the advancing times. Today it is called "salvage" and has its place in the world of free enterprise — a place freer than most.

With the arrival of steam navigation, deep-sea towing became possible, and this led to deep-sea salvage and rescue as we know them today. The first tugs were employed by the Dutch at Rotterdam to tow sailing vessels in and out of the harbor. Soon they were towing ships across the English Channel and saving them many days' sailing. At Key West, where a dozen small schooners often raced out of the harbor at the blast of a conch shell, only one seagoing tug, the *Cable,* is now on duty. Yet this one vessel keeps twenty-four-hour watch over three wave lengths of distress and commercial radio, and her crew never ventures out of range of her whistle. A dozen such vessels are on station in American and Canadian waters, and many more are keeping vigil on the western shores of Europe and the British Isles.

Today's salvage vessel is a floating workshop, manned by the same dauntless breed of men who labored with little more than their bare hands in the old wrecking schooners. In many parts of the world these modern salvors wait and watch. When gales blow and seas run high, they are ready to answer any signal of distress. When risks are great and conditions desperate, they will still venture forth. And they are capable of swift and efficient action. After a single hurricane in 1951, the American salvage ship *Rescue,* based in the West Indies, refloated thirteen vessels that had gone aground in the same storm.

The salvage ship is a powerful, diesel-driven, seagoing tug, unglamorous and squat, designed to take all the ocean can give and survive it. It is usually from 700 to 1,100 tons burden, approximately 200 feet long, with 4000 horsepower engines and a cruising range of up to 2000 miles. Its crew is expert in the arts of keeping a modern ship afloat. Its equipment includes firefighting and rescue gear, air compressors and pumps, boilers, tools for cutting away plating or making patches under water, anchors, high explosives, a derrick and towing equipment, diving gear and lifeboats.

Risk, both physical and financial, remains a necessary ingredient of the business. Lloyd's of London, to minimize the difficulties, created the well-known "No cure, no pay" contract, which many salvage craft carry ready for use. Under its terms the salvor agrees to make no claim for reward unless he saves the endangered vessel. It was this contract which the British salvage tug *Turmoil* used in its renowned dash to save the freighter *Flying Enterprise* during the 1950s. After ten days of heroic struggle, during which people throughout the world waited attentively and hoped, the freighter sank almost within sight of land. The *Turmoil* received nothing for its gallant struggle. The owners of the *Flying Enterprise,* however, presented the salvage crew with a financial token in admiration for their heroic work.

In the great room at Lloyd's, where marine underwriters sit primly at their desks, accepting risks from the brokers, a large bulletin board carries announcements of all mishaps reported by ships at sea. When a serious accident takes place, the bell of the *Lutine* is rung, and the casualty is announced by a "caller" standing upon the rostrum, dressed in the traditional scarlet cloak. The underwriters who have insured the vessel cable the agent of Lloyd's nearest the wreck to go to the scene and report on what he finds. Sometimes they also cable the nearest salvor to go to the wreck and take charge.

At this point there may be a special kind of bargaining among the underwriters. One who has insured the damaged vessel, fearing that it may prove to be a steep loss, may wish to cut his loss by paying another underwriter a fixed amount of cash to take on the uncertain risk. The other will take on the risk if he feels the original holder has overestimated the loss involved — or if he feels he can pass the risk along to a third party at a profit.

This transfer of the insurance obligation is known as reinsurance. In practice, it depends on each man's estimate of the likelihood of getting the casualty safely afloat or of her being smashed by the first bad weather. It also requires a knowledge of the ship's construction, her captain and the salvage firm at work on her. The last underwriter to accept the risk makes the profit or takes the loss, though he may cut his loss or increase his profit by salvaging the wreck.

When a crippled ship is safely in port, the salvors cable Lloyd's to have its owner or insurer post a bond. If none is posted, the salvor may take legal action to determine the amount of his compensation; but usually the bond is forthcoming. The claim for salvage is then arbitrated, with both sides preparing briefs and arguing as in a court trial, and a just settlement is arrived at. It is recognized on both sides that this procedure fosters the salvage industry and breeds energetic and resourceful men, whereas a system of daily wages would lower the whole standard of the service.

The bell of the *Lutine,* which hangs in the great hall at Lloyd's, is a constant reminder of the hazards of marine underwriting. The *Lutine* was a British frigate which sailed from Yarmouth Roads bound for Hamburg in October 1799, during the French Revolutionary Wars. She carried a large amount of gold, including £140,000 to pay English troops fighting in Holland, some private shipments of gold and silver consigned to merchants in Hamburg and 1,000 bars of gold and 500 of silver in miscellaneous shipments. She ran into a great storm and sank on the shoals off the coast of Holland. There were no survivors.

Lloyd's paid the insurers £900,000, a staggering sum, and the wreck — in theory, at least — belonged to them. The Dutch government claimed it, however, and offered fishermen one-third of any gold they could raise. In this way, about £72,000 was brought up, and one Dutch wrecker worked vainly for eight years to reach the treasure vault of the sunken ship. By 1857, Lloyd's had prodded the British government into obtaining rights to the sunken gold and silver from the Dutch; and in the next five years, Lloyd's wreckers raised about £40,000, along with the ship's bell. Many efforts have been made to reach the remaining treasure, but all have ended in disappointment. The vessel's magazine collapsed on top of the vault, and the shifting sandy bed of the sea has completely engulfed the wreck.

So general was the ignorance of and prejudice against wrecking down through the years that salvage techniques received little or no attention from shipmasters, owners and naval authorities. At the start of World War II, the United States Navy had no salvage division and no trained salvage men. The British Admiralty was caught in more or less the same condition, but it quickly took over salvage and rescue in waters adjacent to its shores by posting naval officers on all private salvage craft. Other Allied countries maintained rescue vessels, but the early months of the war saw half of them sunk or captured by Germany. The earliest convoys from America sailed with a British salvage tug in their wake. When a ship was torpedoed, the other vessels sailed around it and continued on their way, leaving the stricken ship for the rescue tug coming along behind. When a salvor with a casualty in tow approached land, a small corvette was sent out to meet the pair and escort them in.

When the United States recognized that it must enter the war, Admiral William Sullivan was sent to England to study British methods of rescue and repair. On his recommendation, the United States Navy took over the New York firm of Merritt-Chapman & Scott as the nucleus of its salvage division, and contracted for a number of modern rescue tugs to be built. A salvage school was set up at San Diego, California; and the first class for training salvage men had just begun when the disaster at Pearl Harbor rocked the world. The new salvage cadets were rushed to Honolulu to learn their work on the job, and a new class was enrolled in the school.

American rescue vessels saved 498 ships during the war years, with cargoes valued at $675,640,967, and assisted several hundred more in times of emergency. Legal salvage awards for this work were paid into the Treasury of the United States.

Among the exploits of the salvage fleet was its last minute aid to the Allied invasion of France on D-day in June 1944. Huge concrete blocks called Phoenix Units had been secretly constructed in England and were to be floated across the Channel to the French beaches, where they would be used to make two artificial harbors. These hollow blocks, almost as tall as three-storied buildings, were filled with water and sunk offshore for concealment. Shortly before D-day, one of the units broke loose and drifted out to sea. So well had the invasion plans been concealed that the salvage division knew nothing about them until suddenly called upon to go out and bring back the runaway Phoenix Unit.

When final preparations for the invasion were completed, it was suddenly discovered that the pumps which were to raise the units had not arrived. The invasion plans were in serious trouble. Without the artificial breakwaters to shelter the landings, the invasion could not take place. But the salvage men knew what to do. Their lives had been spent in handling emergencies, and this was just one more call to improvise. Dismay was soon replaced with grim humor as the rescue tugs gathered from all directions, carrying the heavy-duty, portable pumps they used in emptying the holds of flooded ships. The salvage men worked in shifts twenty-four hours a day and floated sixty-five Phoenix Units in thirteen days. D-day came off as planned.

Eighteen salvage ships sailed with the invasion. They carried pontoons to keep sinking vessels afloat, coils of lifting and towing cable, air compressors, diving suits, portable generators and pumps, steel plates, girders, underwater cutters and many other first-aid appliances for ships in peril. Most important of all, they carried skilled and courageous men to use them.

In European waters, ocean salvage has become a great international business, employing fast, powerful vessels that keep watch twenty-four hours a day. To reach the more important northern ports of Europe, shipping must sail past southwest Ireland, western England and northwestern France. In winter some of the worst weather in the world sweeps these coasts. When an S O S call is identified, each salvor puts to sea at top speed. The work is highly competitive: as in the days of the old wreckers, the first tugmaster to reach the distressed vessel arranges for the business. The ability of a salvage tug to get away from the wharf fast and plow into a gale at top speed is an important factor in obtaining business, as well as in a successful rescue.

Among the noted European salvors after World War I was the Italian vessel *Artiglio* of the Società Recuperi Maritimi in Genoa. Her gay and intrepid crew were called on to destroy many a dangerous sunken wreck. Among the *Artiglio*'s exploits was the recovery of a million pounds in gold from the strong room of the Peninsular and Oriental steamship *Egypt* off the coast of Brittany in 1929. But her men had little time to enjoy their fame, for a sunken shipload of ammunition near St. Nazaire, on which they were working soon afterward, exploded and annihilated the ship and the crew.

Another well-known European craft is the *Seefalke,* which carries a German crew but is based at a French port, from which she ranges over 6,000 miles of seaway. Near Vlaardingen in the Netherlands is based the *Zwarte Zee,* the finest and largest salvage vessel in Europe and perhaps in the world. She is the flagship of the L. Smit International Towing Service, which in 1957 was operating nineteen large rescue tugs. The savage Bay of Biscay and adjacent waters are protected by tugs of a French firm, Compagnie de Remorque et de Sauvetage.

Great Britain has produced the remarkable London Salvage Association, an unofficial but powerful arbiter of salvage matters not only in that country but in areas throughout the world. Supported by shipowners and underwriters to protect their interests, the association maintains representatives in all important seaports. One of these representatives is usually on hand after every major accident at sea, ready to advise the shipmaster and to make certain that the salvors bring efficient methods and proper equipment into play. The association has a splendidly equipped vessel of its own, which has seen many years of valiant service.

The top-ranking British salvors are the Overseas Towage and Salvage Company of London and Metal Industries, Limited, of Scotland.

A brilliant piece of salvage turned in by the British was the recovery of £2,379,000 in gold bars from the trans-Pacific liner *Niagara,* which sank on June 19, 1940, in 428 feet of water off the coast of New Zealand after striking a mine. The underwriters took charge and sent a specially equipped vessel, which carried a deep-sea observation chamber that could be lowered as much as 500 feet into the sea. From this chamber, rimmed with glass portholes and lamps, the salvors directed the placing of explosives, blasted holes in the side of the wreck and cleaned out the debris after each blast. Finally they opened the *Niagara's* strong room and, with a heavy grab bucket, scooped up the bars of gold.

Impressive as today's salvage craft may be, they lack the glory of the lifesaving mission. That portion of the wreckers' calling has passed to the lifeboat men. In the United States the lifesaving stations are manned by the Coast Guard; in Great Britain, by the Royal National Institution for the Preservation of Life from Shipwreck; and elsewhere by similar agencies.

The United States Coast Guard responds to calls for help from ships in trouble in the interest of saving human life and, in a lesser degree, saving property. Coast Guard aircraft may search the seas for victims of an air disaster, or fly a disabled seaman fom his ship to a hospital on shore; its versatile cutters may dash to the aid of a disabled craft and tow it to port, or stand by through an emergency as long as there is danger. But the Coast Guard moves out of the picture as soon as an adequately equipped salvage ship, representing private industry, arrives to take over.

In Great Britain, the Royal National Lifeboat Association permits its men to do salvage work and to use the lifeboat gear on such missions if they wish, providing that they remember the real purpose of a lifeboat is to save life.

Among the heirs of the early wreckers are the men who retrieve sunken materials from the sea bottom — as commercial undertakings, scientific explorations or sporting ventures. Known wrecks in American coastal waters since the beginning of World War II are claimed by the United States government; permission to attempt their salvage must be obtained from official sources or from the underwriters. Sinkings which took place before 1939 are the property of anybody who can reach them, provided the salvor can prove they have actually been abandoned by their rightful owners.

A diver may come upon a modern vessel lying on the bottom in more or less the same condition as when she sank. But no wreck over a hundred years old — in the Caribbean area, at least — has escaped the torpedo shipworm, which eats away every vestige of wood and leaves only the hardest substances such as metals and crockery. These are soon camouflaged with a coating of whitish coral cement. Then come the coral polyps, which slowly cover the remains with a yellowish crust. Hurricanes churn the shallow seas to the bottom, and build up or carry away tons of the sandy floor. It takes an expert even to recognize the presence of an ancient wreck. Often the only identifying feature is an anchor or the coral-encrusted barrel of a gun.

It is a romantic fact that of all substances, only gold and pewter are unharmed by long immersion in the sea. Other metals suffer from exposure to sea water, which acts as an electrolyte, setting up oxidation and similar chemical conversions. Silver often becomes silver sulphide; iron converts to crystalline magnetite; and copper and brass may form copper chlorides and acetates. Most material recovered from shipwreck sites requires expert cleaning and restorative treatment, or it will disintegrate. Many priceless objects retrieved by amateurs have been lost in this way.

While World II was still fresh in the public mind, persons close to American government circles, seeing quick profits for a trifling investment, quietly obtained the right to salvage some of the more valuable sunken wartime cargo vessels. Unfavorable publicity stopped this speculation, and most of the hastily formed corporations were dissolved. But a few legitimate ventures did proceed, among them the raising of the cargo of the *Edward S. Luckenbach.*

During the preparations for the invasion of North Africa, the staging area for concentration of American ships was just within the entrance of the Gulf of Mexico, about thirty miles north of Key West. Among the freighters assembled there was the *Luckenbach,* loaded with 10,000 tons of ore: one-sixth of the total supply of tungsten then available, as well as zinc, antimony and tin ore valued at approximately four and one-half million dollars in the postwar market. The ship sank in seventy feet of water. She was presumed to be the victim of a German submarine; but divers who later surveyed the wreck as it lay on the floor of the gulf found close beside it three other vessels which were evidently wrecked at the same time: the American destroyer *Sturtevant*, the Dutch freighter *Gunbor* and an American minesweeper. The divers believed that the minesweeper had laid a protective mine field and had then been trapped in it with the three other vessels.

The *Luckenbach* lay in a position that made her a hazard to ships entering or leaving the gulf. The navy quickly sent a salvage vessel to break up the *Luckenbach* with dynamite, so that other vessels could pass safely above her, and at the same time to raise as much of the tungsten as could be hastily salvaged.

After the war a dummy corporation reportedly obtained rights to salvage the *Luckenbach* and her remaining cargo for $800; but the plan was discovered and publicized, and the deal was off. Meanwhile, a wildcat wrecker in Key West is said to have located the sunken vessel and to have helped himself to about two hundred thousand dollars worth of ore, which he disposed of by means of forged manifest papers. The Federal Bureau of Investigation learned about it and went into action. Evidently someone tipped off the plunderer, for he fled the neighborhood with such haste that most of his personal effects were left behind.

A New York salvage company then purchased all rights to the wreck, surveyed it and set up a salvage operation on the spot. Equipment, divers and salvage men were assembled at Key West. Working from a reconstructed ferryboat, they scientifically raised the remaining cargo and machinery of the sunken freighter. First, the steel hull and the exposed machinery were broken up with explosives and raised as scrap metal. When the ore cargo had been laid bare, an arrangement called an air lift was brought into play. This mechanism, first used in France, comprised a heavy steel pipe reaching down to the wreck, a rubber hose and a pump capable of drawing 105 cubic feet of air a minute through the pipe. With this simple equipment, the ore was sucked up from the sea bottom. A diver remained below to regulate the intake of air and to control the pipe while the lift was in operation.

More colorful, perhaps, is the work of the skin divers — scientists and sportsmen equipped with masks, oxygen tanks and flippers — who go down to the reefs in search of the remains of Spanish galleons, buccaneer sloops and pirate vessels. The prospect of looting such wrecks is as enthralling today as ever. Teenagers on the American keys and the Bahamian cays often go through a spell of it, and even serious-minded adults can be found poking about the sea bottom with electronic equipment and underwater cameras, hunting historic shipwrecks and vanished cities.

Sportsmen-explorers with the means of financing their own ventures have done some interesting work of this kind. An outstanding example is Edward A. Link, chairman of the board of the Link Aviation Company. Like many yachtsmen on the Florida coast, Link became interested in the underwater world. But he went a little further in his interest than most: he learned deep-sea diving and gathered together the most complete collection of modern equipment to be had, some of which he designed and manufactured himself. His first ship, the *Sea Diver,* was a treasure hunter's dream. It carried a battery of electronic locating devices — a magnetometer, which detects the presence of iron beneath several feet of sand or coral; sonar, which locates masses projecting from the sea bottom; underwater television; an electronic detector, which notes the presence of any electric conductor; a fathometer, which records the depth of water; Loran, which is used in obtaining exact fixes on shipwreck sites, and an automatic pilot for steering the ship — as well as power diving machines that tow divers underwater and a double-ended diving boat to be launched from the ship's deck when approaching a reef. This boat carried deep-sea diving gear and had air compressors arranged to keep several divers supplied with air simultaneously. By 1960, Link had sold the *Sea Diver* and was building a new ship, bigger and even better equipped.

Link is interested in the marine archaeological project of the

Smithsonian Institution at Washington, D.C.; he makes it an annual grant of funds and participates personally in as much of its work as his business will permit. The goal of the Smithsonian project is to find and explore historic shipwrecks, and to collect, preserve and study the objects removed from them. With Mendel L. Peterson, curator of naval history at the Smithsonian — and sometimes on his own — Link has ventured into strange and exciting areas. His foot was the first in modern times to tread the lost pirate city of Port Royal, Jamaica, which sank in an earthquake in 1692 and carried down into the sea about 2,000 people. Link found the old walls of the town at a depth of twenty to forty feet underwater and buried under six feet of mud and silt. He brought up objects of metal, glass and pottery.

After a painstaking search of the site where Columbus' flagship, the *Santa Maria,* went down off the coast of Hispaniola, Link found and brought up a weird, ghostly anchor. It was of an unusual shape and construction, which identified it as having been made in the same locality and at about the same time as when the *Santa Maria* was built. Experts have declared that the anchor must be that of the *Santa Maria* herself or else of another ship built at about the same time in about the same locality and lost on the same bit of seacoast — a string of coincidences which is possible but not probable.

The treasure hunter who forages not for science but for profit is, alas! no longer on the road to sudden fortune. If successful, he must report all taxable treasure on his federal income tax return. State laws also must be observed; Florida, for instance, has a law securing to the state twelve and a half percent of any treasure trove recovered in its waters.

In British colonial waters, sunken treasure still belongs to the Crown. Local government officials seem to have discretion as to whether the finder may keep it or not. Young Teddy Tucker learned this to his dismay in 1955, when he made what has been called the most important discovery of sunken treasure in this century.

In waters holding over 300 known shipwrecks, Tucker, exploring undersea in skin-diving equipment, found some ancient cannon in a coral pocket in a reef near Hamilton, Bermuda. As he thought over his find, he regretted that he had not searched the site more thoroughly. When Edward Link visited Hamilton in the *Sea Diver,* Tucker told him his story and asked for help in searching again for the ancient wreck. Link responded promptly; and together they sailed for the site, about twelve miles out, and dived on the wreck. Judging from the variety of guns it carried, it appeared to be the remains of a pirate or buccaneer vessel. Mendel Peterson, of the Smithsonian, who sometimes accompanies Link on his expeditions, has given as his opinion that the ship probably sank sometime between 1592, the date of the oldest coin found in the wreck, and 1609, when the colonists led by Sir George Somers settled at Bermuda. He reasons that the colonists would have salvaged the wreck so close to their shores if they had known of it.

Tucker, with the advantages of Link's modern equipment, was able to spend ten thrill-packed days on the site. It was his show, and Link modestly assumed the role of interested bystander. Working head down, without weights, in about twenty-five feet of water, Tucker spent forty or fifty hours underwater, until a shift of weather forced him to abandon the search. At times he stayed down as long as five hours at a stretch. Within this brief period he brought up nine gold objects; 200 silver coins; eighty artifacts (including brass dividers, a timing glass, several pewter porringers and a steel breastplate); a bar of gold stamped PINTO, thought to be from the Pinto River in Colombia; and an exquisite, emerald-studded gold cross about six or seven inches high. The requirements of everyday life — Tucker's job and the demands of Link's business affairs — made it impossible for either man to wait the change of weather and ended their adventure.

Tucker was offered $25,000 for the gold cross; but being a law-abiding Britisher, he reported his finds to the government of Bermuda. He was permitted to keep them, provided he would sell only to the government anything he wished to dispose of. Most of the objects were placed in a museum, and Tucker was given 10 per cent of all admissions.

Generally speaking, wrecking as it was known as late as the nineteenth century has passed. Its precocious offspring include the Coast Guard, the lifesaving services, the gentlemen-sportsmen with masks and flippers, and the international fleet of great rescue tugs. With all our progress, approximately six thousand ships each year experience a major mishap or a breakdown, and require the presence of trained and competent salvage or repair men. Such men are there, ready and waiting, along all the seacoasts of the world.

The old wreckers would roar with glee at the magnificent seamanship of their modern successors, probably surpassing that of men in any other branch of maritime activity. Their eyes would shine with pleasure at the wonderful machines and equipment at their disposal. But they would growl with dismay at the common theory that these machines have made ocean salvage what it is today. They know better. Technology has supplied marvelous tools to aid magnificent ships; but the method, the principles, the comprehension of salvage work — the very sense and feel of it in the blood — were all theirs to bequeath to the modern world.

And it would be a cosmic jest for the old wreckers, to regale them on their celestial voyages, if they knew that the wrecking licenses which the Admiralty court at Key West discontinued with such ceremonious finality had returned, this time on a world-wide scale. They are known now as commissions; and every skipper, before he may command a salvage craft, must earn his ticket or rating as a rescue tugmaster. This done, he is no longer a stranger and an opponent. He may sit down, a comrade and peer, in the honored company of deep-water ship captains — at last.

Aft Word

Today the old frontiers have vanished, and we are off and away to the moon! Behind us are the dry years of sophistication, when men had seen everything, thought everything and been everywhere. The surfeit of learning has been digested, and men stir to a new humility as they peer out into untried space through the mists of unthought ideas — the eternal frontier.

One day, when the discoverers and pioneers have gone, and little spaceships of trade and commerce are abroad in the skies, there will be shipwrecks on the high seas of space. Because of inaccurate charts, inexperienced navigators, sun storms, jet streams and comets' tails, aircraft will run aground on the rings of Saturn. They will turn turtle where there is neither up nor down, and will be swept by magnetic currents onto the shoals of the Milky Way.

When that time comes, a new breed of wreckers will take ship and ride a radio beam through the wild blue yonder. They will locate the luckless wreck, dragging its anchor on the Pleiades because its pilot had been fooling around Venus instead of watching the stars. As in former times, the captain will shout to them to go back where they came from: their charges are exorbitant, and they don't know anything about his vessel, anyway. The wreckers will flash into orbit and circle the wreck until the captain sees that his situation is hopeless and signals them aboard. Then they will bail him out with the little dipper, toss him a cable and tow him to a wrecking platform — out where the North Star isn't north and the Southern Cross isn't south. There he will find atmosphere and learn to breath again, and can wait for an earth-bound tug to come and tow him home.

You say the romance of wrecking is dead? Just wait awhile! You haven't seen anything yet!

Selected Bibliography

"A Plaine Description of the Bermudas," in *Tracts and Other Papers* (coll. by Peter Force). Washington: Wm. Q. Force, n.d. Vol. III.

A True Relation of That Which Happened to the Spanish Fleet in America. London: 1623.

Accounts of Shipwrecks and Other Disasters at Sea. Brunswick: Joseph Griffith, 1823.

Adamson, Hans C., *Keepers of the Lights.* New York: Greenberg, 1955.

An Exact and Perfect Relation of the Arrival of the James and Mary. N.d.

Awful Calamities or the Shipwrecks of 1839. Boston: J. Howe, 1840.

Baarslag, Karl, *S O S, To the Rescue.* New York: Oxford University Press, 1935.

Bangs, Mary Rogers, *Old Cape Cod.* Boston: Houghton Mifflin, 1920.

Banks, Charles Edward, *The History of Martha's Vineyard.* Boston: Dean, 1911.

Bowen, Frank C., *From Carrack to Clipper.* London: Halton & T. Smith, 1927.

Brookfield, Charles M., and Griswold, Oliver, *They All Called It Tropical.* Miami: Data Press, 1949.

Browne, Jefferson B., *Key West: The Old and the New.* St. Augustine: The Record Company, 1912.

Cappick, Marie, *The Key West Story.* Key West: The Coral Tribune, 1957.

Chapelle, Howard I., *The Baltimore Clipper.* Salem: Marine Research Society, 1930.

———, *History of American Sailing Ships.* New York: W. W. Norton, 1935.

Clark, Arthur H., *Clipper Ship Era.* New York: G. P. Putnam's Sons, 1910.

Coffin, Robert P. T., *Captain Abby and Captain John.* New York: Macmillan, 1939.

Cooper, Earnest Read, *Storm Warriors of the Suffolk Coast.* London: Heath Cranton, 1937.

Curry, Robert, *Bahamian Lore.* Paris: Lecram Press, 1928.

Dalton, J. W., *Life Savers of Cape Cod.* Boston: Barta Press, 1902.

Dalyell, Sir J. A., *Shipwrecks and Disasters.* Edinburgh: A. Constable, 1812.

d'Escalente Fontaneda, Hernando, *Memoir of d'Escalente Fontaneda Respecting Florida.* Coral Gables: Glade House, 1944.

Dickinson, Jonathan, *Jonathan Dickinson's Journal* (ed. by Evangeline W. Andrews and Charles McL. Andrews). New Haven: Yale University Press, 1945.

Dow, George Francis, *Pirates of the New England Coast.* Salem: Marine Research Society, 1923.

Duffy, James, *Shipwreck and Empire.* Cambridge: Harvard University Press, 1955.

Durkin, Joseph T., *Stephen R. Mallory.* Chapel Hill: University of North Carolina Press, 1954.

Edwards, Bryan, *History of the West Indies.* Charleston: E. Marford, Wellington, 1810.

Ellms, Charles, *Shipwrecks and Disasters at Sea.* New York: R. Marsh, 1836.

———, *Tragedy of the Seas.* Cincinnati: Israel Post, 1841.

Evans, Capt. Stephen H., *The United States Coast Guard, 1790–1915.* Annapolis: U.S. Naval Inst., 1949.

Exquemiin, Alexandre, *The Pirates of Panama.* New York: Frederick A. Stokes, 1914.

Fairburn, William Armstrong, *Merchant Sail.* Center Lovell, Maine: Fairburn Marine Educational Foundation, 1945–1955.

Forbes, R. B., *Notes on Some Few of the Wrecks and Rescues.* Boston: Little, Brown, 1889.

Freuchen, Peter, *Book of the Seven Seas.* New York: Messner, 1957.

Garcilaso de la Vega (*El Inca*). *The Florida of the Inca* (trans. and ed. by John Grier Varner and Jeannette Johnson Varner). Austin: University of Texas Press, 1951.

Gardner, Arthur H., *Wrecks Around Nantucket.* Nantucket: Inquirer and Mirror Press, 1915.

Gibbs, James A., Jr., *Pacific Graveyard.* Portland: Oregon Historical Society, Binfords & Mort, 1950.

Gifford, John, *Rehabilitation of the Florida Keys.* Coral Gables: University of Miami Press, 1934.

Gilmore, Rev. John, *Storm Warriors or Life Boat Work on the Goodwin Sands.* London: Macmillan, 1874.

Harllee, William Curry, *Kinfolks.* New Orleans: 1934.

Hassam, John T., *The Bahama Islands.* Cambridge: John Wilson & Son, 1899.

Holman, H., *Handy Book for Ship Owners.* London: 1891.

Hopkins, Manley, *Handbook of Average.* London: 1859.

———, *Port of Refuge.* London: King & Co., 1873.

Houghson, Shirley Carter, *The Carolina Pirates and Colonial Commerce.* Baltimore: Johns Hopkins Press, 1894.

Hoyt, Capt. John C., *Annual Report,* January 1, 1850. Board of Underwriters of Port of New York, 1850.

Jackson, William Richard, Jr., *Early Florida Through Spanish Eyes.* Coral Gables: University of Miami Press, 1954.

Jenkin, A. K. Hamilton, *Cornish Seafarers.* London: J. M. Dent & Sons, 1932.

———, *Cornish Homes and Customs.* London and Toronto: J. M. Dent & Sons, 1934.

Karraker, Cyrus Harreld, *The Hispaniola Treasure.* Philadelphia: University of Pennsylvania Press, 1934.

Kittredge, Henry C., *Shipmasters of Cape Cod.* Boston: Houghton Mifflin, 1935.

———, *Mooncussers of Cape Cod.* Boston: Houghton Mifflin, 1937.

Lawson, J. Murray, *Yarmouth, Past and Present.* Yarmouth: Herald Office, 1902.

———, *Record of Shipping of Yarmouth.* Yarmouth: 1876.

Lincoln, Joseph, *Cape Cod Yesterdays.* Boston: Little, Brown, 1935.

Livermore, Charles W., *Ye Antient Wrecke of the Sparrowhawk.* Boston: A. Mudge & Son, 1865.

Luna y Arellano, Tristan de, *The Luna Papers* (ed. and trans. by H. I. Priestly). Florida State Historical Society (Yale University Press), 1928.

Marvin, Judge William, *A Treatise on the Law of Wreck and Salvage.* Boston: Little, Brown, 1858.

Masters, David, *Crimes of the High Seas.* New York: Henry Holt, 1936.

———, *Divers in Deep Seas.* London: Eyre & Spottiswoode, 1938.

———, *Epics of Salvage.* London: Cassel, 1953.

———, *When Ships Go Down.* New York: Henry Holt, 1935.

———, *Wonders of Salvage,* New York: Dodd Mead, 1924.

McFee, William, *The Law of the Sea.* New York: J. B. Lippincott, 1950.

Meier, Frank, *Hurricane Warning.* New York: E. P. Dutton, 1947.

———, *Fathoms Below.* New York: E. P. Dutton, 1943.

Moore, Col. E. S. C., *British America.* London: Kegan Paul, Trench, Trübner, 1900.

Morison, Samuel Eliot, *Maritime History of Massachusetts.* Boston: Houghton Mifflin, 1921.

Moseley, Mary, *Bahamas Handbook.* Nassau: Nassau Guardian, 1926.

Mowat, Farley, *The Grey Seas Under.* Boston: Little, Brown, 1958.

Narrative of the Loss of the Pulaski. Providence: H. H. Brown, 1839.

Newell, G. R., *S.O.S. North Pacific.* Portland: Binfords & Mort, 1955.

Nicholl, John, *An Houre Glasse of Indian Newes.* London: Nathaniell Butter, 1607.

Norris, Martin, Jr., *The Law of Salvage.* Mt. Kisco: Baker, Voorhis, 1958.

Peggs, A. Deans, *A Short History of the Bahamas.* Nassau: Deans Peggs Research Fund, 1959.

Peterson, Mendel L., *History Under the Sea.* Washington: Smithsonian Institution, 1954.

———, *The Last Cruise of H. M. S. Loo.* Washington: Smithsonian Institution, 1955.

Powles, Louis Diston, *Land of the Pink Pearl.* London: S. Low, Marston, Searle & Rivington, 1888.

Preston, Howard W., *Rhode Island and the Sea.* Providence: R. I. State Bureau of Information, 1932.

Rattray, Jeannette Edwards, *Ship Ashore.* New York: Coward-McCann, 1955.

Riesenberg, Felix, *Yankee Ships to the Rescue.* New York: Dodd Mead, 1940.

Rowe, William Hutchinson, *Maritime History of Maine.* New York: W. W. Norton, 1948.

Sanders, Lt. Comdr. R. E., *The Practice of Ocean Rescue.* Glasgow: Brown, Son & Ferguson, 1947.

Scott, David, *Seven Fathoms Deep.* New York: Henry Holt, 1932.

Shaw, Edward Richard, *Legends of Fire Island Beach.*

Siebert, Wilbar Henry, *Loyalists in East Florida.* Florida State Historical Society (Yale University Press), 1929.

———, *Legacy of the American Revolution to the British West Indies and Bahamas* (pamphlet). Columbus: Ohio State University Bull., 1913.

Smith, Fitz-Henry, Jr., *Storms and Shipwrecks in Boston Bay.* Boston: Bostonian Society Publication, II, 2d Series, 1917.

Snider, C. H. J., *Under the Red Jack.* London: M. Hopkinson, 1928.

Snow, Edward Rowe, *Strange Tales from Nova Scotia to Cape Hatteras.* New York: Dodd Mead, 1949.

Stick, David, *Graveyard of the Atlantic.* Chapel Hill: University of North Carolina Press, 1952.

Strabel, Thelma, *Reap the Wild Wind.* New York: Triangle Books, 1941.

Toxopeus, Klaas, *The Flying Storm.* New York: Dodd Mead, 1954.

Tracey, William, *A Candid and Accurate Narrative.* Portsmouth: 1785.

Twelve Hours on the Wreck. New York: T. C. Butler, 1844.

Vercel, Roger, *Salvage.* New York: Harper & Bros., 1936.

Vignoles, Charles Blacker, *Observations upon the Floridas.* New York: E. Bliss & E. White, 1823.

Voyages and Cruises of Commodore Walker During the Spanish and French Wars. London: A. Millar, 1760.

Wilkinson, Henry C., *Bermuda in the Old Empire.* London: Oxford University Press, 1950.

Wolfe, Reese, *Yankee Ships.* Indianapolis: Bobbs-Merrill, 1953.

Wryde, J. Saxby, *British Lighthouses.* London: T. F. Unwin, 1913.

Young, Desmond, *Ship Ashore.* London: J. Cape, 1933.

Notes

CHAPTER 1

1. Anonymous, *Twelve Hours on the Wreck* (New York: T. C. Butler, 1844), pp. 26-27, including a reprint of the original newspaper account written by Reverend Doctor Cutler, of St. Ann's Church, Brooklyn.

2. *Ibid.*, p. 23.

3. Charles Ellms, *The Tragedy of the Seas* (New York: Israel Post, 1841), p. 329.

4. *Ibid.*, p. 126.

CHAPTER 2

1. Cited in Thelma Strabel, *Reap the Wild Wind* (New York: Triangle Books, 1941), p. 249.

2. *Curry* v. *Barque Howard*, Florida Supreme Court, File No. 0861. Cited in Dorothy Dodd, "The Wrecking Business on the Florida Reef, 1822–1860," *Florida Historical Quarterly*, XXII, No. 4 (April 1944), 199. Thelma Strabel, in *Reap the Wild Wind*, identifies the wrecking ship as the *Thistle* and the captain as Jesse MacDonald.

3. T. Frederick Davis, "Pioneer Days. Indian Key and Wrecking," *Florida Historical Quarterly*, XXII, No. 2 (October 1943), 57-61.

4. John James Audubon, *Journal.* From extracts reprinted in "Three Florida Episodes," *Tequesta, the Journal of the Historical Association of Southern Florida*, II, No. 5 (January 1946), 56-62 *passim.*

CHAPTER 3

1. Martin J. Norris, *The Law of Salvage* (Mt. Kisco: Baker, Voorhis, 1958), pp. 5-6.

2. Reverend John Gilmore, M. A., *Storm Warriors or Life Boat Work on the Goodwin Sands* (London: Macmillan, 1874).

3. *Ibid.*, p. 7.

4. *Ibid.*, p. 8.

5. *Ibid.*

6. *Ibid.*, p. 6.

7. Anonymous, *Voyages and Cruises of Commodore Walker During the Spanish and French Wars* (London: A. Millar, 1760), I, 232-37.

8. Justice Joseph Story in *Case of Schr. Emulous*, 1 Sum. 216, quoted by William C. Marvin in *A Treatise on the Law of Wreck and Salvage* (Boston: Little, Brown, 1858), p. 109:

> [Salvage] is compensation for labor and services, for activity and enterprise, for courage and gallantry actually exerted, and not for the possible exercise of them, which under other circumstances might have been requisite. It is allowed because the property is saved. . . .

CHAPTER 4

1. Marie Cappick, *The Key West Story* (Key West: Coral Tribune, 1957).

2. Robert A. Curry, *Bahamian Lore* (Paris: Lecram Press, 1928), pp. 42-43.

3. A. Deans Peggs, *A Short History of the Bahamas* (Nassau: Deans Peggs Research Fund, 1959), p. 9.

CHAPTER 5

1. Do. d'Escalente Fontaneda, *Memoir of Do. d'Escalente Fontaneda Respecting Florida*, written in Spain about 1575, trans.

by Buckingham Smith (Washington, 1854). A revised edition was published by the University of Miami and the Historical Association of Southern Florida (Miami, 1944).

2. John Nicholl, *An Houre Glasse of Indian Newes* (London: Nathaniell Butter, 1607), in the Massachusetts Historical Society Collections.

3. William Armstrong Fairburn, *Merchant Sail* (Center Lovell, Maine: Fairburn Marine Educational Foundation, 1945–1955), p. 157.

4. *Ibid.*, p. 156.

5. Mary Rogers Bangs, *Old Cape Cod* (Boston: Houghton Mifflin, 1920), p. 170.

6. Cyrus H. Karraker, *The Hispaniola Treasure* (Philadelphia: University of Pennsylvania Press, 1934), p. 95.

CHAPTER 6

1. Anonymous, *An Exact and Perfect Relation of the Arrival of the Ship James and Mary, Taken from a Gentleman who was on board the said Ship the whole Voyage* (n.d.), from collections of Maritime Museum, Newport News, Virginia.

2. Cyrus H. Karraker, *op. cit.*, p. 44.

3. Anonymous, *An Exact and Perfect Relation, supra* note 1.

CHAPTER 7

1. Colonial Records of North Carolina, coll. and ed. by William L. Saunders, secretary of state (Raleigh: P. M. Hale, printer to the State, 1886), IV, 1300-1310.

2. *Ibid.*

CHAPTER 8

1. Edward Rowe Snow, *Strange Tales from Nova Scotia to Cape Hatteras* (New York: Dodd, Mead, 1949), p. 218.

2. Joseph Mitchell, "Dragger Captain, a Profile," *The New Yorker*, January 11, 1947.

3. Mary Rogers Bangs, *op. cit.*, p. 182.

4. Adapted from Joseph Lincoln, *Cape Cod Yesterdays* (Boston: Little, Brown, 1935), p. 237.

5. *The Humane Society of the Commonwealth of Massachusetts, Charter and By-Laws,* incorporated February 23, 1791 (Boston: T. R. Marvin & Son, 1880), pp. 10-11.

6. Fitz-Henry Smith, Jr., *Storms and Shipwrecks in Boston Bay* (Boston: Bostonian Society Publications, 2d Series, 1917), II, 32-33.

CHAPTER 9

1. Reverend George Patterson, D.D., "Sable Island: Its History and Phenomena," *Proceedings and Transactions of the Royal Society of Canada* (Ottawa: John Durie & Son, 1895), XII, 3-49.

2. *Ibid.*, p. 36.

3. *Ibid.*, p. 37.

4. *Ibid.*, p. 38.

5. Farley Mowat, *The Grey Seas Under* (Boston: Little, Brown, 1958), pp. 75, 76.

CHAPTER 10

1. Jeannette Edwards Rattray, *Ship Ashore* (New York: Coward-McCann, 1955), p. 64.

2. *Report of the Commissioners to Investigate the Charges Concerning the Wrecks on the Monmouth Coast* (Trenton: Sherman, 1846).

3. Charles E. Averill, *The Wreckers* (Boston: F. Gleason, 1848), p. 8.

CHAPTER 11

1. Reese Wolfe, *Yankee Ships* (Indianapolis: Bobbs-Merrill, 1953), p. 32.

2. A. Deans Peggs, *loc. cit.*

3. Charles Blacker Vignoles, *Observations Upon the Floridas* (New York: E. Bliss and E. White, 1823), p. 125.

4. John Nicholl, *op. cit.*

CHAPTER 12

1. Dorothy Dodd, "The Wrecking Business on the Florida Reef, 1822–1860," *Florida Historical Quarterly*, XXII, No. 4 (April 1944), 176.

2. *Florida Historical Records, Survey of Spanish Land Grants in Florida* (Tallahassee: State Library Board, 1941), V, 83-90.

3. *United States Senate Executive Journal III,* pp. 312, 313.

4. Marie Cappick, *op. cit.*

CHAPTER 13

1. House Document 53, 17th Cong. 2d Sess. (78), p. 7.

2. *Memorial. The legislative council of Florida to the President of the United States* (n.d.), MS. in Florida State Library.

3. William P. DuVal to E. Livingston, October 7, 1831, Senate Report 242, 30th Cong., 1st Sess. (512), p. 94.

4. 4 United States Statutes at Large, 132, 133.

5. Jefferson B. Browne, *Key West: The Old and the New* (St Augustine: The Record Co., 1912), pp. 207-210.

6. *Supra* note 4, 292, 293.

CHAPTER 14

1. Jefferson B. Browne, *op. cit.*, pp. 62-63.

2. Henry Ewbank, 1 Sumner, 417. Cited in William C. Marvin, *A Treatise on the Law of Wreck and Salvage* (Boston: Little, Brown, 1858), p. 140n.

CHAPTER 15

1. Jefferson B. Browne, *op. cit.*, pp. 38-40.

CHAPTER 16

1. Howard I. Chapelle, *The Baltimore Clipper* (Salem: Marine Research Society, 1930), p. 5.
2. John James Audubon, *op. cit.*, p. 62.
3. Stephen R. Mallory, *Congressional Globe*, U.S. Senate, 35th Cong., 2d Sess., pt. 2, p. 1190, February 21, 1859.
4. *Key West Gazette*, March 21, 1831.
5. Adapted from Marie Cappick, *op. cit.*

CHAPTER 17

1. This account follows the news report in the *Key West Register* of April 9, 1929. Certain of the names have been corrected, however, to follow an editorial on the incident in the *Key West Inquirer* of February 28, 1835.

CHAPTER 20

1. Napoleon B. Broward, *Autobiography, Platform, Letter and Short Story of the Steamer Three Friends*, reprint of campaign literature (Miami: Ruth Leach Carson and James M. Carson, 1938).
2. *New London Day*, February 18, 1907.

CHAPTER 21

1. C. Nordhoff, "Wrecking on the Florida Keys," *Harper's New Monthly Magazine*, XVIII, 577-586 (April 1859). A few details have been added from other sources.
2. *Ibid.*
3. *Key West Inquirer*, June 18, 1836.

Index